The Arjuna Way

NAVIGATING YOUR LIFE'S DEEPEST QUESTIONS
THROUGH SEVEN PROVEN PATHS FROM THE
BHAGAVAD GITA

MAHESH HARVU

WICK LIGHTS PRESS

WICK LIGHTS
PRESS

WICK LIGHTS PRESS

ISBN 979-8-9932969-0-6

Praise for The Arjuna Way

The Arjuna Way is not just a book I read – it is one I experience. It takes the timeless wisdom of the Bhagavad Gita and makes it deeply relevant for the dilemmas and choices that confront us today. Each chapter invites the reader to pause, reflect, and discover how ancient insights can shape the way we think, act, and lead.

What resonated with me most is how the author helps us see Arjuna's struggles as our own – reminding us that moments of confusion, fear, and moral conflict are part of every human journey. The book shows a path to clarity, conviction, and purposeful action.

Having spent over four decades working at the grassroots, influencing public policy, and teaching leadership at Cornell University, I see this book as a meaningful companion for anyone seeking to lead with authenticity and courage. It is one I will return to, and I hope many leaders, students, and seekers will engage with it deeply.

— Dr. R. Balasubramaniam
Author of 'Power Within: The Leadership Legacy of Narendra Modi' and 'Leadership Lessons for Daily Living'

The Arjuna Way offers wisdom rooted in the spirit of the Bhagavad Gita, grounded and tested in the author's own life experience. So much practical advice is found in these pages, on the basics of the spiritual life, the search for wisdom, daily morality and worship, in the good times of life and hard times as well. Mahesh Harvu has done a great act of service in making this book available in today's troubled world. It will be helpful for everyone, but particularly for young people finding their way in today's confusing world.

— Francis X. Clooney, SJ
Parkman Professor of Divinity, Harvard University

The Arjuna Way delivers what contemporary seekers need: a clear path from confusion to clarity without requiring blind faith or withdrawal from worldly responsibilities. Most importantly, Mahesh's systematic approach shows how spiritual maturity enhances rather than diminishes daily life engagement. This isn't just another Gita interpretation; it's a complete reimagining of how ancient wisdom functions as a transformative force in modern life.

— Jonathan Edelmann (D.Phil., Oxford University)
Fellow, International Society for Science and Religion
jedelmann.com

As a classic religious text, the Bhagavad Gita serves as an eternal source of wisdom, ever responding to the needs of the era. Mahesh Harvu, in his book *The Arjuna Way,* offers a relevant contemporary reading of the Gita based on his real-life experience in leadership and policy. The wisdom in this book will be of service for those in search of the contemporary relevance of Hindu wisdom in answering the questions of the purpose of life, mortality, devotion, duty, and spirituality. Harvu offers an exemplar of how a present-day Western Hindu turns to the Gita for guidance in life.

— Alan Brill
Cooperman Ross Professor in honor of Sr Rose Thering
Seton Hall University

Dedicated to YOU, the courageous spiritual inquirer

My life has been a continuous scaffolding of learning. At every step, I've received support from simple ties to strong ropes and robust studs, each one a manifestation of divine grace working through countless souls. Without them and the knowledge gained, I'm just another speck of dust in this magnificent universe, yet with them, I'm part of something far greater.

SECRET OF THE ARJUNA WAY

DISPEL IGNORANCE THROUGH KNOWLEDGE

नष्टो मोह: स्मृतिर्लब्धा त्वत्प्रसादान्मयाच्युत |
स्थितोऽस्मि गतसन्देह: करिष्ये वचनं तव

naṣhṭo mohaḥ smṛitir labdhā tvat-prasādān mayāchyuta
sthito 'smi gata-sandehaḥ kariṣhye vachanaṁ tava

Chapter 18 | Verse 73 of The Bhagavad Gita

ARJUNA SAID

KRISHNA, WITH YOUR GUIDANCE AND GRACE, MY IGNORANCE IS
DISPELLED, and I am situated in knowledge. I am now free from
doubts, and I shall act according to your guidance.

Spoken after receiving divine guidance from Krishna of the
Gita, Arjuna's declaration here isn't just his victory—it's the
blueprint to address our life's challenges. The Arjuna Way leads
to this exact realization.

CONTENTS

2. WORSHIP AND PRAYERS

3. THE SEEKER'S PATH

7. CONFRONTING MORTALITY

8. NOW IT'S YOUR TURN

|| श्री वीरविठ्ठलो विजयते ||

Sri Sri Sugunendra Theertha Swamiji

Jagadguru Srimanmadhwaachaarya moola mahaa samsthaanam
Srimad Upendra Theertha Peetham, Sri Puthige Matha,Udupi - 576 101,Karnataka, INDIA
Email : puthigeshree@gmail.com, www.sreeputhige.org

Foreword

We are delighted to offer our blessings and endorsement for "The Arjuna Way: Developing Your Spiritual Core," a timely work that illuminates the path from confusion to clarity using the eternal wisdom of the Bhagavad Gita and Upanishads.

As we write this foreword during our fourth Paryaya (2024-2026), which we have dedicated as the "Vishwa Gita Paryaya" to promote the universal teachings of the Bhagavad Gita, we find remarkable synchronicity in Sri Mahesh Harvu's endeavor. His work aligns perfectly with our mission to make the Gita's profound life-management principles accessible to seekers across the globe. In our current paryaya, we are offering the Koti Gita Lekhana Yajna (one crore handwritten Bhagavad Gitas) and conducting the World Gita Conference.

The Sri Puthige Matha, established over 800 years ago as one of the Ashta Mathas founded by Jagadguru Sri Madhvacharya, has been blessed to preserve and propagate the Dvaita philosophy the doctrine of divine distinction that recognizes both the transcendent nature of the Supreme and the individual soul's eternal relationship with Krishna.

We owe our gratitude to Sri Upendra Tirtha, the foremost disciple of Sri Madhvacharya, in whose lineage devotees find their authentic spiritual path. The message in our paryaya is consistent that Gita provides solutions to emotional and professional challenges faced by contemporary humanity.

The Arjuna Way

Sri Mahesh Harvu, a devoted follower and ardent devotee of our Krishna Vrundavana in New Jersey, exemplifies the modern seeker on the path of

|| श्री वीरविठ्ठलो विजयते ||

Sri Sri Sugunendra Theertha Swamiji

Jagadguru Srimanmadhwaachaarya moola mahaa samsthaanam
Srimad Upendra Theertha Peetham, Sri Puthige Matha,Udupi - 576 101,Karnataka, INDIA
Email : puthigeshree@gmail.com, www.sreeputhige.org

inquiry of the ultimate truth. For over two decades, he has been instrumental in initiating and nurturing numerous spiritual programs at Krishna Vrundavana, demonstrating his commitment not merely as a student of spiritual principles but as an active facilitator of community spiritual growth. His sincere participation in our interfaith initiatives and spiritual inquiry programs reflects the very spirit of tattva vichara (philosophical inquiry) that forms the foundation of authentic spiritual development.

We like "The Arjuna Way" and its balanced approach to spiritual development. This method resonates deeply with the Dvaita tradition's emphasis on both bhakti (devotion) and jnana (knowledge) as complementary paths to spiritual realization. Krishna's teachings to Arjuna constitute the ultimate life-management scripture.

The author writes about developing critical spiritual thinking rather than blind acceptance. This approach aligns perfectly with the Dvaita tradition's commitment to rigorous philosophical inquiry. Sri Madhvacharya himself established our philosophical system through meticulous scriptural analysis and logical argumentation, demonstrating that authentic faith strengthens rather than fears intellectual examination.

"The Arjuna Way" exemplifies how Gita-based wisdom can transform everyday challenges into opportunities for spiritual advancement. The Dvaita understanding that the phenomenal world is as real as the spiritual realm means that our professional duties, family obligations, and social responsibilities are not obstacles to overcome but sacred territories where Krishna consciousness can be cultivated. This perspective transforms the workplace into a temple and every interaction into potential seva (service).

‖ श्री वीरविठ्ठलो विजयते ‖

Sri Sri Sugunendra Theertha Swamiji

Jagadguru Srimanmadhwaachaarya moola mahaa samsthaanam
Srimad Upendra Theertha Peetham, Sri Puthige Matha,Udupi - 576 101,Karnataka, INDIA
Email : puthigeshree@gmail.com, www.sreeputhige.org

This work focuses on transforming knowledge into practical wisdom, and that resonates with our tradition's understanding that authentic spiritual progress must be measurable in daily life. We believe that our dharmic responsibilities in this world serve our ultimate spiritual evolution.

As devotees and seekers engage with this profound work, we suggest approaching it as you would any sacred study-with reverence for the source texts, and commitment to consistent practice. The seven paths outlined provide a structured approach to spiritual development that honors both individual inquiry and traditional wisdom. Most importantly, allow these teachings to awaken your innate devotion to Sri Krishna, for it is through such bhakti that all spiritual practices find their ultimate fulfillment.

As we continue our mission to spread the universal message of the Bhagavad Gita during this Vishwa Gita Paryaya, we are grateful for dedicated individuals like Sri Mahesh Harvu who contribute to making Krishna's timeless wisdom accessible to modern seekers.

Udupi Sri Krishna has blessed our Puthige Matha with continuous darshan for eight centuries, and we pray for His divine grace to all.

H.H. Sri Sri Sri Sugunendra Theertha Swamiji
30th Pontiff
Jagadguru Sri Madhvacharya Moola Maha Samsthanam
Sri Puthige Matha, Udupi
International President, Religions for Peace
Currently serving the Fourth Paryaya (2024-2026)

18-09-2025
Thursday

Vishwavasu
Bhadrapada
Krishna Dwadashi

vii

Phone : 0821-2422536

ಶ್ರೀ ಬ್ರಹ್ಮತಂತ್ರ ಸ್ವತಂತ್ರ ಪರಕಾಲಸ್ವಾಮಿ ಮಠ

ಕೃಷ್ಣವಿಲಾಸ ರಸ್ತೆ, (ಜಗನ್ಮೋಹನ ಅರಮನೆ ಸಮೀಪ), ದೇವರಾಜ ಮೊಹಲ್ಲಾ,
ಮೈಸೂರು - 570024.

SRI BRAHMATANTRA SWATANTRA PARAKALA SWAMY MUTT

Krishnavilasa Road (Near J.M. Palace), Devaraja Mohalla, Mysore - 570 024, Karnataka State, INDIA

ಶ್ರೀ ಲಕ್ಷ್ಮೀಹಯವದನ ಲಕ್ಷ್ಮೀನಾರಾಯಣಾಭ್ಯಾಂ ನಮಃ	Sree Lakshmi Hayavadana Lakshmi Narayanabhyam Namaha
ಶ್ರೀಮತೆ ರಾಮಾನುಜಾಯ ನಮಃ	Sreemathe Ramanujaya Namaha
ಶ್ರೀಮತೇ ನಿಗಮಾಂತ ಮಹಾದೇಶಿಕಾಯ ನಮಃ	Srimathe Nigamantha Maha Desikaya Namaha
ಶ್ರೀ ಬ್ರಹ್ಮತಂತ್ರ ಸ್ವತಂತ್ರ ಪರಕಾಲ ಗುರು ಪರಂಪರಾಯೈ ನಮಃ	Sri Brahmatantra Swatantra Parakala Gruruparamparayai Namaha

Date: October 6th, 2025

sri

ACHARYA'S DIVYA SANDESHAM

"The Arjuna Way" is one of the finest works, and is based on the Bhagavad Gita and Upanishads, with the practical realities of contemporary life needed nowadays – from youth to old age.

This book is written by Shri Mahesh Harvu, who is one of the best disciples of the founder of the Sri Brahmatantra Swatantra Parakala Jeeyar under the guidance of Sri Vedantha Deshikar.

In this book, the author's real knowledge is unimaginable and he also distinguishes between spirituality, religious practice, and cultural tradition – reflects not just for all of India but also all over the World readers.

The blessings of Lord Sri Lakshmi Hayagreeva and Sri Brahmatantra Swantantra Parakala Guruparamparas Anugraham to Shri Mahesh Harvu's family.

By Acharya's Order,
E.V.Veeraraghavachar
SRI KARYAKARTHA
Sri Brahmatantra Swatantra
Parakala Swamy Mutt, Mysore

narayana smrtyaha
H.H. Srimad Abhinava Vageesha
Brahmatantra Parakala Swamiji
Sri Brahmatantra Swatantra
Parakala Swamy Mutt
Mysore, Karnataka State, India

ix

Who Was Arjuna

IN THE ANCIENT EPIC OF THE BHAGAVAD GITA, shared around 5,000 years ago, Arjuna stands as one of history's most compelling spiritual seekers, not because he was perfect, but because he was profoundly, wonderfully human.

Arjuna possessed everything our society considers impressive: exceptional talents, worldly success, and noble lineage. He was a celebrated warrior-prince, skilled beyond measure, disciplined in his practices, and blessed with divine Krishna as his charioteer.

Yet when facing life's most crucial decision, whether to fight in a righteous war against his cousins, this accomplished warrior became paralyzed entirely by doubt and confusion.

The Moment of Crisis

Standing on the battlefield of Kurukshetra, Arjuna surveyed the opposing army and saw not just enemies, but beloved teachers, respected elders, and family members. Despite his training, despite his righteousness, despite having divine guidance right beside him, he found himself overwhelmed by questions that had no easy answers. His concerns were both practical and profound:

- What will be the real consequences of this war?

- How can I harm those I love and respect?

- What does it truly mean to do the right thing?

- How do I act when I can't see the bigger picture?

We see this extraordinary quality in an ordinary human struggle. Arjuna experiences the fundamental tension between knowing and doing, between emotion and wisdom. He shows remarkable clarity in some moments and profound confusion in others.

Doesn't that sound familiar?

In that moment of total confusion, Arjuna made the most courageous decision of his life. He laid down his weapons, turned to Krishna, and said, "I am confused about my duty. Please teach me what is best for me."

The Art of Authentic Seeking

What makes Arjuna truly special isn't his impressive resume— it's his willingness to admit confusion in the face of life's complexity and his exceptional ability to truly listen for guidance.

Throughout the Gita, Arjuna demonstrates a rare ability: the capacity to quiet his mental chatter and genuinely absorb Krishna's wisdom. His questions aren't defensive or argumentative. They stem from genuine curiosity. Instead of pretending he has all the answers or defending his position, he creates space for real learning to happen.

If there's one lesson from Arjuna's transformation, it's this: the willingness to say "I don't know" as a means to open the door to genuine understanding. His deep, receptive listening—not the half-hearted listening most of us do while preparing our response—allowed him to receive Krishna's most profound teachings. By the end of their dialogue, Arjuna could declare:

My confusion is dispelled, and I have regained my memory. I stand firm, free from doubt, and am prepared to act according to your instruction.

Your Connection to Arjuna

Arjuna's struggles mirror the inner battles we all face. The battlefield may be different, but the essence remains the same. We all encounter moments when life's complexity paralyzes us, when we must make important decisions without being able to see all the consequences.

THE ARJUNA WAY draws from the same timeless wisdom that transformed a confused warrior into an awakened being. The ancient guidance that helped him find clarity during chaos is available to help you navigate your own complex decisions and challenging moments.

YOUR JOURNEY BEGINS BY DEMONSTRATING A SIMILAR COURAGE AS ARJUNA — THE WILLINGNESS TO ADMIT UNCERTAINTY AND REMAIN OPEN TO GUIDANCE.

Introduction

THERE COMES A MOMENT IN EVERY SEEKER'S life when the surface of existence no longer satisfies, and you find yourself questioning everything you've been told about spirituality, religion, and what it means to live a meaningful life.

Perhaps you feel like you're living two lives: one where you go through the motions of traditional religious practices to appease family and society, and another where you're dealing with the real challenges of modern life, wondering if these two worlds can ever come together. Perhaps this split originated from your upbringing, leaving you to wonder how to bridge these separate worlds.

You get busy dealing with real-world challenges, the way the material world works, and when things don't go the way you prefer, you find yourself attributing it to karma or feeling helpless while hoping that an invisible God will do justice at some point, but deep down, you know these explanations don't really satisfy you anymore.

Like Arjuna on the battlefield, you find yourself at a crossroads, not just of circumstances, but of your very ability to address or deal with the circumstance. The old answers no longer work. The inherited beliefs feel hollow. The mechanical rituals provide no real nourishment. You're ready for something authentic that speaks to the very core of who you are.

But where do you start? How do you finally stop living two lives? How do you bring these divided worlds into one integrated life? How do you distinguish between what's real and what's just tradition? What's the difference between blind faith and genuine spiritual development? How do you know if your prayers actually mean anything, or if you're talking to yourself?

THE ARJUNA WAY starts exactly where you are, with these honest questions and the real challenge of making clear decisions when you're pulled in different directions. We begin with the basics: What is spirituality? How is it different from religion? What role should tradition play in your life? What does it actually mean to connect with the divine? What does prayer really mean, and how can you develop a faith-based discipline that's realistic and helps you connect with your daily reality?

Instead of giving you more things to believe, this book helps you develop something much more valuable: the ability to discern truth for yourself. You'll learn to distinguish between practices that genuinely build your spiritual strength and those that merely make you feel comfortable. Between teachers who help you grow and those who want to keep you dependent. Between devotion that transforms you and rituals that waste your time.

As we clear away this confusion together, something remarkable happens. You start developing what I call your spiritual core, that inner strength and clarity that doesn't waver when life gets challenging. This isn't about escaping the world or spending hours in meditation. It's about becoming the kind of person who can handle whatever comes with wisdom, compassion, and genuine confidence.

You'll learn to see people for who they truly are, beyond just their surface behavior. You'll learn to make decisions from a place of inner knowing rather than fear or confusion. This applies when you're facing relationship challenges, navigating difficult choices in your professional life, or trying to balance competing demands from family and career. When someone tries to manipulate you or when you face a difficult choice, you'll have the spiritual maturity to respond appropriately.

This development happens naturally as you work through the practical exercises and insights drawn from the Bhagavad Gita and Upanishads. These aren't ancient relics. They're tested methods for building the kind of inner strength that serves you in relationships, at work, in family, and in every other area of life.

Whether you're naturally skeptical or naturally inclined to believe, whether you come from a religious background or consider yourself secular, we'll start with what's real and build from there. No blind faith required, just honest inquiry and a willingness to develop the spiritual capacity that's already within YOU.

YOUR JOURNEY FROM CONFUSION TO CLARITY BEGINS ON THE NEXT PAGE.

Author's Note

THE BOOK IS DIVIDED into *seven distinct paths,* each containing *multiple explorations* that expand on spiritual aphorisms. The number **seven** holds profound symbolic significance in spiritual philosophy, as it is a powerful symbol of cosmic order, spiritual evolution, and ritual completeness, exemplified in concepts such as the seven worlds, seven chakras, seven seers, and the seven sacred vows of marriage.

Each exploration constitutes a chapter, unfolding a systematic learning journey and follows a consistent four-part structure:

1. **Opening** - Introduction to the concept

2. **Let's Deep Dive** - Detailed Exploration

3. **Summary** - Key takeaways

4. **Start Today: Your First Step** - Practical Application

Learning Integration:

Following the traditional Gita and Upanishadic method of *sravana* (listening), *manana* (contemplation), and *nidhidhyasa* (practice), the book creates a complete learning cycle:

- **Chapter content** facilitates *sravana* (absorption of knowledge)

- **Start Today** sections encourage *manana* (reflection and contemplation)

- **Reflection Exercises** enable *nidhidhyasa* (contemplation and practical application)

Sanskrit terms appear in *italics*, accompanied by their English meanings. Gita verses are in *italics*. A comprehensive glossary serves as a quick reference guide to the Sanskrit terms.

PART ONE

The Spiritual Essentials

Understanding Divinity

BEYOND THE THRONE IN THE SKY

DEBATES ABOUT DIVINITY often begin with familiar images: perhaps a mystical figure sitting on a celestial throne, sorting through countless prayers like emails in an inbox, deciding which ones to answer based on some mysterious criteria. The throne-in-the-sky concept is deeply embedded in popular culture and certain traditions, but it's not the only way to understand DIVINITY.

Our journey in these pages will explore a different conception of the divine, rooted in the profound wisdom of the Upanishads and the Bhagavad Gita. The Upanishadic understanding doesn't place divinity somewhere "out there" in a heavenly realm, separate from our world. Instead, it recognizes divinity as an all-pervasive energy that constitutes the fabric of existence, a dynamic interplay of fundamental elements and qualities that manifest in infinite forms throughout the cosmos.

By shifting our perspective from a personified deity to this expansive vision of divine energy, we open ourselves to a deeper relationship with the sacred dimension of life. We begin to see divinity not just in designated holy places or special moments, but in the extraordinary miracle of ordinary existence—every breath, every interaction, and every moment of awareness.

Let's Dive Deeper

Before fully grasping this understanding of divinity, we must set aside some of our habitual ways of thinking. When contemplating the divine, our minds naturally gravitate toward concrete images and human-like figures. Nothing is wrong with these visual representations, as they can be powerful focal points for devotion and contemplation. But the Upanishadic vision invites us to look beyond these forms to the formless energy that gives rise to all forms.

When you look at the ocean, you might focus on a particular wave, appreciating its unique shape and movement. But that wave is inseparable from the vast body of water from which it arises. Similarly, specific divine forms or representations can be understood as expressions of a boundless divine energy that transcends yet includes all particular manifestations.

The Upanishads and the Gita offer a sophisticated framework for understanding this divine energy, not through simplistic definitions or dogmatic assertions but through a careful exploration of the fundamental elements and qualities that constitute existence. They invite us to recognize divinity not as something foreign to our experience but as the very ground of our being.

Let's begin our exploration of divinity as cosmic energy — a perspective that may expand our spiritual horizons in unexpected and transformative ways.

What Is Divinity? The Cosmic Energy

In the vision of the Upanishads and the Bhagavad Gita, divinity isn't a heavenly figure managing the universe from afar. It's not an entity that receives and responds to prayers based on merit or worthiness. While meaningful to many, the concept of a celestial manager doesn't capture the profound understanding of divinity in these ancient texts.

Instead, divinity is understood as a form of energy: a dynamic, all-pervasive presence that constitutes the very fabric of existence. If you're struggling to visualize this concept, imagine a vast, boundless field of energy or light. Divine energy isn't just a physical force but encompasses all dimensions of reality: physical, mental, emotional, and spiritual.

To help us comprehend this abstract concept, the ancient texts describe divinity in terms of attributes and characteristics. Rather than defining divine energy by its appearance, they identify what it consists of and how it manifests throughout the cosmos. The sacred isn't something separate from the world but is the essential nature of everything.

The Two Types of Energy

According to the Bhagavad Gita, cosmic energy manifests in two fundamental forms. The first is what the Gita calls "material energy," or what we might consider inferior energy. This comprises the physical elements and forces that make up the tangible universe, everything that can be perceived with our senses.

The second form is what we might call the "superior energy" or the soul energy. This is the consciousness or awareness that animates living beings and the knowing principle that enables us to experience, be aware of, and recognize ourselves as existing. While distinct from material energy, this soul energy isn't separate from the divine; instead, it's a higher expression of the same cosmic energy.

These energies aren't separate. They're different aspects or expressions of the same fundamental divine reality. But distinguishing between them helps us understand how the divine manifests in various dimensions of existence.

The Eight Fundamental Components

The Bhagavad Gita provides a fascinating framework for understanding the composition of the divine energy. According to this sacred text, eight fundamental components form the foundation of the entire cosmic universe:

Earth, water, fire, air, space, mind, intellect, and I (or ego).

Notice how Gita's list begins with the physical elements—earth, water, fire, air, and space, which correspond roughly to the states of matter and the medium in which they exist. These are the building blocks of the material world, the tangible reality we experience through our senses.

But the list doesn't stop there. It continues with mind, intellect, and "I" elements that belong to the realm of consciousness and awareness rather than the physical realm. The mind perceives and feels; the intellect discerns and decides; and the "I" or ego provides the sense of individual identity and agency.

By including physical and conscious elements in this list, the Gita suggests that divinity encompasses both matter and consciousness, that is, the known and the knower, the object and the subject. Divinity isn't just the stuff of the universe; it's the awareness that experiences it. These eight components, which the Gita refers to as *dravya* or substance, form the foundation upon which all existence is built. They're not separate from divinity but constitute its fundamental nature.

The Twenty Emotions and Infinite Combinations

The Gita describes twenty different emotions or qualities from these eight fundamental components. These aren't just human feelings but cosmic principles manifesting in various forms and degrees throughout existence. These twenty emotions span the entire spectrum of our lived experience. They include:

- The ability to analyze things in their proper perspective

- The capacity to discriminate between the spiritual and the material

- The faculty to make decisions in states of confusion

- The quality of forgiveness and the virtue of compassion

- The adherence to truth and honesty

- The capacity for sensory restraint and self-control

- The ability to manage sorrow, affliction, joy, and delight

- The experience of confronting death

- The quality of fearlessness in overcoming difficulties, and many more.

These twenty qualities aren't rigidly separate categories but fluid aspects of the divine energy that intermingle and combine in countless ways. They are primary colors that blend to create an infinite palette of hues, tones, and shades. The combinations and permutations of these twenty qualities, emerging from the eight fundamental components, are limitless in number.

When we consider all possible combinations of these elements and qualities, we catch a glimpse of the boundless nature of divinity. The divine isn't limited to a single form or expression. Still, it manifests in endless variety throughout the cosmos, from the grandeur of galaxies to the intricate dance of subatomic particles, from the majesty of mountains to the mystery of consciousness.

Packaging Infinity: The Supreme

When we combine all these eight fundamental components, twenty different emotions or qualities, and their infinite permutations and combinations, and try to conceptualize them as a whole, we arrive at what we can call the divine or the supreme.

The Upanishads and the Gita refer to this as *paramatma* or divinity. It is not a separate being from the world, but the essential nature of all that exists. Of course, putting a conceptual "box" around this infinite reality is only a way of speaking about it. By its very nature, our limited minds cannot contain or fully comprehend the divine. It's boundless, endless, without beginning or end. Any definition or description we offer can only point toward this reality without fully capturing it.

For this reason, the Upanishads often describe the divine through paradox and negation. It is "not this, not that" (*neti neti*), bigger than the biggest, smaller than the smallest, farther than the farthest, yet closer than our breath. These seemingly contradictory statements aren't meant to confuse but to liberate our minds from the limitations of ordinary thinking, opening us to a more direct apprehension of divine reality.

From Formless to Form: Understanding Gods

Once you understand divinity as this infinite cosmic energy, you might wonder how we get from this formless conception to the many gods and deities in Hindu traditions. Here's where things get interesting.

When we define a name and form for divinity, or even just for some subset of its characteristics, we create what we might call a deity, or what the Sanskrit language terms a *deva*. Naming and forming divine aspects help us relate to infinite aspects in ways our minds can grasp.

Think of it this way: divinity is akin to a vast, universal library containing all knowledge, wisdom, and possibilities. Each deity is like a specialized section of this library, helping us access and understand particular aspects of this infinite knowledge. While the entire library may overwhelm us, we can engage meaningfully with specific sections based on our current needs and interests. Yet, each section remains fundamentally connected to and inseparable from the whole.

If we attempt to give a name and form to the entire set of divine characteristics (the omnipresent, omnipotent, all-knowing reality), we might refer to it as *ishvara* or *bhagavan*, as described in the Gita. These terms indicate divinity with a personal form that encompasses everything.

On the other hand, if we prefer to keep the concept impersonal without a specific name and form, we might use terms such as *paramatma* (the Supreme Soul) or *brahman* (the Absolute), as described in the Upanishads.

Another name for a divinity with an all-encompassing personal form is *narayana*, which means "the abode of everything," the space where everything and everyone dwells. When this same supreme deity emphasizes qualities of motherhood, compassion, forgiveness, and nurturing aspects of a loving mother, we refer to the deity as *lakshmi*.

The Emergence of Specific Deities

The fascinating aspect of this approach is how it helps us understand the emergence of numerous deities across traditions. Take *rudra* (often interpreted as *shiva*) as an example. The eleven sense faculties are collectively responsible for all our emotions and experiences. These include five subtle sense organs (sight, hearing, smell, taste, and touch), five physical organs of action (speech, hands, feet, organs of procreation, and excretion), and the mind. When given a name and form, the set of characteristics becomes *rudra*.

Similarly, when we focus on just one aspect of divine function, like removing obstacles, we create another specific deity. By giving a name and form to this particular characteristic, we obtain *ganesha* or *ganapati*, the deity traditionally associated with clearing paths and removing impediments. This same divine function appears in different Hindu traditions; those who maintain unwavering devotion to the supreme being *narayana*, for instance, associate *vishwaksena* with removing obstacles.

The development of specific deities isn't arbitrary or merely cultural; it reflects a profound understanding of how the human mind works, since we connect more easily with specificity than with abstraction. By giving names and forms to particular aspects of divinity, we create connection points, allowing us to relate to cosmic principles in a personal and meaningful way.

Over centuries, various combinations of divine characteristics have been attributed to human-like forms, resulting in the rich pantheon of deities found in many Hindu traditions. Each deity represents a subset of divine attributes, making infinite divinity accessible to finite human understanding.

When we invoke these deities, we're not just engaging with imaginary figures but connecting with specific aspects of a greater reality. When we think of *narayana*, we contemplate the all-powerful, all-encompassing divine. When we invoke *lakshmi*, we connect with divine compassion and abundance. Each deity provides a doorway to particular aspects of the divine that may be especially relevant to our needs or circumstances.

Through this personification process, we arrive at the concept of "God" as a "giver on demand"—we make requests to specific manifestations of divinity, hoping they'll respond to our prayers.

Experiencing the Divine in Daily Life

What might appear as an abstract or philosophical perspective has profound practical implications for how we live and experience our daily lives. When we recognize divinity as the fundamental energy constituting all of existence, we begin to see the sacred dimension in ordinary experiences.

The divine isn't sequestered in temples or accessible only through special rituals or practices. It's the ground of being present in every moment, breath, and interaction. The challenge isn't to find the divine but to remove the veils that prevent us from recognizing what is already here.

Recognizing divinity as the fundamental energy transforms our relationship with ourselves, others, and the world. We begin to see that the same divine energy that constitutes our being also constitutes everything and everyone else. The boundaries that seem to separate us from each other and the rest of existence are revealed as relative rather than absolute.

Acknowledging our divine nature doesn't mean denying our individuality or the world's apparent multiplicity. Instead, it means recognizing that our expressions are unique manifestations of the same underlying reality, like waves arising from and returning to the same ocean.

Living with this awareness doesn't require us to withdraw from the world or engage in elaborate spiritual practices (though such practices can certainly support our journey). It is an invitation for us to be present in what is, to recognize the extraordinary miracle of ordinary existence, and to relate to all beings with the reverence appropriate to their divine nature.

Summary: Divinity as Cosmic Energy

Let's recap what we've explored in this chapter:

- According to the Upanishads and the Bhagavad Gita, divinity isn't a heavenly figure managing the universe from afar but a cosmic energy constituting the fabric of existence.

- This divine energy manifests in two forms: material energy (comprising physical elements) and soul energy (comprising consciousness).

- Eight fundamental components: earth, water, fire, air, space, mind, intellect, and I form the foundation of the cosmic universe.

- Twenty different emotions or qualities span the entire spectrum of experience from these eight components.

- The combinations and permutations of these components and qualities are infinite, reflecting the boundless nature of divinity.

- When we conceptualize all of this, we arrive at what the ancient texts call *paramatma*, the supreme, all-encompassing, transcendent, and inherent reality.

- When we give names and forms to specific aspects or subsets of divine characteristics, we create deities (*devas*) that help us relate to particular facets of the infinite.

- Major deities like *rudra (shiva), ganesha, and vishwaksena* represent different combinations of divine attributes, making the abstract concrete and the infinite accessible.

- The cosmic energy perspective of divinity transforms our relationship with ourselves, others, and the world, inviting us to recognize the sacred dimension in ordinary existence.

The divine isn't something to be sought elsewhere but the very ground of our being, not a distant authority but the innermost essence of all that exists. By shifting our perspective from a personified deity to this more expansive vision of divine energy, we open ourselves to a deeper, more intimate relationship with the sacred dimension of life.

Start Today: Your First Step

If there's one action I encourage you to take right now, it's this: **Practice Conscious Connection with the Elements.**

Conscious connection invites you to experience your intimate relationship with the fundamental components of existence. By consciously connecting with these elements, you begin to recognize yourself not as separate from the cosmos but as an integral expression of the same divine energy that constitutes all of reality.

Here's how to begin:

Think of this as a 5-10 minute check-in with yourself and the world around you. Find a spot where you won't be interrupted: your bedroom, a quiet corner, anywhere you can be for a few minutes. Get comfortable. Sit however feels natural, though keeping your back reasonably straight helps you stay alert. Take a few deep breaths and let yourself settle.

Think about the qualities and characteristics that matter most to you right now. What draws you? The strength to face difficulties? Is it compassion? Courage? Wisdom? Forgiveness? The ability to remain calm in chaos? The capacity for unconditional love? The joy that lifts others?

Notice how these relate to the twenty emotions and characteristics we discussed earlier in this chapter. Feel these qualities—notice which ones resonate most deeply with you. Then ask yourself: If I were to give these characteristics a name and form, who or what would embody them?

Maybe it's Krishna, a beloved teacher, someone in your own life, or even a force of nature. *Let the name and form emerge naturally from the qualities you've been contemplating.*

Here's the provocative question: Does it make a difference if we approach divinity from the elements and energies first, building toward a name and form? Or does it feel different when we start with the name and form and try to understand the elements behind it?

When you start with a specific deity or person, you might see them as separate, as something "out there" to aspire to. But when you work from the inside out, from elements to characteristics to form, something shifts. You realize you're not worshipping something foreign. You're recognizing different expressions of the same cosmic energy that constitutes you.

We will revisit this practice in a slightly different manner in the chapter on Theism. The intention in this chapter is to help you get started and understand divinity from the core, ground up, and not just as a personified individual.

Now, try something different: We're going to notice what's already there. One element at a time.

- **Earth:** Feel your body. Not in an abstract way, but really feel it. Your bones support you. Your muscles hold you upright. The physical aspects that make you who you are. All these solid parts of you? They came from the earth and will return to it. You're literally made of the same stuff as the ground beneath your feet. *Think: "The earth and I are the same thing."*

- **Fire:** Pay attention to the warmth of your body. That's energy, the same kind of energy that makes the sun shine and cooks your dinner. Your body constantly transforms food into energy, burning fuel to sustain life. *Recognize: "I'm carrying the same fire as the sun."*

- **Mind:** Watch your mind doing its thing for a moment. Thoughts, feelings, sensations are all happening right now. That capacity you have to notice, to feel, to experience? It's connected to the same intelligence that keeps planets orbiting and seasons changing. *Notice: "My awareness is part of a cosmic awareness."*

After connecting with these elements, please take a moment to feel them all at once. You're not just a body or just a mind. You're this amazing, unique arrangement of universal elements and energies. Finish by saying thanks, however that feels natural to you. Thanks for being alive. Thanks for this moment of recognition. Thanks for being part of this wild, interconnected universe.

Try this for a few days, just once a day. Don't make it complicated. You might notice something shift. That stranger at the airport may seem a little less strange, or your morning coffee tastes different when you realize you're connected to the water in it, the fire that heated it, and the air around it. The line between "ordinary" and "extraordinary" starts to blur.

You don't have to get it perfect. You don't have to achieve anything. You're just recognizing what's already true. You've always belonged to this cosmic whole. Separation was never absolute.

REMEMBER, DAILY PRACTICE ISN'T ABOUT ACHIEVING SOME SPECIAL STATE OR EXPERIENCE. IT'S SIMPLY ABOUT RECOGNIZING WHAT'S ALREADY TRUE—YOUR INTIMATE CONNECTION WITH THE DIVINE ENERGY THAT CONSTITUTES ALL EXISTENCE.

Getting Closer to God

REMEMBER THE LAST TIME you were with someone you truly trusted? That wonderful feeling when you can just be yourself, no need to watch your words, maintain appearances, or worry about being judged. There's a special kind of freedom in those relationships, a space where you can laugh out loud, share your wildest ideas, or even cry without embarrassment. The masks come off, and a genuine connection happens.

I've been thinking a lot lately about how our relationship with the divine could be exactly like that, but it often isn't.

For many of us, our approach to spirituality has been shaped by a sense of formality and distance. We've been taught to approach God with carefully chosen words, proper behaviors, and a sense of unworthiness. But what if that's not what God wants from us at all?

What if the divine is waiting for us to drop the formalities and show up authentically with all our doubts, messiness, confusion, and joy?

Let's Dive Deeper

In the Bhagavad Gita, there's a decisive moment that perfectly captures this idea. Arjuna, the great warrior, suddenly realizes he's been taking his closeness with Lord Krishna for granted. He's made mistakes, spoken carelessly, and perhaps even been disrespectful. In a moment of profound humility, he pleads for forgiveness, saying: "Krishna, pardon me like a father pardons a son, a friend forgives a friend, a lover pardons a loved one."

This simple statement reveals something extraordinary—that our relationship with the divine can take multiple forms, each offering a different kind of intimacy. When we understand these various dimensions of connection, we open ourselves to a spiritual relationship that's richer, more authentic, and more transformative than we ever imagined possible.

Let's explore these models of divine relationship together and discover how they might transform your spiritual journey.

The Father-Son Relationship: Divine Guidance with Playful Trust

Think about a child with a loving father. What freedom that child enjoys! They can be silly, stubborn, curious, or even naughty and still be completely secure in their father's love. There's no need for the child to be perfect or to hide their true nature. They are, and that's enough.

When we relate to the divine as a loving father (or parent), we step into that same freedom. We no longer need to approach spirituality as if we're constantly being evaluated or judged. Instead, we can bring our whole selves, including our questions, our resistance, and even our spiritual tantrums into the relationship.

When my son was 5 years old, I recall how he would run around, occasionally checking in with me before dashing off on another adventure. At one point, he fell and scraped his knee. Without hesitation, he came straight to me, and I scooped him up, comforted him, and then sent him back out to play once the tears had dried. There was complete trust between us; my son knew his father would provide protection and freedom.

Our relationship with the divine can mirror this beautiful dynamic. We can run freely through life, exploring and growing, knowing we can return for guidance, comfort, and wisdom when needed. The divine parent doesn't demand perfection; only genuine connection is required.

This father-son aspect of the divine relationship also permits us to be playful in our spirituality. Prayers don't have to be solemn and serious all the time, and meditation isn't always about stillness and silence. Sometimes, our spiritual practice can be joyful, spontaneous, and even a bit naughty, like a child playing in the presence of a loving parent.

Arjuna's relationship with Krishna often reflected this dynamic. He would sometimes question Krishna's wisdom, occasionally resist his guidance, and freely express his confusion and delight in their interactions. Yet, through it all, Krishna maintained a patient love and continued to guide Arjuna toward greater understanding. To cultivate this aspect of divine relationship in your own life, you might:

- Approach prayer with childlike directness rather than formal language

- Bring your questions and doubts honestly before God

- Trust in divine guidance even when the path forward seems unclear

- Allow yourself to experience spiritual joy without self-consciousness

- Rest in the security of unconditional love

When was the last time you approached the divine with the trusting openness of a child? What might change if you allowed yourself that freedom?

The Friend-Friend Relationship: Divine Companionship with Honest Exchange

Now imagine sitting with your closest friend. You know, the one you can tell anything to without fear of judgment. With this person, there's no need for pretense or impression management. You can share your wildest dreams, darkest thoughts, or just the mundane details of your day. There is a comfortable equality between you and mutual respect that allows for complete honesty.

This is the second model Arjuna presents: friendship with the divine. And it's revolutionary when you think about it—the idea that we might approach God not from a position of subservience but as a trusted companion walking alongside us through life.

True friendship has remarkable transparency. There are no secrets, no need for formal protocols, political diplomacy, or false correctness between genuine friends. Friends speak truthfully to one another, knowing the relationship is strong enough to withstand honesty. There is an openness and authenticity that allows both parties to be fully themselves.

Krishna and Arjuna exemplified this spiritual friendship. Throughout much of the Gita, they're in a chariot together, side by side, facing life's challenges as companions. Krishna didn't demand formal worship or subservience from Arjuna; instead, they conversed freely, sharing ordinary moments and extraordinary insights.

When we cultivate a friendship with the divine, something remarkable happens: God becomes accessible in a whole new way, no longer a distant power to be appeased, but a close companion on our daily journey. We begin to share our thoughts freely, listen attentively for divine wisdom, and walk through life with an awareness of the sacred presence beside us.

I've experienced this myself during difficult decisions in my life. Rather than approaching prayer with formal petitions, I've had honest conversations with the divine, laying out my confusion, asking for clarity, and sometimes even expressing frustration. And in that space of authentic exchange, I've often found wisdom emerging not as a thunderous command from above but as gentle insight from a trusted friend.

This model of divine friendship offers several unique spiritual benefits:

- It enables honest communication without fear of judgment

- It creates space for questioning and spiritual exploration

- It infuses ordinary moments with sacred presence

- It provides companionship in life's lonely passages

- It establishes a foundation of trust and mutual respect

To develop this dimension of divine relationship, you might practice:

- Conversational prayer to share daily experiences

- Mindful awareness of divine presence in ordinary activities

- Honest expression of doubts and struggles

- Attentive listening for spiritual insight

- Cultivating gratitude for divine companionship

How might your spiritual life change if you approached the divine as your closest friend? What would you talk about? What questions would you finally feel comfortable asking?

The Lover Relationship: Divine Devotion with Complete Absorption

The third relationship model takes us into even deeper intimacy, that of the devotee as lover and the divine as beloved. The lover relationship is perhaps the most intense and all-consuming spiritual relationship, characterized by complete absorption in the divine.

Think about being deeply in love. In that state, the beloved is never absent from your thoughts. You carry them everywhere, seeing reminders of them in the most unexpected places. Their absence brings sorrow; their presence brings joy. You would do anything for them, and your love is expressed through kindness, generosity, and devotion. The relationship between the spiritual lover and the divine beloved is a profound connection that transforms every aspect of life.

The story of Andal and Ranganatha (one of Krishna's manifestations) is a beautiful tale of divine devotion. Andal, a young woman in ancient South India, dedicated her entire being to Lord Ranganatha. She filled her home with his images and spoke to him as if he were physically present in her life. "He is my only beloved," she would say with complete conviction. Her face would light up when composing poetry for her divine husband, and every action, including weaving garlands and writing hymns, was an act of love. She would wear the garlands herself before offering them to the Lord, symbolizing their special bond. Her absorption in Ranganatha was so complete that, according to tradition, she eventually merged with her beloved, transcending her physical form to unite with the divine in eternal union.

Arjuna experienced this lover's devotion to Krishna. The divine was always in his thoughts, shaping his perceptions and decisions. He felt genuine sorrow when Krishna was not present and deep pleasure in his company. This complete absorption transformed Arjuna's entire way of being in the world. The spiritual lover relationship represents devotion or *bhakti*. It is characterized by:

- A single-minded focus on the divine

- Emotional intensity in spiritual practice

- Willingness to sacrifice for the beloved

- Constant remembrance of divine presence

- Profound longing for communion

- It represents a love that consumes the devotee, turning all thoughts and actions toward the divine

To cultivate this lover's relationship with God, you might:

- Practice constant remembrance through sacred mantras

- Keep images or symbols that evoke divine presence

- Express devotion through sacred music, poetry, or dance

- Develop practices that nurture divine communion

- Surrender personal desires in favor of divine will

Have you ever experienced moments of this lover's devotion to the divine? Perhaps in moments of profound beauty in nature, during deep meditation, or in times of intense gratitude? How might you nurture that connection in your daily life?

The Parent-Child Relationship: Divine Nurturing with Role Reversal

The fourth relationship offers a fascinating reversal. It is the relationship where the divine becomes the child, and the devotee becomes the parent. This unusual dynamic creates yet another dimension of spiritual connection.

Imagine the tenderness a parent feels for their child, the protective care, the generous giving, the willing sacrifice. In this relationship, the devotee experiences that same nurturing love toward the divine, creating a unique bond of care and offering.

In this relationship, the devotee dotes on the divine child, protects, and gives their best. Just as a parent feeds their child before eating themselves, the true devotee first offers to the divine before partaking of it. The devotee focuses on nurturing and honoring the divine presence in their life.

We find examples of this parent-child dynamic with the divine in many homes. Devotees care for the idol of baby Krishna with tender attention, bathing the image, dressing it in tiny clothes, offering food, and singing lullabies.

At the Sri Krishna Temple in Udupi, India, the priest carefully performs the bathing and decoration (*abhisheka*) ritual for Lord Krishna, his face displaying the same concentrated care you might see on a mother bathing her infant. When the priest finishes the sacred bathing ceremony, he gently dries and dresses Krishna, softly chanting mantras. There is something profoundly moving about witnessing this expression of spiritual love—the divine not as a mighty overlord but as a beloved child receiving tender care. This relationship offers several spiritual benefits:

- It cultivates generosity and selflessness

- It transforms material consumption into a sacred offering

- It develops nurturing qualities in the devotee

- It creates an intimate, protective connection with the divine

- It establishes rituals of care that sanctify daily life

To develop this dimension of spiritual relationship, you might practice:

- Making offerings of food before eating

- Dedicating a sacred space in the home for divine "care."

- Offering the first fruits of your labor or creativity

- Developing rituals that honor and nurture divine presence

- Approaching spiritual practice with protective attention

How might this reversal of roles, in which you see yourself as the caretaker of the divine, shift your understanding of spirituality? What qualities might it develop in you?

Fusion: The Multidimensional Divine Relationship

The brilliance of Arjuna's plea to Krishna lies in its recognition that divine relationships are not one-dimensional. We need not choose between these models of connection. We should adopt a mature spiritual life that embraces all four dimensions, allowing them to enrich and balance one another.

Think about your closest human relationships. With your partner, parent, child, or dearest friend, you likely move fluidly between different modes of relating. Sometimes, you need guidance; sometimes, you offer it. There are moments of playful companionship, periods of passionate connection, and times of nurturing care. The relationship breathes and shifts according to circumstances and needs.

Our relationship with the divine can have this same dynamic flexibility. There will be seasons when we most need the guidance of a divine Father, times when the companionship of a divine Friend sustains us, periods when the passion of a spiritual lover animates our practice, and moments when the care of the divine Child grounds us in sacred service.

By cultivating all four relationships, we develop a resilient spiritual life that responds to our changing needs. We create space within our divine connection for the full range of human experience, from dependency to equality, passion to nurturing.

I've noticed this in my spiritual journey. During times of confusion or major life decisions, I naturally gravitate toward the father-child relationship, seeking guidance and direction. In my daily life, friendship provides companionship and conversation. In moments of deep meditation or profound gratitude, I experience the lover's absorption. And in my regular practice of offering and service, I embody the parent caring for the divine child.

When we integrate these relationships, all barriers between ourselves and the divine begin to dissolve. We move beyond formal religious observance into true spiritual intimacy. In this relationship, we can be completely authentic with the divine and experience the sacred as fully present in our lives.

Summary: The Path of Devotion (*bhakti*)

As explored in this chapter, our relationship with the divine doesn't need to be one-dimensional or defined by formality. Through Arjuna's simple plea for forgiveness, we discover four powerful models of divine connection, each offering a distinct quality of spiritual intimacy.

- As children of divine parents, we find freedom, guidance, and unconditional love. We learn to bring our whole selves (playful, questioning, authentic) into our spiritual lives.

- As friends with the divine, we discover sacred companionship in daily life. We create space for honest exchange, mutual respect, and sharing life's journey.

- As lovers of the divine, we experience the transformative power of complete absorption. Our hearts and minds center on the beloved; every aspect of life expresses devotion.

- As parents to the divine child, we cultivate generosity, care, and selfless offering. We learn to give our best and to find the sacred in acts of nurturing attention.

- When we integrate these four dimensions, we discover what Arjuna found in his relationship with Krishna—that true devotion (*bhakti*) transcends religious formalities and creates a direct, heart-to-heart connection with the sacred.

- This multidimensional relationship frees us from the constraints of perfectionism in our spiritual lives. We no longer need to approach the divine with flawless performances or carefully crafted words. Instead, we bring our authentic selves (messy, imperfect, and real) into a relationship of genuine intimacy.

The path forward isn't about striving for spiritual perfection but rather deepening our capacity for spiritual connection. It's about removing the barriers we've placed between ourselves and the divine, including the masks we wear, the formalities we maintain, and the distance we create out of fear or unworthiness.

As we cultivate these four relationships with God, we discover that the divine has been waiting for us to draw near, not as distant worshippers but as beloved children, trusted friends, passionate lovers, and caring parents. In this sacred intimacy, we find the divine presence and our true selves reflected in the loving gaze of the eternal.

Start Today: Your First Step

If there's one action I encourage you to take right now, it's this: **Begin a daily practice of honest conversation with the divine.** I encourage you to engage in a frank discussion with the divine on a daily basis.

Here's how to begin:

Set aside time—perhaps in the morning before the day's demands take place or in the evening as you reflect on your journey. Find a quiet space where you won't be interrupted and speak to the divine as you would to someone with whom you share deep intimacy.

Practice isn't a formal prayer with prescribed words. It is heart-to-heart communication in which you bring your authentic self—your joys and struggles, your questions and insights, your gratitude, and your needs. Consider exploring each of the four relationship models we've discussed:

- **The Child** - Speak to the divine as a child would to a loving parent. Share your needs, questions, struggles, and joys with simple directness. Allow yourself to be vulnerable, seek guidance, and express trust.

- **The Friend** - Converse with the divine as you would with a trusted friend walking alongside you. Share the details of your day, ask for advice, express your honest thoughts, and listen for wisdom that might emerge in the silence between your words.

- **The Lover** - Express your devotion and longing for divine connection. Speak from your heart about what draws you to the divine. Allow yourself to experience the emotional depth of spiritual connection through words, sacred music, or silent communion.

- **The Parent** - Approach the divine as a beloved child in your care. Express your commitment to service, willingness to offer your best, and desire to nurture the divine presence in your life and the world.

- **Fusion** - Allow yourself to flow naturally between these different relationships, noticing which feels most appropriate at different moments or for various aspects of your life.

Don't worry about getting it "right." Begin this practice when you're ready and watch the barriers between you and the divine gradually dissolve, revealing the intimate connection that has been waiting for you all along.

REMEMBER THAT THE ESSENCE OF THESE RELATIONSHIPS IS FREEDOM FROM FORMALITY AND CONSTRAINT. THE DIVINE IS NOT SEEKING PERFECT WORDS BUT AN OPEN HEART.

Om Tat Sat

THE ULTIMATE SPIRITUAL MASTER KEY

WE OFTEN NAVIGATE COUNTLESS practices, *mantras*, and teachings in search of meaning and connection. It can feel overwhelming, especially when spiritual texts span thousands of pages written over centuries. But what if three simple syllables contain the fundamental essence of all spiritual wisdom?

om tat sat may sound deceptively simple, but within these three syllables lies a profound spiritual technology that can transform your everyday experience. These ancient Sanskrit words aren't just another mantra or ritual phrase, but the fundamental building blocks of spiritual understanding. Think of them as the primary colors that create all other hues or the introductory notes that form every possible melody.

This chapter explores how these three syllables can serve as your spiritual compass, guiding you through life's complexities toward greater peace, awareness, and connection. Whether you're just beginning your spiritual journey or have been walking this path for decades, understanding *om tat sat* offers a refreshingly direct approach to living with spiritual consciousness.

Let's Dive Deeper

Before we dissect each syllable of *om tat sat*, let me share an analogy that might help us grasp its significance. Imagine you're admiring a magnificent skyscraper. Your attention naturally goes to its impressive height, architectural style, and how it catches the light. Rarely do you think about the cement, steel, and basic materials that make the building possible.

Similarly, when we look at the world around us, we focus on the apparent forms of people, animals, plants, objects, even our bodies and thoughts, rather than the fundamental energy that makes their existence possible. *om tat sat* directs our attention to this fundamental substance underlying all creation.

In the Bhagavad Gita, Krishna emphasizes the importance of these syllables, particularly in chapter 17, verses 24-27. He explains that spiritual aspirants begin their actions, whether routine daily activities, charitable works, or meditative practices, by uttering *om*. They recognize the divine essence (*tat*) in all things and cultivate a state of equilibrium and truth (*sat*) throughout their activities.

Let's explore each of these powerful syllables individually to understand how they work together as a complete spiritual technology.

The Power of *om*

We arrive at the concept of vibration or sound energy when we reduce the universe's infinite manifestations to their most basic form. Everything you experience, including your body and thoughts, emerges from vibrational patterns. *om* represents this primordial sound from which all creation springs.

The syllable *om* is the "seed mantra" because, like a seed containing the potential of an entire tree, *om* includes the essence of all mantras and all creation. The Mandukya Upanishad states this authoritatively in its first verse, declaring that *om* encompasses all that has been, all that is, and all that will be.

Think about this for a moment. The chair you're sitting in, the device you're reading this on, and your own body—beneath the apparent diversity lies a unified field of energy that the ancient sages perceived and named as *om*. When you utter this syllable, you connect with the fundamental vibration of existence itself.

Krishna emphasizes the power of *om* in chapter 8, verse 13 of the Gita, stating that a spiritual seeker who departs from the body while uttering *om* attains the supreme goal of merging with divinity. Far from being a mystical exaggeration, this statement points to the profound reality that aligning your consciousness with the fundamental vibration of existence dissolves the illusion of separation.

When you begin any activity, such as starting your workday, preparing a meal, or entering meditation, uttering 'om' attunes your awareness to the fundamental energy that underlies all creation. It's like tuning an instrument before playing music, ensuring your actions resonate with the universe's natural frequency.

The Recognition of *tat*

The second syllable, *tat*, means "that" in Sanskrit. In this context, "that" refers to the divine reality within and beyond us. It points to the paradoxical truth that divinity is present in all things, yet simultaneously surpasses them. Chapter 9 of the Bhagavad Gita elaborates on this concept in multiple verses.

When you add *tat* to your awareness, you acknowledge that whatever you're doing isn't isolated or separate from the greater cosmic reality. You recognize that your actions, thoughts, and experiences are both expressions of divinity and offerings to divinity.

Acknowledging this connection creates a remarkable shift in perspective. Instead of being completely identified with the ups and downs of your experiences, successes, and failures, as well as the pleasures and pains, you begin to observe these experiences more objectively. In chapter 17, verse 25, Krishna guides us to add *tat* to *om* when performing any action, creating the invocation *om tat*.

Imagine you're having a difficult conversation with someone. Without *tat* consciousness, you might become entirely entangled in reactive emotions and thoughts. With *tat* awareness, while still fully present in the conversation, you maintain a subtle recognition that both you and the other person are expressions of the same divine reality.

The *tat* consciousness doesn't make you passive or disengaged. Quite the contrary. You become more fully present but with a quality of awareness that separates you from the temporary conditions of the moment.

The concept perfectly illustrates what it means to avoid getting "tangled in the spaghetti or the roller coaster of ups and downs." You still experience the full range of human emotions and challenges, but you don't become completely defined by them. Like watching waves on the ocean, you observe the changing conditions while remaining connected to the unchanging depth.

The Stability of *sat*

The third syllable, *sat*, completes this spiritual technology. *sat* refers to that which is real, authentic, and unchanging, pointing to the existence and the quality of aware presence that recognizes existence. When you invoke *sat*, you anchor yourself in stability and equilibrium, regardless of external circumstances.

Consider the distinction between being tossed about by ever-changing conditions versus maintaining inner steadiness through life's inevitable fluctuations. *sat* consciousness cultivates this inner steadiness. The quality of *sat* doesn't prevent you from responding appropriately to changing circumstances, but helps you respond from a place of centered awareness rather than reactivity.

Krishna emphasizes in chapter 17, verses 26-27, that actions performed with this quality of *sat* become auspicious and elevating, while actions performed without faith in this underlying reality become "a*sat*" or unreal. Krishna's statement isn't a moral judgment but a practical observation about the quality of consciousness we bring to our activities.

When you add *sat* to *om tat*, completing the invocation as *om tat sat*, you're aligning with the full spectrum of spiritual consciousness: the fundamental energy of creation (*om*), the recognition of divine presence in all things (*tat*), and the stability of truth and existence (*sat*).

om tat sat in Daily Life

Now that we understand the individual syllables, how do we apply this wisdom in our everyday lives? The beauty of *om tat sat* is that it doesn't require elaborate rituals or exceptional circumstances. Instead, it applies to any action, thought, or situation.

Here's a simple practice: Before beginning any significant activity in your day, whether it's starting work, having a meaningful conversation, making a decision, or even just preparing a meal, mentally or softly recite the mantra *om tat sat*. As you do, bring awareness to each syllable:

> With *om*, connect to the fundamental energy of existence

> With *tat*, recognize the divine presence within and beyond the activity

> With *sat*, establish yourself in stability and truth.

Incorporating *om tat sat* doesn't need to be time-consuming or obvious to others. It can be as brief as a few seconds of conscious awareness. The power isn't in the external utterance, but in the internal alignment it creates.

As you continue this practice, you might notice subtle but significant shifts in your experience:

- Actions performed with *om tat sat* consciousness tend to feel more aligned and purposeful

- Challenging situations become opportunities for growth rather than sources of suffering

- A quiet sense of peace begins to permeate even busy or challenging days

- The distinction between "spiritual" activities and "ordinary" activities begins to dissolve

Remember Krishna's guidance that this simple invocation can be used during this lifetime and even at the moment of death. It's not just a practice for special occasions, but a fundamental orientation to life.

Summary: The essence of *om tat sat*

As we conclude our exploration of *om tat sat*, let's gather the essential insights:

- *om tat sat* represents the fundamental building blocks of spiritual reality. Like the raw materials that form magnificent buildings, these three syllables contain the essence from which all spiritual wisdom emerges.

- *om* connects us with the primordial vibration from which all creation manifests. When we invoke *om*, we attune ourselves to the fundamental energy of existence itself.

- *tat* points to the divine reality that pervades everything while transcending everything. Recognizing *tat*, we maintain awareness of the greater cosmic reality even as we engage with specific experiences.

- *sat* anchors us in truth, existence, and stability. It allows us to maintain equilibrium through changing circumstances, responding from centered awareness rather than reactivity.

- Together, these three syllables form a complete spiritual technology that applies to any aspect of life. Whether in formal spiritual practices or everyday activities, "*om tat sat*" helps us align with the deeper reality underlying all experiences.

- While spiritual traditions have numerous mantras, practices, and teachings, *om tat sat* contains their essential substance. Just as we recognize that all buildings, despite their diverse appearances, are composed of the same basic materials, we see that all spiritual wisdom ultimately points to the same fundamental reality.

The beauty of *om tat sat* lies in its simplicity and accessibility. It doesn't require exceptional circumstances or elaborate rituals. It can be practiced at any moment, bringing the quality of spiritual consciousness to every aspect of life.

As we recognize and align with *om tat sat*, the distinction between "spiritual life" and "ordinary life" gradually dissolves. We begin to experience all of life as an expression of the same divine reality—diverse in form but unified in essence.

Start Today: Your First Step

If there's one action I encourage you to take right now, it's this: **Begin incorporating *om* into your daily life.** Of the three syllables, *om* is the foundation—the seed from which everything else grows.

Here's how to begin:

Choose three specific transition moments in your day—perhaps when you first wake up, before starting work, and before dinner.

At each of these moments, take three conscious breaths and mentally or softly recite 'om' with each exhalation.

As you do this, don't worry about getting it "right" or having any particular experience. Bring your awareness to the sound and vibration, allowing it to resonate through your consciousness.

After practicing with *om* for a week, add *tat* to your practice for another week, reciting *om tat* at your chosen transition moments. Finally, complete the sequence by adding *sat* in the third week, reciting the complete *om tat sat*.

Regular invocation begins to create subtle shifts in your awareness throughout the day. You may find that even during busy or challenging moments, the resonance of *om tat sat* continues to influence your experience, bringing a quality of presence and peace that wasn't there before.

REMEMBER, SPIRITUAL PRACTICE ISN'T ABOUT DRAMATIC EXPERIENCES OR PERFECT PERFORMANCE. IT'S ABOUT CONSISTENTLY ALIGNING WITH THE DEEPER REALITY THAT'S ALWAYS PRESENT. OM TAT SAT OFFERS A DIRECT AND ACCESSIBLE PATH TO THIS ALIGNMENT, AVAILABLE WHENEVER YOU CHOOSE TO RECALL IT.

Breaking Free

THE ART OF TRANSCENDING KARMA

I ONCE HEARD A BEAUTIFUL STORY about a disciple approaching his spiritual teacher one day after a meditation session. The disciple's face showed signs of frustration. "Master," the disciple said, "I've been working diligently on my career for years. Each time I start a new project, I tell myself this time will be different. I prepare more carefully, collaborate more openly, and manage my time better. Yet somehow, each project ends with the same challenges and disappointments. Why keep repeating this cycle despite my best efforts to change?"

The teacher looked at his student compassionately and replied, "You're trying to escape *karma* by changing your external actions. But true freedom comes not from changing what you do, but from changing your relationship to what you do." "I don't understand," the disciple admitted.

"When you act with yourself at the center, thinking ' my project,' 'my success,' 'my failure,' you remain bound to the wheel of *karma*. The action may change, but the actor remains attached to the fruits," the teacher explained. "Instead, try shifting the center from yourself to the divine. See yourself as an instrument rather than the doer."

The teacher's wisdom profoundly illuminated the disciple's understanding, just as it transformed my perspective when I initially encountered it. It captures the essence of how we all become trapped in patterns that seem impossible to break, repeating the same mistakes, experiencing the same obstacles, and riding an emotional roller coaster that always brings us back to the starting point.

While we've all heard about *karma*, few of us have the practical tools to overcome it. In this chapter, I aim to share what I've learned about breaking free from these binding patterns not through dramatic life changes or complex spiritual rituals, but through a simple shift in perspective that can transform even our most ordinary actions into pathways to liberation.

Let's Dive Deeper

Let's discuss *karma* in simple terms.

At its core, *karma* is just the law of cause and effect. You act, and that action creates consequences. These consequences become causes for future effects, creating an endless chain reaction. It's like throwing a pebble into a pond where the ripples continue outward, affecting everything they touch and eventually returning to the point of origin.

The challenge is that no one can remain inactive, even for a moment. As Krishna explains in the Bhagavad Gita, we're all constantly engaged in physical, verbal, or mental action. Even choosing to do nothing is, in itself, an action with consequences. We're in an inescapable tsunami of cause and effect.

Over the years, I've sat through countless lectures on *karma*, nodding along as teachers explained the problem in intricate detail. But I always left with the same question: "Okay, I understand I'm bound by *karma*, but what can I DO about it?" Maybe you've wondered the same thing.

The complexity deepens when you realize that your actions, your causes and effects, aren't determined solely by what you do. Others' actions also influence them. Think about the last time you argued with someone. If asked why you responded angrily, you might point to something they said or did that triggered you. And if they were asked, they'd point to something else as their trigger. It's an intricate web where we receive countless effects and creators of numerous causes. In traditional texts, *karma* is of three types:

- *sanchita karma*: Consider *sanchita karma* your cosmic ledger and savings account—every accumulated deed from previous incarnations is stored until the moment is right for its expression.

- *prarabdha karma*: Think of this as the "monthly withdrawal" from your karmic account — the portion of *sanchita karma* you're assigned to experience in your current life.

- *agami karma:* Every action you perform today creates *agami karma*—newly formed cause-and-effect relationships that contribute to your karmic inventory. Some of it you'll experience immediately, and some will be deposited into your *sanchita karma* for future "withdrawal."

Do you see the dilemma? The karmic structure appears deliberately constructed to maintain our endless entrapment. The more we try to work through our *karma*, the more *karma* we create! It's like emptying the ocean with a teaspoon while a river flows into it.

As Krishna states in the Gita, the ways of *karma* are profound and complex. We are continually stuck in a web of actions involving countless entities across time. No wonder it feels impossible to break free!

The Secret: Shifting the Center of Gravity

Here's where things get interesting. Despite the complexity of this karmic web, transcending it isn't as difficult as you might think once you understand the secret. And that's what I want to share with you now.

I've noticed something fascinating in my spiritual journey: the most profound spiritual truths are often elementary. It's their implementation that poses the challenge. Compare this to non-spiritual traditions, where God is usually portrayed as increasingly complex and distant. In authentic spirituality, the divine becomes more straightforward and accessible, allowing you to experience it within yourself and everything around you.

Let me explain this approach to transcending *karma* through a concrete example. Let's consider a charitable act of donation. You might assume that such a noble deed wouldn't trap you in the cycle of cause and effect, but that's not the case. Even acts of charity create *karma*; they might give you a smoother ride on the karmic wheel, but they won't let you off the hook.

When you donate, there are typically five components involved:

The Subject: That's you, the person donating.

The Recipient: The person or organization receiving your donation.

The Donation Itself: The money, food, or item you give.

The Means: How you're donating, such as serving food with your hands, taking your car to the orphanage, etc.

The Cause: Your reason for donating—in memory of someone, to help others, or with an expectation of some benefit.

Take a closer look at each component, and you'll see why *karma* is inescapable through conventional means.

- In the first component, the subject is "you" with an inherent sense of "I, me, mine." When this identification exists, you're attached to the act, and *karma* ensues.

- With the recipient, you might think in terms of "my temple," "the orphanage I support," or "the person I wanted to help." Again, there's an attachment to you, and *karma* follows.

- For the donation itself, the thoughts are "I gave my money" or "I bought this item and gave it." Once more, attachment and *karma*.

- The means of donation bring thoughts like "I'm donating with my hand" or "my car." Attachment and *karma* continue.

- Finally, the cause of donation might be "in memory of my mother" or "so that my family remains healthy." These thoughts also create a sense of attachment and *karma*.

- Even in such a noble act, you can see how attachment to the self can perpetuate the cycle of cause and effect, leaving one to feel as though there is no escape.

    Here's the secret to breaking free: change the center of gravity from yourself to the divine.

In all the steps I outlined above, you are the gravitational center. Even when the focus seems to be on someone else, such as the recipient of your donation, that person is still connected to you. You're chained to *karma* as long as you remain the central figure in the equation. The key to transcending *karma* lies in shifting this focus away from yourself and toward the divine. Let me show you how this works in practice.

Two Practical Methods for Transcending *karma*

There are two straightforward ways to introduce the divine into your actions and shift the center of gravity:

Method 1: Explicit Divine Connection

In this approach, you perform the same five steps of your action but explicitly bring the divine (I'll use Krishna as an example, but you can substitute whatever name or concept of the divine resonates with you) into each one, both in thought and words:

> Instead of saying, "I'm donating," think and say, "With Krishna's grace, I'm able to donate."
>
> Instead of saying "I'm giving it to so-and-so," consider rephrasing it as "With Krishna's grace, there is an opportunity to help so-and-so."
>
> Instead of saying "I'm donating food/money," consider rephrasing it as "With Krishna's grace, I can provide for others."
>
> Instead of saying "I'm donating with my hands/car," consider saying, "With Krishna's grace, I have the strength and means to make this donation."
>
> Instead of "I'm donating in memory of my mother," consider saying, "With Krishna's grace, I can do something to remember my mother." If you donate for good health, change it to "I surrender to Krishna, the energy that supports and sustains me."

By inserting the divine into each step, you shift the center of gravity away from yourself. Now, the effects of your actions don't bounce back to you, but they flow to the divine, who, as the supreme consciousness, can absorb the burden of cause and effect.

I've practiced this method during activities as ordinary as eating a meal. Instead of thinking, "I'm eating this food to satisfy my hunger," I shift to "Through divine grace, this nourishment is being received to sustain my body." The activity remains the same, but my relationship with it undergoes a complete transformation.

Method 2: om tat sat

For those who find the first method too elaborate, there is an even more straightforward approach: recite and meditate on the phrase *om tat sat*. This powerful mantra is, in many ways, the only prayer you need. I explore the profound meaning and origins of *om tat sat* in greater detail in a separate chapter of this book, where you'll discover its roots and transformative power.

With this method, you still perform the five steps of your action, but before each one, you silently say, *om tat sat*. This has the same effect as moving the center of gravity from you to the divine, thereby sparing you from the cause and effect of that action.

I often use this more straightforward method when I'm in situations that require my full attention or when I'm engaged in multiple activities in quick succession. Before entering a meeting, sending an important email, or even starting my morning routine, I silently recite *om tat sat* and find that it immediately shifts my perspective from self-centered action to a divine-centered flow.

What About My Past *karma*?

At this point, you might wonder, "This is great for future actions, but what about all the *karma* I've accumulated from my past? What about my *sanchita karma*?"

It's a valid question. After all, we're not just dealing with new *karma* we might create today — we're also experiencing the effects of actions from our past. How do we address this accumulated karmic debt?

Once again, Gita offers a simple yet profound solution: surrender. Krishna says,

Abandon all varieties of dharma (duty) and simply surrender unto me alone. I shall deliver you from all sinful reactions. Do not fear

While the solution is simple, implementing it requires genuine spiritual maturity. True surrender to the divine means developing the discipline and conviction that you are and will be cared for by a higher power. It means handing over the reins of your life. Surrendering to the divine never implies resignation or inactive acceptance of circumstances. Instead, it means clarifying the difference between having a goal and becoming attached to results.

Set your goals, define the steps or objectives to achieve them, and execute them with determination. But don't become attached to the outcome. Why? Because when you surrender, you change the center of gravity from yourself to the divine. And if the divine is in control, how can you dictate what should happen?

I experience the power of this surrender in life's most straightforward and most complex decisions and activities. The principle remains the same: surrendering attachment to outcomes transforms everything.

For instance, when taking a work flight, instead of clutching the armrest with anxiety about landing time or obsessing over the meeting that awaits me, I practice surrender. "I release my attachment to a smooth journey and a perfect presentation," I silently affirm. The flight becomes peaceful rather than stressful, and I arrive with clarity and a sense of presence.

Similarly, I follow the same practice on a larger scale when facing a significant financial decision. After researching and taking action to find options for a path forward, I surrender the outcome completely. When things don't go as expected, instead of disappointment, I take the next set of actions and explore the available options. A more suitable outcome becomes available, usually one that better meets my needs in ways I couldn't have anticipated.

The relief and clarity that come with surrender are accessible in both trivial and transformative moments. In all scenarios, surrendering attachment to outcomes has revealed possibilities beyond my limited perspective.

That's the paradox of surrender: by releasing control in small and significant matters, you gain access to solutions beyond your imagination. Your past *karma* loses its grip because you've fundamentally changed your relationship with it. You're no longer the one who needs to "pay the debt" or "reap the reward," you've surrendered that burden to something greater than yourself.

Summary: The Road to Freedom

Let's bring these insights together.

- *karma* is the universal law of cause and effect that keeps us bound in cycles of action and reaction.

- As long as we remain at the center of these actions by claiming ownership, expecting results, and acting from ego-identification, we stay trapped in the karmic web.

- The pathway to freedom isn't through avoiding action (which is impossible) but through transforming our relationship to action. We change the fundamental dynamic by shifting the center of gravity from ourselves to the divine. Actions still occur, but they no longer bind us with karmic chains.

We can implement this shift through two practical methods:

- **Explicit Divine Connection:** Consciously bringing the divine into each component of our actions, recognizing that all doing, all capacity, and all opportunity flow from grace rather than from our limited selves.

- ***om tat sat***: Utilizing this powerful mantra to consecrate our actions to the divine, we create a simple yet effective shift in consciousness.

- For accumulated *karma* from our past, the solution is surrender. Completely releasing our attachment to outcomes and our sense of ownership over actions, trusting in divine wisdom rather than our limited understanding.

- Freeing yourself from karmic bonds through divine-centered action doesn't involve evading duties or withdrawing from meaningful participation. It's about shifting perspective from self-centered to divine-centered. It's about recognizing that you're not the ultimate doer but an instrument of something greater. And in that recognition lies your liberation.

Don't wait until some distant future to implement these practices. Begin overcoming the *karma* of your past actions through surrender, and transcend the *karma* of your current and future actions through the two methods I've described. With divine grace, free yourself from the shackles of *karma* today.

Remember, breaking free from *karma* isn't a one-time event but an ongoing practice. There will be moments when you forget and slip back into ego-centered action. That's natural. Notice when this happens, adjust your perspective, and continue. With consistency, this shift in consciousness becomes increasingly natural, until it becomes your default way of being in the world.

The next time you find yourself caught in what seems like karmic patterns, which are repeating the same mistakes, encountering the same obstacles, and feeling trapped in cycles, remember to shift your focus. Introduce the divine into your actions, surrender the outcomes, and watch as the chains of *karma* begin to loosen. Your path to freedom isn't in avoiding life but in transforming how you relate to it.

Start Today: Your First Step

If there's one action I encourage you to take right now, it's this: Shift your thinking from **"I am doing this"** to **"Through divine grace, this is being done."**

Choose a routine activity that you'll perform today— something you do almost every day without much thought. It might be making your morning coffee, commuting to work, preparing dinner, or even just brushing your teeth.

Here's how to begin:

Before you start this activity, pause for a moment. Take a deep breath and silently say, *om tat sat*. As you perform each step of the action, shift your thinking from "I am doing this" to "Through divine grace, this is being done." For example, if you're making coffee:

- Before reaching for the coffee maker: *om tat sat*

- As you pour the coffee: *om tat sat* or "Through divine grace, I'm fortunate to have this cup of coffee."

Notice how this subtle shift feels. Does the action feel different? Is there a sense of lightness or ease that wasn't there before? Are you less concerned with the outcome (whether the coffee turns out perfectly) and more present with the process itself?

Don't worry about getting it perfect. Shifting your perspective represents an ongoing discipline, and like all worthwhile skills, requires patience and consistent effort to master. Start with just this one activity today. Tomorrow, you might choose the same activity or a different one. Gradually, you can expand this practice to more areas of your life.

Here's why recalibrating your relationship to action through this basic technique yields extraordinary results: it begins to rewire your neural pathways around the action. Instead of automatically falling into the "I am the doer" mindset, you create a new pattern that acknowledges a greater reality at work through you. With repetition, this new pattern becomes stronger until it begins to apply automatically to more and more of your activities.

Your freedom from karmic bonds doesn't require you to change what you do, but only how you relate to the doing. And that transformation begins with the very first action you take. Begin with a single step and watch how it gradually transforms your relationship with action, outcome, and ultimately, *karma* itself.

REMEMBER, YOU DON'T TRANSCEND KARMA THROUGH GRAND GESTURES BUT THROUGH CONSISTENT, MINDFUL SHIFTS IN YOUR EVERYDAY ACTIONS.

The Purpose Of Life

A SPIRITUAL EXPLORATION

"WHAT IS MY PURPOSE IN LIFE?" We ask this question in quiet moments, during significant life transitions, or when facing challenges. Many spiritual traditions offer the answer "to attain *moksha*" (spiritual liberation), but this concept can feel abstract when you're just starting your spiritual journey. There's much more to discover about life's purpose, especially insights that can help you right where you are today.

In this chapter, we'll dive beneath the surface of conventional wisdom. We'll explore the purpose of life not through dogmatic assertions but through spiritual inquiry, approaching it like students of both ancient wisdom and modern science. Together, we'll examine what drives us as human beings, what gives our existence meaning, and how understanding our purpose can transform our daily lives.

Our exploration isn't about criticizing others' viewpoints or promoting a single answer. Instead, it's about peeling back the layers to discover something more nuanced and practical than you might expect. The beauty of spiritual inquiry lies in its openness, allowing us to hold faith and reason together as complementary forces rather than opposing ones.

Let's Dive Deeper

When we discuss life's purpose from a spiritual perspective, we don't dismiss faith. Quite the contrary, just as scientists maintain faith in their ability to discover truth through experimentation, spiritualists maintain faith in authentic scriptures validated through experience and universal applicability. Both paths require confident trust in the process of inquiry itself.

Look around you at the vast universe with its incredible complexity and beauty. Isn't there something awe-inspiring about how it all works? Amid good and evil, happiness and sorrow, ups and downs, a mysterious equilibrium exists. Even through challenges and tribulations, things eventually settle into a new normal. Such universal equilibrium offers us our first clue about life's purpose.

At its core, divinity seems to have one fundamental characteristic—the drive to evolve, expand, and grow. Could this same impulse also be our primary purpose? Let's explore what this means for our lives and how it connects to the ancient wisdom of the Upanishads and the Bhagavad Gita.

The First Purpose: Material Growth

Our first purpose in life mirrors the fundamental nature of divinity itself: to evolve, expand, and grow. We see this everywhere in the physical world. We nurture children for growth, cultivate plants to flourish, and pursue education for career advancement. Our growth impulse is woven into the very fabric of existence.

Think about your own life for a moment. Aren't you constantly engaged in some form of growth? At work, at home, with family, with friends. In all these spheres, we're naturally drawn toward expansion. We seek promotion, celebrate our child's academic achievements, and work toward financial stability. Through these material values, we find purpose.

The ancient texts refer to this aspect of purpose as *artha*, which involves pursuing material prosperity and growth. It's not something to be ashamed of. It's a legitimate and necessary dimension of human existence. The desire for material security and development is deeply ingrained in our nature, reflecting the divine impulse toward growth and expansion.

The Second Purpose: Continuous Desire

But something interesting happens as we evolve and extract material value from life. We develop an urge to do something more than what we have. We don't stop growing, acquiring, or achieving. There's a continual quest for more, an almost unsatisfying thirst that keeps us in constant motion.

It's like water finding the path of least resistance, seeping through every available crack in our consciousness. Even the most spiritual among us, the saintliest figures, experience this continual quest. The only difference might be that their quest is directed toward subtle values, transforming learning into knowledge and wisdom rather than toward material gain.

But don't be mistaken. This restless seeking, at its core, is another manifestation of divinity and constitutes our second purpose in life. Ancient texts refer to this aspect as *kama*—the pursuit of desire and gratification. Like material value, none of us can escape this purpose, which is a continual quest for fulfillment.

The Pause of Introspection

Fundamental to both purposes we've discussed is the belief that we'll find happiness and satisfaction through the acquisition and fulfillment of desires. Indeed, many people spend their entire lives pursuing material growth and the gratification of continual desires, thinking these will bring freedom and perpetual joy.

But a fortunate few pause along this journey. Through introspection and self-reflection, they ask more profound questions: How much can I evolve and grow? To what end? After I achieve gratification by fulfilling one desire, do I stop, or am I immediately on to the next thing? Where does this all end?

When these questions arise, you're still driving on the road of life, but you've hit what we might call a "rumble strip," those ribbed patterns on highways designed to alert motorists to potential dangers. These questions alert you to the potential pitfalls of endlessly pursuing physical or material value and mental gratification.

Some might become dejected at this point, thinking that the only recourse is complete renunciation, the cessation of all desire for material growth and mental gratification. They believe that complete detachment lies at the heart of freedom.

The Third Purpose: The Guiding Principle or *dharma*

But the path prescribed by the Gita is more practical. It acknowledges that we live in a world where material value and gratification are inescapable. Instead of renouncing these aspects of life, we're encouraged to pursue them with a guiding principle called *dharma*.

According to the Gita and Upanishads, this guiding principle serves as the guardrail of our lives as we pursue material growth and fulfill our desires. *dharma* is like the balancing pointer in a weighing scale, bringing equilibrium to our pursuits. As Krishna says in chapter 7, verse 11, action in *dharma* brings serenity and strength.

What exactly is *dharma*? It's demonstrated and executed through our behavior and refers to our righteous duty in whatever role we play. An individual assumes different roles in life, and the righteous duty associated with each may vary. *Dharma* depends on the role and considers both the context and the object in action.

Effectively, *dharma* incorporates both objective and subjective perspectives. The situation in which an action is performed is vital in determining if it aligns with *dharma*. The same action may be perceived as right by one individual and wrong by another. Only through a holistic view can one see the action as Dharmic.

Only time will tell if our principle is correct when we apply dharma. Judging *dharma* requires us to be impartial rather than emotional, and that's a challenging task, since we're often victims of our emotions in the heat of the moment.

Becoming Dharmic or developing the "muscle" of *dharma* requires us to observe our own lives continuously. When we do this, the actions we perform to fulfill our purposes of material growth and mental gratification are executed in harmony. We then approach what Krishna describes in chapter 2, verse 70— being tranquil in the midst of surging waters.

The two purposes of life—material growth and the fulfillment of desires are fundamental to our existence. However, they gain meaning when grounded in *dharma*. At this juncture, we realize that the rumble strip on life's highway has awakened us. Without specific, deliberate effort, we seem to effortlessly cruise on the road, even with the dualities of pain and pleasure, ups and downs.

We continue to evolve and seek mental gratification, but these impulses are now channeled and streamlined by the guardrails of *dharma*. When this happens, we align with the natural rhythms of the universe. We are attached yet detached. We experience peace and feel liberated. We work not because someone asked us to, but because it's our inherent nature, like a river flowing simply because that's what rivers do.

The Fourth Purpose: The Wrapper of *moksha*

Some eventually realize that material growth and mental gratification, when underpinned by *dharma*, constitute true liberation, which is actual *moksha*. The insight reveals that *moksha* isn't a distant destination but the underlying reality that has always been present. Through the brush of *dharma*, knowledge, and righteous action, we clear away the cobwebs to merge with this wrapper.

The purpose of life, my friends, is to evolve and grow through a continual quest, supported by the tip of the Dharmic scale, to realize the ever-present essence of liberation, known as *moksha*.

Our Upanishads and Gita refer to material value, *artha*, and mental gratification, *kama*, which are supported by the guiding principle of *dharma*. All these are functioning under the various manifestations of the underlying framework of a liberated state, called *moksha*. Such a framework is known as *purushartha*, the objective of human life.

Summary: The Four-Fold Purpose

As we conclude our exploration, let's gather the essential insights about life's purpose:

- Life's purpose isn't singular but multi-dimensional. It encompasses four interconnected aspects known as *purushartha* in the ancient wisdom traditions: *artha*, *kama*, *dharma*, and *moksha*.

- The first purpose (*artha*) is to evolve, expand, and grow in material terms, pursuing prosperity, security, and achievement. The pursuit mirrors the expansive nature of divinity itself and is a legitimate dimension of human existence.

- The second purpose (*kama*) is the continuous quest to fulfill desires, the restless seeking that keeps us in constant motion. The continuous pursuit is a manifestation of divinity and a necessary aspect of human experience.

- Both these purposes gain meaning and balance when guided by *dharma*, the principle of righteous duty that varies according to our roles and contexts. *dharma* brings equilibrium to our pursuits, ensuring they don't veer into harmful extremes.

- When material growth and fulfillment of desires are pursued with Dharmic awareness, we naturally align with the fourth purpose, *moksha*. Rather than a distant destination, *moksha* is the state of liberation that has always been present as the underlying essence of existence.

- Purushartha's framework allows us to remain engaged in the world while maintaining inner freedom. We can pursue growth and fulfill our desires while remaining tranquil amidst life's inevitable ups and downs, being both attached and detached, active yet peaceful.

Understanding this comprehensive view of life's purpose helps us avoid the pitfalls of excessive worldliness and impractical renunciation. It offers a middle path that balances our material needs with our spiritual potential, providing a more effective approach to living.

Start Today: Your First Step

If there's one action I encourage you to take right now, it's this: **Begin practicing Dharmic awareness in your daily life.**

Dharmic awareness isn't about drastically changing your external circumstances, but rather about bringing a new quality of attention to your existing pursuits.

Here's how to begin:

Each day, take a few moments to reflect on your various roles, such as those of a professional, parent, friend, or citizen. Ask yourself: "What is the righteous duty associated with these roles today? How can I fulfill my material needs and desires while aligning with *dharma*?"

Start small. Choose one situation each day where you consciously apply Dharmic awareness. It might be a challenging conversation at work, a parenting decision, or a matter of how you spend your resources. Before acting, pause to consider what you want and what action would reflect righteous duty in your current role and context.

As you practice this Dharmic awareness, notice how it affects your relationship with material pursuits and desires. Do you feel less frantically attached to specific outcomes? Are you more peaceful in the face of challenges? Are you clearer about which desires to prioritize?

Over time, regular dharmic awareness can transform your experience of life's purpose. You may find yourself naturally balancing material growth and the fulfillment of desires with a growing sense of inner freedom, experiencing the "wrapper" of *moksha* even as you remain fully engaged in the world.

REMEMBER, THE PURPOSE OF LIFE ISN'T TO ESCAPE LIFE'S CHALLENGES BUT TO NAVIGATE THEM WITH WISDOM. IT'S NOT ABOUT REACHING A DISTANT DESTINATION BUT ABOUT RECOGNIZING THE LIBERATION THAT HAS ALWAYS BEEN BENEATH THE SURFACE OF EVERYDAY EXPERIENCE.

Purposeful Living

THE FOUR MINDSETS

A FRIEND CAUGHT ME OFF GUARD recently when she sighed and asked, "Is this all there is? Just moving from one life stage to the next?" That question stuck with me. Many of us navigate life by responding to whatever comes our way. We handle careers, relationships, and responsibilities without pausing to consider how we might approach each moment with greater intention and purpose.

Our default is to think of life as a predictable timeline: study when young, work and raise a family in middle age, retire, and then prepare for the end. But what if I told you there was a more dynamic and fulfilling way to approach your journey?

The ancient wisdom of the Bhagavad Gita offers us exactly that, providing a framework for moving through life and actively shaping our experience at any point along the way. And the best part? It doesn't require you to abandon your responsibilities or make dramatic changes. Instead, it invites you to adopt a perspective that extracts meaning and purpose from your current situation.

This chapter will reimagine the traditional concept of the four *asramas* (life stages) as mindsets that can be accessed at any point in life. Reimagining life stages as mindsets transforms ancient teachings into tools for modern living, allowing you to draw on different approaches as your circumstances require.

Let's explore how this wisdom can transform not only your perspective on life's journey but also your experience of each step along the way.

Let's Dive Deeper

The Bhagavad Gita describes four *asramas*, or life stages: the student (*brahmacharya*), the householder (grihastha), the forest dweller or retiree (*vanaprastha*), and the renunciate (*sannyasa*). Traditionally, these stages were viewed as sequential periods that we pass through as we age. We learn in youth, build and maintain in adulthood, step back in later years, and ultimately let go in our final stage.

But what if we viewed these not as fixed periods tied to specific ages but as mindsets—mental frameworks we could consciously adopt at any point in our lives? Reimagining these stages of life doesn't involve discarding tradition but seeing its more profound relevance to our everyday experience.

When we make this shift, we move from being passengers on a predetermined timeline to becoming the center of our existence, surrounded by four distinct mindsets we can draw upon as needed. Such a perspective liberates us from rigid thinking, allowing us to live with greater intention and flexibility.

The Student Mindset: Perpetual Growth

There's something magical about learning. Possibilities suddenly open up before you, creating excitement. That's the essence of the student mindset, an orientation toward growth, curiosity, and discovery that serves us throughout our lives.

At its core, the student mindset embodies self-discipline, curiosity, and a commitment to growth and development. While we typically associate this mindset with youth and formal education, it represents something more universal: our lifelong capacity to learn and evolve.

The Gita speaks about this in chapter 6, verse 16, advising moderation in all aspects of life to maintain the balance and focus essential for learning:

> *Yoga is not for one who eats too much or too little, sleeps too much or too little. Yoga destroys all sorrow for the one who is moderate in eating, recreation, work, sleep, and wakefulness*

The Gita's guidance reminds us that the student mindset requires intentional balance. By practicing moderation in our daily habits (whether in what we consume, how we rest, or how we spend our time), we create the optimal conditions for continued growth. In practice, adopting the student mindset might look like this:

- Approaching unfamiliar situations with genuine curiosity rather than pretending to have all the answers

- Creating dedicated time for learning, even if it's just 15 minutes a day

- Practicing humility when receiving feedback, seeing it as valuable data rather than criticism

- Cultivating discipline in daily habits to support mental clarity

- Seeking out mentors and teachers who can guide your development in areas that matter to you

I've met 80-year-olds who embody this mindset beautifully. They are constantly reading, asking questions, and trying new hobbies. I've even met 30-year-olds who have closed themselves off to new ideas, convinced they already know everything worth knowing. The student mindset isn't about age or formal education; it's about maintaining an open, disciplined approach to growth that serves as the foundation for all other mindsets.

The Householder Mindset: Engaged Responsibilities

We all know that feeling when responsibility sits heavily on our shoulders, whether for family, work, or community. That's the householder mindset in action. Perhaps the most demanding of the four, this mindset centers on fulfilling our duties and responsibilities toward others. It involves the practical work of building security, contributing to collective well-being, and nurturing relationships.

Far from being limited to those actively raising families, this mindset represents our engagement with the world around us and how we contribute, provide, and participate in the ongoing flow of life. The householder mindset drives the economy, sustains communities, and ensures the continuation of society itself. The Gita emphasizes the importance of performing these duties righteously, not abandoning them even when they become difficult. In contemporary terms, adopting the householder mindset might involve:

- Taking responsibility for your financial well-being and that of your dependents

- Contributing meaningfully to your community through work, service, or leadership

- Building and maintaining healthy relationships with family, friends, and colleagues

- Managing resources wisely with consideration for future needs

- Creating systems and structures that support not just your life but the lives of others

The principles of this mindset can be adopted at any stage, even though they are commonly associated with the period between the ages of 25 and 50. I've known teenagers who demonstrate remarkable responsibility in caring for siblings or contributing to family expenses and elders who continue to serve their communities long after the traditional "retirement" age.

The householder mindset reminds us that engagement with worldly responsibilities isn't a distraction from spiritual growth but can be a profound spiritual practice when approached with the right attitude.

The Retired Mindset: Thoughtful Observation

The essence of the retired mindset is not withdrawal from life, but rather the deliberate cultivation of a perspective that allows for wiser engagement.

The retired mindset represents a step back from active involvement, allowing for the development of capacity for thoughtful observation. Rather than disengagement, it cultivates the ability to separate from a situation's immediate emotional pull, allowing one to see it more clearly.

Cultivating thoughtful observation helps us develop an "observer consciousness," the ability to witness our thoughts, feelings, and reactions with greater objectivity. Through practices like meditation, as described in chapter 6, verse 10 of the Gita, we strengthen this inner observer:

A yogi should always try to concentrate the mind on the Supreme Self; they should remain in seclusion, alone, with the mind and body controlled, free from desires and possessions

The retired mindset teaches us to choose based on wisdom rather than emotional reactivity. This mindset can be cultivated at any age, even though it is traditionally associated with the period after primary household responsibilities have been fulfilled (often after age 50):

- Developing the habit of pausing before reacting to challenging situations

- Creating moments of solitude for reflection and self-observation

- Seeking to understand the broader context and implications of decisions

- Establishing regular meditation or contemplative practice

- Offering guidance based on experience rather than imposing solutions

The retired mindset doesn't require giving up family or material attachments entirely, but it does involve creating the space necessary to develop a more contemplative relationship with life. It's about being in the world but not entirely consumed by it.

I've known young professionals who set aside time each morning for meditation and reflection, cultivating this mindset amid busy careers, and parents who create small pockets of contemplative space within active family lives. The retired mindset is accessible to anyone willing to prioritize perspective alongside activity.

The Renounced Mindset: Inner Detachment

Perhaps the most misunderstood of the four, the renounced mindset isn't about abandoning life but about approaching it with profound freedom. Often mistaken as simply "giving everything up," this mindset represents our capacity for deep contentment and freedom from attachment.

It's not about physically abandoning people or possessions but developing an inner detachment that allows for full presence without desperation. In chapter 18, verse 66, Krishna expresses this as surrender to the divine:

> Abandon all varieties of dharma and surrender unto me alone. I shall deliver you from all sinful reactions. Do not fear

The renounced mindset represents our capacity for deep contentment and freedom from attachment. We learn to redirect our focus from the results to the process itself, seeing outcomes as "the divine's will," thereby freeing ourselves from the burden of trying to control everything. In daily life, cultivating the renounced mindset might look like this:

- Approach every action with gratitude to the divine

- Take out the focus from constant acquisition and accumulation

- Developing comfort with uncertainty and impermanence

- Practicing acceptance of situations beyond your control

The elements of this mindset can be integrated at any age, even though they are traditionally associated with later stages of life, particularly after the age of 70. I've known young adults who approach life with complete surrender to the process and business leaders who make bold decisions without fear because they've released their attachment to outcomes.

Inner detachment enables us to approach every person and situation with equanimity, not indifference, but a calm acceptance that is independent of specific outcomes.

Fusion: The Dance of Mindsets

Now, here's where things get interesting. The true power of these four mindsets emerges not when we rigidly adhere to one but when we learn to move fluidly between them as circumstances require. Like a dancer who knows when to step forward and when to step back, we can develop wisdom to recognize which mindset best serves a given situation. Consider how these mindsets might flow together in everyday life:

- You encounter a challenging work situation and first adopt the student's mindset to learn everything you can about the problem

- You shift to the householder mindset as you take responsibility for addressing the issue

- The retired mindset helps you step back to observe patterns and consider implications

- Finally, the renounced mindset allows you to act decisively without attachment to specific outcomes

The fluid movement between mindsets creates a simultaneously engaged and detached life, one that is both active and contemplative, and responsible and free. Rather than moving sequentially from one stage to another, we become the center around which these mindsets revolve, drawing on each as needed.

I've observed this fluidity in the most effective leaders, parents, teachers, and friends. They know when to learn, when to act, when to reflect, and when to let go, moving skillfully between these states as wisdom dictates.

Summary: Living from the Center

As we've explored in this chapter, reimagining the four asramas as mindsets transforms them from a rigid timeline into a dynamic toolkit for purposeful living. Viewing life stages as accessible mental frameworks offers several powerful benefits:

- First, it frees us from age-based expectations, allowing us to access the wisdom of each mindset regardless of our chronological age or life circumstances. Whether you're 25 or 75, you can draw on the student's curiosity, the householder's responsibility, the retiree's perspective, and the renunciate's freedom.

- Second, it encourages balance and wholeness. Rather than overidentifying with a single approach to life, we recognize the value of different orientations and develop the flexibility to move between them. The balanced approach prevents the common pitfalls of being perpetually burned out from responsibilities or completely disengaged from meaningful contributions.

- Third, it offers practical guidance for navigating life's challenges. When faced with difficult situations, we can consciously choose the mindset that best serves that moment, rather than reacting out of habit. The conscious selection of mindsets leads to wiser decisions and more skillful actions.

- Finally, it aligns our outer lives with our inner development. Instead of waiting for external circumstances to change before we can grow spiritually, we recognize that our inner orientation can transform our experience at any moment. True purpose comes not from what we do but how we approach it.

By viewing these ancient teachings as mindsets rather than sequential life stages, we transform them from historical curiosities into practical tools for navigating the complexity of modern existence. We free ourselves from rigid age-based expectations and are open to living with greater purpose, flexibility, and fulfillment at every stage of life.

The question isn't whether you've reached a particular stage of life. The question is whether you're accessing the full range of mindsets available now. The power to maximize your time on earth is not in some distant future; it's available right now in the mindset you choose to adopt today.

Start Today: Your First Step

If there's one action I encourage you to take right now, it's this: **Conduct a personal mindset audit.**

Here's how to begin:

Set aside a few uninterrupted minutes today. Find a quiet space, take a few deep breaths, and ask yourself these questions:

- Which of the four mindsets (student, householder, retired, renounced) do I naturally gravitate toward daily?

- Which mindset seems most foreign or challenging to me?

- What situation would benefit from a different mindset than the one I'm currently applying for?

- What's one small way I could practice my least-accessed mindset today?

Write down your answers. Your written reflection serves as your entry point into more conscious living. It doesn't require purchasing special equipment, attending a retreat, or mastering complex spiritual practices. It asks you to pause and notice the mental frameworks already shaping your experience.

Your self-assessment isn't just an intellectual exercise but a practical tool for breaking out of unconscious patterns. By identifying which mindsets you overuse and which you neglect, you gain immediate insight into why certain aspects of life might feel out of balance. Don't wait for the "right time" to begin this practice. The wisdom of the Gita reminds us that our mindsets are available to us at every moment.

REMEMBER, THE JOURNEY TOWARD MAXIMIZING YOUR PURPOSE BEGINS WITH A SINGLE STEP OF AWARENESS, REGARDLESS OF AGE OR CIRCUMSTANCE. TOMORROW, YOU MIGHT SEE YOUR LIFE THROUGH ENTIRELY NEW EYES.

Devotion

THE FIVE-FOLD PATH

SPIRITUAL SEEKERS FREQUENTLY share a common set of concerns: "I do everything right. I meditate daily, I attend retreats, and I've read all the right books. But something still feels missing. It's like I'm going through the motions without experiencing the transformation I keep reading about."

Have you felt something similar? That gap between spiritual practice and genuine spiritual experience is something many of us encounter. We follow the instructions and check all the boxes, and yet somehow miss the essence.

That familiar struggle points us toward one of the most profound teachings in the Bhagavad Gita. Within all the verses of timeless wisdom that Krishna shares with Arjuna, he explicitly highlights five extraordinary qualities that mark true devotion. Five characteristics that, when cultivated together, enable us to perceive what remains hidden from ordinary awareness, and that is the divine presence which permeates all existence.

In this chapter, we'll explore each of these five qualities in depth, examining not only what they mean individually but also how they weave together to create a comprehensive path to spiritual awakening. More importantly, we'll discover how to bring them alive in the laboratory of your everyday experiences, within your relationships, work, challenges, and joys.

Let's Dive Deeper

What makes these five qualities so remarkable is that they're not abstract theological concepts or complicated rituals. They're practical principles that transform your daily life experience. When approached with sincerity, this five-fold wisdom places you firmly on the path of *bhakti* (devotion), where the artificial boundary between the spiritual and the mundane dissolves.

1. Performing Duties for the Divine's Sake

How many parts have you divided your life into? Most of us have created these invisible compartments: life, family life, social life, and then, somewhere off to the side, spiritual life. We have our "spiritual time" (maybe in the mornings or during prayers) and then our "regular life" (everything else). Sound familiar?

The first principle of devotion challenges this entire arrangement. It invites you to perform all duties with divine consciousness and to recognize sacred purpose woven into even the most ordinary activities.

It's not about quitting your job to become a monk or adding hours of spiritual practice to your day. It means transforming your perception of the activities you're already engaged in. When you're preparing dinner, you're not "just cooking" but you're engaging in an act of sacred nourishment. When you're responding to emails at work, you're not "just working" but you're participating in service through your unique talents.

Traditional Indian dancers demonstrate this principle beautifully. Hours before stepping on stage, they begin a ritual of preparation by carefully arranging their costumes, applying makeup with focused attention, stretching their muscles, and mentally rehearsing the dance. For them, preparation is an offering to make themselves worthy of the divine expression that flows through the dance. When approached with reverence, what could be mere entertainment becomes a sacred expression.

Consider the difference between eating a meal while scrolling through social media versus eating with full awareness, recognizing the divine presence in the food, in the act of nourishment, and your very body. The action is identical, but the experience is different. Completely transformed.

Here's the beautiful part—you don't need to change your external life to embrace this principle dramatically. The shift occurs in your perception, allowing you to see the divine purpose embedded within your existing responsibilities.

When Krishna speaks about performing duties for His sake, He's inviting you to recognize that the divine isn't separate from your daily life but embedded right within it. Far from burdening your busy schedule, recognizing divine purpose liberates you, infusing even mundane moments with extraordinary meaning.

What would change if you approached just one routine activity today as sacred service? How might washing dishes or commuting to work feel different if you saw it as an opportunity for divine communion?

2. Wholehearted Dependence on the Divine

In our culture, we pride ourselves on self-sufficiency, on not needing anyone or anything, and on maintaining complete control over our circumstances. We've elevated independence to a supreme virtue. If you're anything like me, you've likely discovered that the illusion of total control can create immense suffering.

The second quality of devotion offers a radical alternative. Now, let's clear up a misconception. Being "wholly dependent on the divine" doesn't mean becoming passive or irresponsible. It doesn't mean sitting on your couch waiting for God to pay your bills.

Instead, it means recognizing the limits of personal control and surrendering to a higher wisdom. It means acknowledging that despite your best planning and efforts, life remains stubbornly unpredictable, and there exists a divine intelligence orchestrating events beyond your limited perspective.

Consider the many stories that emerge during a financial crisis. People who had meticulously planned everything, from their education and career moves to investments and personal lives, operated within carefully constructed timelines. Then, despite all this careful planning, many lost nearly everything. Yet, in those moments of crisis, some discovered something unexpected —a sense of surrender that brought a strange comfort. The acknowledgment that they were not ultimately in control somehow freed them from the crushing weight of believing everything depended solely on their efforts.

Do you recall that beautiful parable often associated with spiritual journeys? A traveler walks through a desert with the divine beside him. Looking back, the traveler notices two sets of footprints in the sand, his own and those of the divine. But during the most challenging stretches, only one set of footprints appears. When the traveler asks why he was abandoned in his time of greatest need, the divine responds: Those single footprints aren't yours but mine. I carried you when you could no longer walk alone.

Such stories resonate deeply because they acknowledge a universal human experience in moments when our strength fails, our resources get depleted, and we can no longer continue on our own power. In those moments, the devoted soul doesn't collapse in despair but leans into faith, trusting that divine support is present even when invisible.

What emerges is an extraordinary psychological and spiritual freedom. You no longer carry the crushing weight of believing everything depends solely on your efforts. You no longer exhaust yourself trying to control uncontrollable circumstances. By relinquishing the illusion of complete self-sufficiency, you open yourself to receiving divine assistance that has always been available but that your self-reliance couldn't access.

The devotee lives in a paradoxical yet liberating state. The devotee puts in complete effort while simultaneously surrendering the outcome, planning prudently while remaining flexible to divine redirection, and working diligently while recognizing that strength comes from beyond oneself.

Where in your life right now might you be clinging too tightly to control? What would it feel like to make your best effort and then release the outcome to a higher wisdom?

3. Complete Devotion to the One

Have you fallen prey to what I call "spiritual buffet syndrome"? Sampling practices from various traditions, accumulating techniques and teachings, without deeply committing to any single path. Our contemporary spiritual landscape practically encourages this approach.

While exploring diverse spiritual perspectives can certainly be enriching (and I've done plenty of that myself), the third quality of devotion suggests that spiritual depth often comes through focused commitment. The Gita teaches that devotees in Krishna consciousness "do not search for the supreme in ritualistic or religious books" because they've found the essence directly. They "don't need any other god" because they've established a primary relationship with the divine, and all paths merge.

Throughout history, we find examples of individuals with profound but straightforward devotional practices. They haven't read hundreds of spiritual books or mastered numerous meditation techniques. However, they maintain consistent daily rituals, such as sitting before a small altar, lighting a lamp, and spending time in silent communion with the divine as they understand it. The depth of spiritual presence in such practitioners is noticeable, not from extensive knowledge but from consistent and focused devotion.

Now, don't misunderstand; this doesn't mean that books, teachers, and spiritual practices have no value. They serve as critical gateways to deeper experience. But at some point, the devoted soul recognizes these as means rather than ends. The goal isn't to accumulate spiritual knowledge or master numerous techniques but to establish direct communion with the divine.

Reflect on how this principle might influence your approach to spiritual practice. Rather than anxiously wondering if you're doing enough, such as reading enough spiritual books, attending enough retreats, and practicing enough techniques, you can focus on deepening your primary relationship with the divine. The question shifts from "Am I doing enough?" to "Am I present enough?"

Complete devotion creates a remarkable simplicity in spiritual life. You no longer feel compelled to chase after every new teaching or practice that emerges. You don't feel guilty about not exploring every potential path. Having found the essence, you're content to delve deeper rather than broaden your scope.

Concentrated devotion generates remarkable spiritual power. It's like a magnifying glass focusing sunlight. Scattered light merely warms, but focused light ignites a flame. The scattered mind, jumping from practice to practice, teaching to teaching, rarely generates enough concentrated energy for transformation.

Complete devotion doesn't mean narrow-mindedness or fundamentalism. You can still appreciate the beauty and wisdom in various expressions of truth. But you've found your primary relationship with the divine and have organized your spiritual life around deepening that connection rather than endlessly diversifying it.

What would happen if you simplified your spiritual practice for the next month? If you focused on deepening one primary connection rather than exploring many, what would be the outcome? What might emerge from that concentrated attention?

4. Freedom from Attachment

The fourth quality of devotion addresses something we all struggle with: the relationship between desire and attachment. However, here's a crucial point: in the wisdom of the Gita, freedom from attachment doesn't mean suppressing desires or living an austere life devoid of enjoyment. It points to something much more profound in your relationship with possessions, outcomes, and experiences.

You've probably noticed that attachment creates suffering in two primary ways. First, when you're attached to having things be a certain way, you resist the natural flow of life and experience anxiety when circumstances don't match your preferences. Second, attachment creates fear of loss. Even when you attain what you desire, you can't fully enjoy it because you're preoccupied with the possibility of losing it. Sound familiar?

Consider the persistent Robin that returns each spring to build its nest. With remarkable dedication, it gathers hundreds of twigs and grass, meticulously weaving them into a perfect home for its young. After nurturing its fledglings through summer, the Robin abandons its nest when autumn arrives. Winter storms may destroy what remains, yet when spring returns, the Robin begins again, building an entirely new nest from scratch. Such instinctive behavior reveals profound wisdom about impermanence: *"The beauty was in the creating, not in the keeping. The attachment would diminish the joy of the process."* It's a powerful demonstration of engaging fully with life while holding its outcomes lightly.

Freedom from attachment doesn't mean indifference or apathy; it means being unattached. It means being unattached to the things that matter. You can still fully engage with life, appreciate beauty, enjoy relationships, and work toward goals. The difference lies in the clinging quality of the mind. Where others might grasp desperately at experiences, possessions, or outcomes, the devotee holds them lightly, recognizing their impermanent nature.

What emerges is a remarkable lightness of being. When you perform all duties for the sake of the divine, see the divine presence in all things, and depend wholly on divine support, attachment to outcomes naturally diminishes. Your primary attachment becomes the relationship with the divine itself, and that cannot be lost or taken away from you.

Reflect on how this principle might impact your perspective on the inevitable life changes. When a relationship ends, a career opportunity falls through, or material possessions are lost, you'll undoubtedly feel the natural human emotions of sadness or disappointment. Yet, you won't be devastated because your core identity and happiness aren't dependent on these external circumstances.

What emerges is a remarkable lightness of being. No longer burdened by the weight of countless attachments and the anxiety they generate, you can move through life with grace and flexibility. You can fully engage with the present moment rather than being perpetually preoccupied with protecting what you have or obtaining what you don't.

The Gita describes this state as one of perpetual bliss. Not because your external circumstances are always pleasant or in your favor, but because your inner state remains anchored in divine connection regardless of outer conditions. True freedom isn't freedom from life's natural ups and downs but freedom from being defined and controlled by them.

What is one attachment that creates suffering in your life right now? How might your experience change if you could hold it more lightly while still fully engaging with it?

5. Absence of Malice Toward All Beings

How do you relate to people who have harmed or opposed you? The fifth quality of devotion addresses this very question. The devoted soul cultivates an absence of malice toward all beings, recognizing that negative emotions such as hatred, resentment, and revenge create a separation from divine consciousness.

You don't become a doormat, unable to establish boundaries or speak truth to injustice. It means refusing to allow negative emotions to take up permanent residence in your heart. It means understanding that harboring malice damages you far more than it affects the target of your resentment.

There are remarkable examples throughout history of people who have faced terrible injustice yet chosen to release hatred. Consider the families of victims who speak of forgiveness after violent crimes or those who advocate restorative rather than retributive justice. Their choice isn't about excusing what happened but about freeing themselves from the corrosive effects of ongoing resentment. They recognize a profound truth: "Holding onto anger won't change what happened, and it will destroy me from within."

Gita offers a practical approach to transforming these negative emotions. It teaches that the devotee overcomes malice by "saturating thoughts with memories and divinities of the supreme." Rather than fighting against hatred or resentment, which often only strengthens these emotions, you redirect attention to divine remembrance.

Gita's approach acknowledges a fundamental truth: where divine consciousness is fully present, malice cannot remain. It's like darkness naturally disappearing when light enters a room; similarly, negative emotions toward others dissipate in the presence of divine remembrance.

There is a more profound metaphysical truth behind this practice—all souls, regardless of their current state of awareness or behavior, originate from the same divine source. Recognizing our shared divine origin doesn't excuse harmful behavior, but it enables you to distinguish between actions and the essential nature of the being performing them.

In practical terms, this absence of malice creates tremendous freedom. The energy that would otherwise be consumed by resentment, revenge fantasies, and hatred becomes available for creative and loving purposes. The mental space occupied by negative rumination clears up, allowing for greater presence and awareness.

Moreover, this quality creates the foundation for genuine forgiveness, not the superficial kind that says "it's okay" when it isn't, but the profound forgiveness that releases both the offender and you from the bondage of past harm. You forgive not primarily for others' benefit, though that may occur, but for your liberation and continued communion with the divine.

Is there someone to whom you harbor resentment or malice? How might your experience change if you redirect your attention from that person's actions to divine remembrance whenever those feelings arise?

Fusion: The Five-Fold Path in Action

We've explored each quality individually, but its true power emerges when you cultivate them together as an integrated path. Each quality reinforces and deepens the others, creating a self-sustaining spiritual ecosystem. Think about how these qualities interact in your own experience:

- When you perform all duties for the divine's sake, don't you naturally become less attached to outcomes? Your focus shifts to sacred action itself rather than its results.

- When you depend wholly on divine support, doesn't it become easier to release malice toward others? You recognize that divine justice operates beyond your limited understanding.

- When you practice complete devotion to the divine, doesn't performing duties for the divine's sake become natural rather than forced? It flows from your relationship rather than from obligation.

- When you cultivate freedom from attachment, doesn't total dependence on the divine become easier? You're no longer clinging to the illusion of complete self-sufficiency.

- When you maintain the absence of hatred, doesn't your devotion to the divine deepen? Negative emotions no longer create separation in your consciousness.

These five qualities, when combined, create a comprehensive approach to spiritual life that integrates action, emotion, attention, relationship to circumstances, and relationship to others. Unlike methods that focus solely on belief, ritual practices, or philosophical understanding, this path transforms your entire being.

The Gita teaches that devotees who cultivate these five qualities "acquire divine vision and behold the cosmic form." The message isn't metaphorical. It points to a genuine transformation in perception. You begin to perceive the divine presence that has always been there but remained hidden from ordinary awareness.

Divine vision doesn't remove you from the world but reveals it as it truly is, infused with sacred presence. The mountains and rivers, the bustling cities, the challenging relationships, and the daily work all reveal themselves as expressions of the same divine reality that we worship in temples and meditation halls.

Summary: The Transformative Power of Devotion

As we've explored in this chapter, the five-fold wisdom of devotion offers a comprehensive path to spiritual transformation that integrates every aspect of your experience. Unlike approaches that separate the spiritual from the mundane, this path sanctifies daily life by finding the sacred within ordinary experience rather than apart from it.

- These five qualities—performing duties for the divine's sake, wholehearted dependence on the divine, complete devotion to the One, freedom from attachment, and absence of malice toward all beings—weave together to create a spiritual practice that transforms not just what you do but how you perceive reality itself.

- When cultivated sincerely, these qualities gradually reveal what has always been present but remained hidden: the divine consciousness that permeates all existence. Divine vision doesn't remove you from the world but shows the world's true nature as a manifestation of sacred presence.

- In a culture that often prioritizes accumulation, independence, diversification of attention, attachment to outcomes, and the right to hold grudges, the five-fold path of devotion offers a radical alternative. It invites you into a way of being characterized by sacred service, trust, focused attention, freedom, and forgiveness.

- The devotional path is not about escaping life but about experiencing its depths. It is not about withdrawing from the world but about engaging with it more fully and consciously. It is not about denying your humanity but about realizing its divine potential.

The ancient wisdom of the Gita reminds us that devotion is not merely one approach among many but the very essence of spiritual fulfillment. Through these five qualities, you find yourself "firmly on the path of *bhakti*," the path of transformative love that reveals the divine presence within and all around you, here and now.

Start Today: Your First Step

If there's one action I encourage you to take right now, it's this: Choose one of the five devotional qualities that resonate most deeply with you at this moment and **commit to consciously practicing it for the next seven days**. Rather than trying to implement all five qualities at once (which might feel overwhelming), focus your attention on the one that feels most relevant to your current life circumstances or spiritual needs.

Here's how to begin:

If you choose "Performing Duties for the Divine's Sake":

- Select one routine activity that you perform daily—perhaps preparing breakfast, or commuting to work.

- Before beginning this activity each day, please take a moment to dedicate it as an offering to the divine in your thoughts.

- Throughout the activity, gently remind yourself of its sacred purpose whenever your mind wanders.

- Notice how this intention shifts your experience of something you've done hundreds of times before.

If you choose "Wholehearted Dependence on the Divine":

- Identify one situation in your life where you're trying to maintain tight control and experiencing anxiety as a result.

- Each day, take a few minutes to release this situation to divine care consciously. You're not abandoning responsibility; instead, you're releasing the anxious grip of believing that everything depends solely on you.

- Notice what changes in your experience of this situation as you practice this surrender.

If you choose "Complete Devotion to the One":

- Simplify your spiritual practice for the next week.

- Rather than dividing your attention among various teachings or techniques, choose one primary practice that connects you most directly with the divine as you understand it. Options include meditation, prayer, reading, chanting, or contemplation in nature.

- Commit to this practice daily, even if just for a few minutes, with complete presence.

- Notice how this focused attention affects the quality of your connection.

If you choose "Freedom from Attachment,":

- Select one attachment that creates suffering in your life— perhaps an expectation about how someone should behave, a desire for a particular outcome, or identification with possession or status.

- Each day, practice holding this attachment more lightly. When you notice yourself clinging, gently remind yourself of the impermanent nature of all things and return to your connection with the unchanging divine presence.

- Notice how this shift affects your anxiety levels and your ability to be present.

If you choose "Absence of Malice Toward All Beings,":

- Identify one person towards whom you harbor resentment, irritation, or judgment.

- When thoughts of this person arise, practice redirecting your attention from their actions or perceived flaws to a state of divine remembrance. You're not excusing harmful behavior but freeing yourself from the corrosive effects of ongoing negative emotions.

- Notice how this practice affects your mental space and energy levels.

Whichever quality you select, approach this practice with sincere intention rather than perfectionism. You'll inevitably forget or struggle at times, and that's part of the process. What matters is your willingness to begin again each time you notice you've strayed from your intention.

At the end of the seven days, take some time to reflect on your experience. How did this focused practice affect your daily life? What insights emerged? How about you continue developing this quality while incorporating others?

REMEMBER, THE DIVINE VISION THAT KRISHNA PROMISES ISN'T SOMETHING DISTANT OR ABSTRACT. IT'S YOUR BIRTHRIGHT, WAITING TO BE REALIZED THROUGH SINCERE DEVOTION. BEGIN TODAY WITH JUST ONE STEP ON THE FIVE-FOLD PATH AND WATCH AS NEW PERCEPTIONS GRADUALLY UNFOLD.

Krishna

THE TWO FACES

THE NAME "KRISHNA" conjures different images for different people. You may envision a playful deity playing the flute, surrounded by adoring devotees. Perhaps you see him as a majestic sovereign, adorned with precious gems and golden ornaments, in all his divine splendor. Or maybe you think of the divine child stealing butter, the mischievous youngster whose pranks delight and entertain. Some might even see him as the perfect friend, the loyal companion who stands by your side through life's joys and struggles.

These popular images of Krishna have captured the imagination of millions for centuries, and for a good reason. They represent one aspect of divinity that resonates deeply with the human heart: the personal, accessible divine that loves and is loved in return.

But then there is this other Krishna standing on the battlefield of Kurukshetra, speaking words of profound wisdom to a warrior frozen by moral crisis. Unlike his more playful manifestation on the battlefield, Krishna doesn't play a flute or dance with devotees. Instead, he delivers the Bhagavad Gita, one of the most profound philosophical texts ever composed. Krishna of the Gita manifests as a sage, a philosopher, a master strategist, and the embodiment of perfect wisdom.

I've always been fascinated by these two faces of Krishna. Far from being contradictory, they represent complementary aspects of understanding and connecting with the divine. In this chapter, I aim to explore the two dimensions of Krishna and what they offer us on our spiritual journey. I believe both are essential—we need both the Krishna of devotion and wisdom to transform our lives truly.

Let's explore together, looking beyond the popular images to discover a richer, more nuanced understanding of Krishna, one that might change how you approach devotion and daily living.

Let's Dive Deeper

Among the most beloved figures in Hindu spirituality, Krishna manifests as the ultimate divine being and, for countless followers, is a Supreme God in his own right. The popular manifestation represents Krishna, the protector, the compassionate being, and the divine hero whose stories have been passed down through generations.

In this form, Krishna plays many roles. He's the mischievous child who steals butter and plays pranks, embodying divine playfulness and joy. He's the divine lover to his devotees, symbolizing the soul's longing for union with God. He's the friend who stands by those who love him, offering protection and fulfilling desires.

The devotional Krishna is typically depicted playing the flute, an iconic image. The music of Krishna's flute symbolizes the divine call that awakens the soul from its worldly slumber, drawing it toward spiritual fulfillment. Images of Krishna, surrounded by adoring devotees, remind us of his role as a divine lover and source of spiritual wisdom and joy.

This Krishna comes to the rescue for countless devotees in prayer and devotion. He is the supreme being who fulfills desires and gives everything for material and spiritual life. What makes this aspect of Krishna particularly accessible is his ability to adapt to each devotee's needs and temperament. For some, he is a child to be nurtured, embodying innocence and spontaneity. For others, he is a parent who provides and protects. For others, he is an approachable friend who understands and supports without judgment.

Krishna's extraordinary versatility as a personal deity lies in how you imagine him in whatever form resonates with your heart. He will be there for you. When we offer prayers with *bhakti* (devotion), Devotees often visualize and connect with this personable and relatable form of Krishna. The relationship is intimate, emotional, and deeply personal.

Krishna: The Sage Philosopher

But then there's the other Krishna—the one who stands on the battlefield, not as a worship deity but as the embodiment of perfect wisdom and strategic brilliance. The battlefield reveals Krishna, as depicted in the Bhagavad Gita, delivering profound teachings to Arjuna when needed.

The Gita's Krishna emerges in a drastically different context from the playful deity of Vrindavan. The setting is a war between cousins, the *Pandavas* and *Kauravas,* a conflict with profound ethical dimensions. On one side stand those who have acted unfairly, unethically, and unrighteously; on the other, they have become victims of injustice despite their righteousness and adherence to dharma.

In this crucible of conflict, we meet a Krishna who is nothing short of a maverick. He is a master of governance, negotiation, and strategic thinking. The Gita's Krishna embodies the ultimate wisdom, not abstract philosophical knowledge, but practical intelligence applied to life's most challenging situations.

What strikes me most about Gita's Krishna is his pragmatic approach. Before making any decisions, he carefully evaluates multiple dimensions: What is the nature of the decision? What impact will it have? What is right versus wrong in this context? Who will be affected? What are the short-term and long-term implications? What are the risks of inaction?

I no longer see Krishna as the mischievous child, divine lover, or deity in this context. Instead, I see him as a sage and philosopher with extraordinary insight, someone who seems to have access to everything in the universe yet remains grounded in practical reality.

Krishna, in his sage manifestation, addresses the full spectrum of human questions, from cosmic inquiries to daily dilemmas:

How does the universe operate?

What are our duties in life?

Why do we experience duality?

What does morality mean in this universe?

What is the true nature of charity?

What should we eat, and how should we live?

Why is discipline necessary?

How can we see beyond immediate appearances?

What ideals should we pursue?

Interestingly, this Krishna is remarkably similar to the sages of the Upanishads, those enlightened teachers who transmitted profound wisdom to students sitting at their feet. Like those sages, Krishna presents a far-reaching vision that penetrates the core of existence. He defines divinity, explains what it means to be human, and describes the nature of the world around us.

The Integration of Devotion and Wisdom

I've come to realize that both aspects of Krishna are essential for a complete spiritual life. We need the first Krishna, the supreme personal deity, to anchor devotion. In his personal form, Krishna is always by our side as a parent, child, and friend. The personal aspect represents our projection of divinity into a relatable form, making the infinite accessible to our finite understanding.

But we need the second Krishna, the sage and philosopher, as a teacher, coach, and guide to show us how to live righteously and seek truth. As a sage and teacher, Krishna offers practical wisdom through the Gita, guiding us in navigating the complexities of human existence.

An interesting tension arises when we consider these two aspects together. When Krishna speaks of God and the Supreme in the Gita, is he referring to himself as a person or something beyond human form? The apparent tension between these two aspects requires careful interpretation.

Historical traditions place Krishna on earth about 5,000 years ago, and in the Gita, he claims he will appear whenever righteousness declines and evil flourishes. A rational mind might question: "If that's true, why hasn't Krishna returned? There's so much unrighteousness in our world. We see children suffering, natural disasters, and innocents dying. What is Krishna waiting for? How much worse must things get?"

While many believe Krishna will reappear in a different incarnation, that's not what the Gita's Krishna meant. The teaching becomes clearer when we understand Krishna primarily as a sage rather than focusing on his identity. The Gita's verses aren't about the individual Krishna but about the timeless wisdom he imparts.

Krishna's promise to return wherever unrighteousness flourishes isn't about an external divine coming to save us. Instead, it's a call for righteousness to manifest through our behaviors and actions. By promising to return wherever unrighteousness flourishes, Krishna invites us to embody the teachings of the Gita in our families, communities, and nations. He's challenging us to exercise our choices and make decisions with the same wisdom he demonstrates and to become embodiments of intelligent knowledge in our own way.

Three Examples from the Gita

Let me share three specific examples from the Gita that illustrate this perspective:

First, Krishna says that very few understand him, stating: "*vasudeva sarvam iti sah mahatma sudurlabah.*" We can interpret this in two ways. One interpretation sees Krishna (son of Vasudeva) standing on the battlefield as the ultimate and all-encompassing supreme being, whom very few recognize.

However, another interpretation, which more accurately reflects the Gita's message, is that Sage Krishna is teaching us that divinity exists in the form of Vasudeva, the Lord of the Vasus, meaning that divinity encompasses all fundamental elements, energies, and senses. The sage reminds us not to let ego convince us we're in control. Very few appreciate that a larger energy manifests and sustains the universe, connecting us all. Which makes more sense: Krishna as an individual personified as the ultimate or as the supreme, representing the all-encompassing nature of divinity?

Second, throughout the Gita, Krishna says everything belongs to him and that we should think of him when performing actions. What does "me" represent here? Is it the individual standing on the battlefield instructing Arjuna? Or is Sage Krishna, the embodiment of wisdom, asking us to approach every choice thoroughly and deliberately, taking an objective view rather than being swayed by emotions? By saying, "Think of me," Krishna asks us to emulate his wisdom, not necessarily worship his person.

Third, when Krishna says, "Surrender everything to me," the Sage Krishna asks us to surrender based on his teachings. He's saying: Perform your actions, then surrender the results to the larger universe, accepting whatever outcome emerges, favorable or not. The act of surrender in this context applies not to Krishna as an individual but to the cosmic order he represents.

Summary: Two Essential Facets

To bring everything full circle, both facets of Krishna are vital for our spiritual journey, though they serve different purposes.

- Most of us are familiar and comfortable with the first aspect—Krishna as God, supreme and all-powerful, the giver of grace. As the supreme deity, Krishna meets our need for devotion and a personal relationship with the divine. Through bhakti, we open our hearts to divine love and grace.

- The second aspect, Krishna as sage, philosopher, teacher, and coach, meets our daily guidance needs. The philosophical Krishna provides practical wisdom for navigating life's complexities. When we follow these teachings and live according to the wisdom of Sage Krishna, we naturally align ourselves with cosmic order and become eligible to receive the grace of Supreme Krishna.

- These two facets aren't contradictory. They are complementary. One speaks to our hearts, the other to our minds and actions. One offers love and grace, and the other provides wisdom and guidance. Together, they offer a comprehensive approach to spiritual life, addressing our need for a transcendent connection and practical wisdom.

- I believe the full transformative power of Krishna's presence comes when we embrace both aspects and open our hearts to divine love while applying divine wisdom to our daily choices and actions.

In essence, the two faces of Krishna remind us that spirituality isn't just about transcendent experiences or intellectual understanding. It combines devotion and wisdom, heart and mind, inner transformation and outer action. It's about loving the divine while also living by divine principles.

Start Here: Your Next Step

If there's one action I encourage you to take right now, it's this: **Practice "wisdom-infused devotion" for the next 21 days.**

Here's how to begin:

Each morning, spend a few minutes in a devotional connection with Krishna as your deity, who loves and protects you. Visualize Krishna in whatever form resonates with your heart—as a divine child, friend, guide, or cosmic protector. Express gratitude, share your concerns, and open yourself to divine grace. The morning devotional practice nurtures the bhakti aspect of your relationship with Krishna.

Then, select one learning from the Bhagavad Gita to carry with you throughout the day as practical wisdom from Krishna, the sage. You might choose to learn about acting without attachment to results, maintaining equanimity in all circumstances, or seeing the divine in all beings. Write this learning on a small card or save it on your phone where you can refer to it frequently. You can refer to any of the learnings from this book as a daily source of guidance.

As you move through your day, consciously apply this teaching to your decisions, interactions, and challenges. When facing a difficult choice, ask yourself: "What would Krishna's wisdom guide me to do in this situation?" When feeling overwhelmed by emotions, please return to the verse and let it center you. Let Krishna's teachings guide your communication and listening skills as you interact with others.

At the end of each day, take a few minutes to reflect on how you applied (or failed to apply) the teaching and how this practice affected your experience. Notice how the devotional and wisdom aspects work together, how devotion opens your heart to wisdom, and how applied wisdom deepens your devotional connection.

Don't worry about getting it perfect. The attempt to combine devotion and wisdom is a powerful spiritual practice. Start where you are, with whatever understanding and capacity you have, and let the practice gradually deepen your experience of the two facets of Krishna. By practicing this wisdom-infused devotion for 21 days, you'll begin to experience Krishna as complementary dimensions of a transformed life.

REMEMBER, LOVING KRISHNA AND LIVING ACCORDING TO HIS TEACHINGS ARE NOT SEPARATE SPIRITUAL PRACTICES BUT AN INTEGRATED PRESENCE IN YOUR LIFE—BOTH THE OBJECT OF YOUR DEVOTION AND THE SOURCE OF YOUR DAILY GUIDANCE.

Becoming Arjuna

THE JOURNEY TO SPIRITUAL AWAKENING

PICTURE A CELEBRATED WARRIOR, suddenly frozen between opposing armies, questioning everything he thought he knew. Arjuna finds himself in precisely this position at the beginning of the Bhagavad Gita, paralyzed by doubt when facing the most crucial decision of his life. It's a feeling we know all too well. Those moments when uncertainty stops us in our tracks.

Let me tell you something that might surprise you. When we study the Bhagavad Gita, we're not just reading about Arjuna's transformation. we have an invitation to become Arjuna. His questions become our questions. His struggles mirror our inner battles. Ultimately, his enlightenment provides us with a roadmap to our awakening.

In this chapter, we'll walk with Arjuna, exploring how his remarkable journey can illuminate our path toward self-discovery and spiritual growth. I'll share with you how the different facets of his character reveal universal human qualities, how deep listening created the space for transformation, and how three great spiritual teachers have interpreted his relationship with the divine in ways that can help you discover your authentic spiritual path.

Let's Dive Deeper

Let's start by getting to know Arjuna a bit better. It's easy to put historical or mythological figures on pedestals, imagining they were born enlightened or somehow fundamentally different from us. But that's not Arjuna at all.

Looking carefully at the Gita, you'll notice that Arjuna is profoundly, wonderfully human. Despite being a legendary warrior and Krishna's brother-in-law, he wasn't automatically wise or enlightened. We wouldn't have the Bhagavad Gita if he had been! The entire text exists precisely because Arjuna found himself confused, conflicted, and in need of guidance, just like you and me.

Throughout the text, Krishna addresses Arjuna by several different names, each highlighting a different aspect of his complex character:

- When Krishna calls him *partha*, he acknowledges Arjuna's noble lineage and sense of duty to his family. Don't we all sometimes feel the weight of our heritage and the responsibilities that come with it?

- The name *gudakesha*, meaning "conqueror of sleep," highlights Arjuna's discipline and vigilance—qualities that we all strive to cultivate in our spiritual practice.

- *kaunteya*, referencing his mother Kunti, reminds us of the values our families instill in us, for better or worse.

- When addressed as *dhananjaya* or "winner of wealth," we're reminded of Arjuna's worldly achievements and successes. We all have moments of victory and accomplishment that shape our sense of identity.

- *savyasachin*, the ambidextrous archer, speaks to Arjuna's exceptional skills and abilities. Each of us has unique talents that define our place in the world.

However, what makes Arjuna truly special and truly relatable is that, despite all these impressive qualities, he still experiences the fundamental human struggle between emotion and reason, between knowing and doing. He shows remarkable clarity and profound confusion in crucial moments. Doesn't that sound familiar?

Arjuna's distinguishing quality isn't his perfection but his readiness to acknowledge his confusion. When he lays down his bow and admits to Krishna, "I am confused," he takes the first crucial step that many of us resist, which is admitting we don't have all the answers. And that's where his transformation begins.

The Art of Deep Listening

If I were to identify the most essential quality that enabled Arjuna's transformation, it would be his exceptional listening ability. And I don't mean the kind of half-hearted listening most of us do while mentally preparing our response or defense. I'm referring to thorough, receptive, and attentive listening.

Think about how often you find yourself nodding along in a conversation while your mind races ahead, formulating what you'll say next. We've all been there. But Arjuna shows us a different way.

Throughout the Gita, Arjuna demonstrates a remarkable ability to quiet his mental chatter and truly absorb Krishna's wisdom. His extraordinary receptiveness allows him to pose penetrating questions that elicit Krishna's most profound teachings. A beautiful dance unfolds between teacher and student here—Krishna's wisdom flowing into the space created by Arjuna's attentive silence.

You might think, "That sounds simple enough," but if you've ever tried to truly listen without mentally interrupting, you know how challenging it can be. Our minds constantly chatter, judging, comparing, and preparing our next brilliant point. What would happen if, like Arjuna, we could temporarily suspend that inner dialogue and receive?

From Listening to Living: Contemplation and Application

But Arjuna didn't just listen passively to Krishna's words and immediately accept them at face value. That's not how fundamental transformation works. After listening, he contemplated what he heard, reflecting deeply on how Krishna's teachings applied to his thought processes and life circumstances.

His thoughtful consideration generated follow-up questions that furthered his understanding. You can almost feel Arjuna turning Krishna's words over in his mind, testing them against his experience and returning with more nuanced inquiries.

Through this cycle of listening, contemplating, questioning, and listening again, Arjuna's fears and doubts gradually dissolved. A renewed sense of purpose and determination replaced them. His confusion gave way to clarity, and his paralysis gave way to action.

Isn't this the process we all go through when integrating new wisdom into our lives? First, we hear something that resonates with us. Then, we consider it in light of our own experience. Questions arise, prompting us to seek a deeper understanding. And finally, transformation occurs if the teaching continues to resonate and we are ready.

Three Paths to Understanding Arjuna: The Great Acharyas

Now, let me share something fascinating about the Bhagavad Gita tradition. Three great spiritual teachers (Sankara, Ramanuja, and Madhwa) offer distinct interpretations that help us understand Arjuna even better and can guide us on our path toward the divine.

Each of these acharyas addresses two fundamental questions we all face on our spiritual journey:

How do we relate to divinity?

In what form do we perceive the divine?

And the beautiful thing is that all three perspectives are valid and valuable. Krishna himself touches on all three approaches in the Gita. Which one resonates most with you depends on your spiritual temperament and inclinations.

Madhwa's Path of Devotion

Let's start with Acharya Madhwa and his philosophy on dualism (*dvaita*). From this perspective, we are an image or reflection of the divine, but always separate from it. The divine remains independent, while we are dependent beings, eternally distinct from ultimate reality.

Suppose Madhwa's approach resonates with you; in that case, you might relate to divinity through a sense of loving dependence and perceive the divine through devotion (*bhakti*) to a specific name and form. This could be Krishna, or another manifestation of God that speaks to your heart.

Following Madhwa's path, becoming Arjuna means connecting with the divine through worship and devotion. You immerse yourself in bhakti, cultivating devotional practices that make you receptive to divine grace. Like Arjuna in chapter 11 of the Gita, you might yearn to witness the divine in a form you can behold and worship.

I've known many people who find immense comfort and inspiration in this devotional approach. There is something profoundly moving about surrendering to a divine presence that's greater than ourselves.

Ramanuja's Path of Integration

Ramanuja offers a perspective of qualified non-dualism (*vishishtadvaita*). From this viewpoint, our relationship with the divine is integrated—neither entirely separate nor completely unified. Think of an apple: the red outer peel, the white flesh, and the core with seeds are all distinct components, yet together, they constitute the apple.

Following Ramanuja's path, becoming Arjuna means recognizing your permanent connection to the divine while acknowledging the existing distinctions. You realize this connection by removing the curtain of ignorance through complete surrender, known as *prapatti*.

In the Gita, Krishna grants Arjuna a divine vision to witness the boundless Universal Form, an all-inclusive, radiating divinity that is both terrifying and majestic. This form embodies the unity of all existence while preserving its distinctions.

Since the human mind struggles to comprehend such a universal form fully, you may rely on a specific deity, sacred object, or name as an anchor point for your devotion, even as you surrender to the larger, universal existence.

Ramanuja's middle path appeals to many seekers who sense their connection to and distinction from the divine, experiencing God as both within and transcendent.

Sankara's Path of Knowledge

Sankara's philosophy represents complete non-dualism (*advaita*), which contrasts sharply with Madhwa's dualism. From this perspective, the individual and the divine are fundamentally the same. In our confused state, we fail to recognize this oneness, but with dispelled ignorance, we realize our true identity with the divine.

Following Sankara's path, becoming Arjuna means relating to the divine through self-reflection and perceiving the divine in everyone and everything. You dissolve into universal consciousness and become one with the divine.

The universal form Krishna reveals in chapter 11 is not something external to be seen with physical or even divine eyes, but an internal reality to be realized through self-reflection. A divine vision is to help you reflect internally. Through complete knowledge (*jnana*), self-inquiry, and contemplation, you attain the divine by realizing that you were never separate from it.

Sankara's non-dual approach attracts those with a philosophical inclination who connect with the idea that, at the deepest level, all apparent differences dissolve into a unified whole.

Becoming Arjuna: Your Journey

So, which perspective speaks to you? Are you drawn to Madhwa's devotional dualism, Ramanuja's integrated qualified non-dualism, or Sankara's unitive non-dualism? Different aspects of each approach resonate with you at various times.

The beauty of the Gita lies in its ability to accommodate all these paths, recognizing that each of us must find our authentic way to the divine. But regardless of which philosophical perspective you prefer, the essential elements of becoming Arjuna remain the same:

- You need to develop the capacity for deep listening without mentally preparing your responses or defenses in advance.

- You must sincerely contemplate how spiritual teachings apply to your own life and circumstances.

- You should acknowledge your confusion when it arises and seek clarity through thoughtful questions.

- You'll gradually transform fear and doubt into purpose and determination as you integrate what you learn.

- And you'll choose a perspective on divinity that aligns with your spiritual temperament and inclinations.

Remember, Arjuna's journey mirrors yours, mine, and the journey of anyone engaged in self-discovery, growth, and spiritual awakening. To become Arjuna, we must be willing to ride the roller coaster of transformation, trusting that clarity will eventually emerge from confusion.

Summary: The Message of the Gita

As we've explored in this chapter, the Bhagavad Gita invites us not merely to study Arjuna but to become Arjuna. We must engage in the process of inquiry, expose our weaknesses, listen deeply, and find our way to spiritual awakening through the path that resonates most deeply with our hearts.

- We've seen how Arjuna's complex character reflects our human nature, with all its strengths and contradictions. We've discovered how his practice of deep listening created space for transformation. We've explored three different philosophical perspectives relating to the divine, each offering a valid approach to spiritual awakening.

- The Gita teaches us that transformation isn't about becoming someone else; it's about becoming more fully ourselves. Arjuna didn't stop being a warrior. He became a more conscious, awakened warrior. Similarly, our spiritual journey doesn't require us to abandon our essential nature but to illuminate it with understanding.

- As you continue your journey of becoming Arjuna, remember that confusion is not a barrier to growth but often a necessary precursor. Just as Arjuna's moment of crisis on the battlefield created the opening for Krishna's teachings, our moments of doubt and uncertainty can be gateways to more profound wisdom.

Choose any perspective that resonates with you and embark on your transformation journey today. Become Arjuna.

Start Today: Your First Step

If there's one action I encourage you to take right now, it's this: **Begin embodying Arjuna's transformative qualities by Practicing Deep Listening.** The foundational practice of attentive hearing forms the basis of Arjuna's journey and can also catalyze your transformation.

Here's how to begin:

Today, choose one meaningful conversation—with a family member, friend, colleague, or teacher and commit to listening with your whole being. As you engage in this conversation:

- **Silence your internal dialogue:** When the other person speaks, resist the urge to prepare your response mentally. Absorb their words without judgment or reaction.

- **Observe without interjecting:** Notice how often you feel compelled to interrupt, correct, or add your perspective. Each time you notice this impulse, gently return to listening.

- **Formulate one thoughtful question:** After they finish speaking, pause to contemplate what you've heard. Then, ask one question that seeks to deepen your understanding rather than advance your viewpoint.

The fundamental practice of deep listening—Arjuna's primary transformative quality will initiate shifts in your consciousness and prepare you for the more profound wisdom that follows.

REMEMBER, JUST AS ARJUNA'S ATTENTIVE LISTENING TO KRISHNA BECAME THE FOUNDATION FOR HIS ENLIGHTENMENT, YOUR PRACTICE OF DEEP LISTENING WILL OPEN THE DOOR TO YOUR TRANSFORMATION. START TODAY. LISTEN DEEPLY. BECOME ARJUNA.

Knowing and Doing

THE FOUR PILLARS

THE WORDS BELIEF (VISHWAS), FAITH (SHRADDHA), Conviction (*tapasya*), and Persistence (*sadhana*) frequently appear in spiritual discussions, often used interchangeably as if they mean essentially the same thing. The interchangeable use of these terms is also evident among those deeply engaged in spiritual or religious practices. Yet understanding the distinctions between these concepts is crucial for anyone seeking to deepen their spiritual journey, particularly for those exploring the wisdom of texts like the Gita and Upanishads.

Think of Belief and Faith as stepping stones on a spiritual path. They're certainly related, and you might need to step on one to reach the other, but they represent distinct stages of spiritual development. Similarly, *tapasya* and *sadhana* are like two different pathways, with one focused intently on the destination, the other savoring the journey.

In this chapter, we'll explore two complementary distinctions that can transform your approach to spirituality. First, we'll examine the progression from Belief to Faith to spiritual inquiry, which represent three different depths of engagement with spiritual knowledge. Then, we'll explore the distinction between goal-oriented practice (*tapasya*) and process-oriented practice (*sadhana*) that represent two different approaches to spiritual effort.

Clarifying these fundamental terms will establish a foundation for deeper spiritual explorations. Let's untangle these common confusions and discover the unique power and purpose of these different spiritual approaches.

Let's Dive Deeper

To truly understand these spiritual concepts, we must look beyond dictionary definitions and explore how they function in lived spiritual experiences. Each represents a distinct way of relating to spiritual truths, a unique quality of knowing, and a different approach to practice.

The language we use shapes our understanding and experience of spirituality. The vocabulary of spiritual traditions has developed with precision over centuries, with each term pointing to distinct aspects of human experience and development.

Consider the distinction between "house" and "home." While often used interchangeably, they refer to different realities—one to a physical structure, the other to an emotional experience of belonging. The distinction matters not just linguistically but experientially.

Similarly, these spiritual concepts represent different approaches that create different inner experiences. Some orient us toward future attainment, others toward present awareness. Some engage primarily with the intellect, others with the heart and emotions, and others with our entire being.

By understanding these nuances, we gain access to a more refined spiritual vocabulary that enables us to discern subtle differences in our inner experiences and approaches. This clarity allows us to be more intentional about our spiritual practices and more precise in our understanding of traditional teachings.

Imagine you're standing at the shore of a vast ocean. Belief is like observing the sea from the beach—you can see it, study its patterns, and understand its nature intellectually. Faith is like wading into the sea up to your knees—you're now experiencing the ocean directly, feeling its power, and surrendering to its movements. Spiritual inquiry is like diving deep beneath the surface to explore the ocean's depths.

Throughout human history, spiritual traditions have recognized these distinctions, though they might use different terminology. In Sanskrit, Belief is called *vishwas*, while Faith is *shraddha*, these are terms that carry nuanced meanings developed over thousands of years of spiritual exploration.

As we examine each concept more closely, consider your spiritual journey. Where do you primarily operate? What is your relationship to both knowledge and practice? These questions are not judgmental but invitations to greater self-awareness as we explore these distinctions further.

Belief and Faith: The Depths of Spiritual Engagement

What is Belief? Understanding vishwas

Let's start with 'Belief,' or *vishwas* in Sanskrit. Belief is a conclusion you reach based on information you've gathered. It's intellectual and rooted in learning.

Think about how beliefs form in your life. You hear something from a trusted source, read about it in books or articles, see patterns that suggest a certain truth, or receive teachings from someone knowledgeable. Based on this accumulated information, you eventually conclude: "Yes, this seems true to me." That conclusion is your Belief.

The key characteristic of Belief is that it doesn't necessarily require direct experience. You can believe in things you haven't personally encountered. For instance, most of us are familiar with Tokyo, even if we've never been there. We believe in historical events we didn't witness. We believe in scientific principles that we haven't personally verified through experiments.

This aspect of not having direct experience is equally valid in the spiritual domain. You might believe in karma, reincarnation, or the existence of divine beings without having direct knowledge of these realities. Your Belief is based on what you've learned and what makes sense to your rational mind.

Belief involves a particular kind of conviction, yet it maintains some openness. When something is a belief, you're usually still willing to consider new information that might modify or even change your understanding. There's still an element of intellectual engagement and potential questioning.

What is Faith? Understanding shraddha

Faith, or *shraddha* in Sanskrit, elevates Belief to a higher level. Faith emerges when you elevate a belief to absolute truth in your mind and heart. It's no longer just a reasonable conclusion but unquestionable, like a personal law or gospel.

With Faith, the tentative nature of Belief solidifies into certainty. What was once "I think this is true" becomes "I know this is true," even without direct evidence or experience.

When Faith is directed toward divine entities or principles, whether a personal deity like Krishna or more abstract concepts of divinity, it naturally expresses itself through worship. Faith-based worship isn't just ritual observance but a means of deepening and strengthening one's faith connection.
Worship involves three key elements: Admiration for the object of worship, Prayer or communion with the divine, Emotional investment, and devotion.

Unlike Belief, which maintains a certain intellectual distance, Faith is deeply emotional. It engages not just the mind but the heart and soul. Faith isn't about weighing evidence or logical consideration, but it's about wholehearted commitment and surrender to what you accept as truth.

When you transition from Belief to Faith, your attitude undergoes a profound shift. With Belief, you still engage in learning and understanding. With Faith, you often stop questioning. The matter is settled in your heart, and your energy shifts from inquiry to devotion and implementation.

Spiritual Inquiry: Understanding *adhyatma*

While Belief and Faith are powerful aspects of spiritual life, they aren't the journey's end. A third step transcends both: spiritual inquiry, also known as *adhyatma*.

Spiritual inquiry occurs when you take your beliefs and faith, and instead of treating them as endpoints, use them as starting points for deeper exploration. Rather than simply accepting what you've learned or even what you've come to hold as unquestionable truth, you begin to inquire more deeply into them.

The process of inquiry isn't about doubt in the negative sense. It's not about undermining Faith but about enriching and expanding it through direct experience and deeper understanding. You begin to ask questions like:

- What does this teaching mean?

- How does it apply in different contexts?

- What's the essence beyond the form?

- Can I experience this truth directly rather than just accepting it?

Spiritual inquiry is characterized by:

- Continuous questioning and exploration

- Peeling away layers of understanding to reach more profound truths

- Connecting the dots between different teachings and experiences

- Seeking direct experience rather than secondhand knowledge

- Enjoying the journey rather than rushing to conclusions

Unlike Belief and Faith, which can sometimes be confined to specific traditions or deities, spiritual inquiry transcends boundaries. For the spiritual seeker engaged in *adhyatma*, divinity is recognized in all things, not just in particular forms or traditions. The personal god worshipped in Faith becomes a doorway to experiencing universal divinity.

A Practical Example: Linking to the Bhagavad Gita

To clarify these distinctions, let's apply them to a concrete example: the Bhagavad Gita, one of the most revered texts in Hinduism.

At the level of Belief (*vishwas*): You might learn that the Gita is a sacred dialogue between Krishna and Arjuna on a battlefield before the Kurukshetra War. You understand that Krishna gave spiritual guidance to Arjuna when he was confused about his duty. You've heard that the Gita is considered a core text of Hinduism, containing profound wisdom about life, duty, and spirituality. All of this constitutes Belief, the intellectual understanding based on what you've learned, even though you weren't present for the original event.

At the level of Faith (*shraddha*), Faith emerges when you elevate your Belief in the Gita to the ultimate truth. You accept Krishna's words in the Gita as divine law. Your relationship with the text and Krishna shifts from intellectual appreciation to emotional devotion and surrender. You might express this Faith through worship, treating Krishna's teachings as absolute and infallible. There's less questioning and more acceptance and implementation.

At the level of spiritual inquiry (*adhyatma*), you take your Belief and Faith in the Gita and use them as foundations for deeper exploration. You might start asking questions like: Who is Krishna in reality? Are the teachings of the Gita applicable only to Hindus, or do they contain universal principles? Can I directly experience the states of consciousness the Gita describes? Why is Krishna portrayed as male, and what does gender mean in the context of divinity?

These questions don't undermine your Faith but deepen it through direct understanding and experience. Through this inquiry, you move beyond merely knowing about the Gita or believing in it. You seek to embody its wisdom and directly experience the truths it points toward. The text transforms from a source of information or an object of devotion into a living guide, leading to a direct experience of divine reality.

tapasya and sadhana: Approaches to Spiritual Practice

What is tapasya? The Power of Conviction

tapasya originates from the Sanskrit root *tap*, meaning "to heat" or "to burn." Traditionally, it refers to austerities or spiritual practices that generate inner heat, literally and metaphorically. Metaphorically, the heat burns away impurities and strengthens one's determination.

In essence, *tapasya* is about performing an action with unwavering conviction toward a specific outcome and continuing for whatever period is necessary to achieve that outcome. The defining characteristic of *tapasya* is its goal-oriented nature—you have a clear destination in mind and direct all your energy toward achieving it.

Think of someone who undertakes a pilgrimage to a sacred mountain, walking hundreds of miles while reciting mantras continuously. Each step is taken with the specific goal of reaching the summit where, according to tradition, a profound spiritual realization awaits. The pilgrim endures physical hardship, sleeps under the stars despite harsh weather, and maintains spiritual practices throughout the journey, all with an unwavering focus on the transformative experience at the destination. The effort itself is valued primarily for what it will eventually yield.

The power of *tapasya* lies in its singular focus and determination. There's a certain nobility and strength in saying, "I will do whatever it takes, for as long as it takes, to reach this goal." This unwavering commitment generates tremendous energy and can indeed lead to remarkable achievements.

Historically, *tapasya* has been associated with rigorous practices, such as extended fasting, maintaining challenging postures for long periods, observing silence for months or years, living in extreme environments like forests or mountains, and repeating mantras a specific number of times.

These practices require discipline, no doubt, but their defining feature isn't the discipline itself but the conviction that drives it and the certainty that the promised outcome is worth any temporary discomfort or sacrifice.

In *tapasya*, the practitioner's attention remains fixed on the horizon, on what will be achieved. Orientation toward a future goal can provide powerful motivation, especially when the path becomes difficult. The anticipated reward sustains effort in the face of challenges.

What is sadhana? The Art of Presence

sadhana presents an entirely different approach. Rather than focusing on a distant goal, *sadhana* is about bringing full awareness to the practice. It involves acting with mindfulness, being fully present in the process rather than fixating on its outcome.

The word *sadhana* comes from the Sanskrit root *sadh*, which means "to accomplish" or "to perfect." However, unlike *tapasya*, where accomplishment lies in accomplishing a future goal, in *sadhana*, the accomplishment is in the quality of attention brought to each moment of practice.

When you engage in *sadhana*, you develop discipline and consistency, but with a crucial difference—the outcome is found in the process. You practice not primarily to get somewhere else but to fully experience where you are. The journey becomes the destination.

Consider someone who sits in meditation each morning not to achieve enlightenment (though that may eventually occur) but to be present with whatever arises in each moment. Or imagine someone who chants not to accumulate a certain number of repetitions but to fully experience the vibration and meaning of each sound as it occurs. The defining characteristics of *sadhana* include:

- Present-moment awareness

- Consistent, regular practice

- Attention to the quality of experience rather than quantifiable results

- Enjoyment of the process itself

- An attitude of discovery rather than achievement

A person engaged in this practice is referred to as a "*sadhak*." One who performs actions with persistence and conviction without linking them to a specific outcome, instead finding fulfillment in the journey itself.

In *sadhana*, attention rests in the present rather than stretching toward the future. Present-moment awareness often brings a sense of peace and contentment that isn't dependent on achieving particular results. The practice becomes its reward.

The Essential Distinction: Outcome vs. Process

The fundamental difference between *tapasya* and *sadhana* lies in where fulfillment is found—in a future outcome or the present process.

With *tapasya*:

- The goal is paramount

- Success is measured by the achievement of specific results

- Motivation comes from anticipated future rewards

- You may endure the present moment for the sake of the future

- There's a clear endpoint or destination

With *sadhana*:

- The process is paramount

- Success is measured by the quality of awareness in each moment

- Motivation comes from engagement with the practice itself

- The present moment is entirely inhabited and valued

- The practice is ongoing, with no final destination

Neither approach is inherently superior, as they represent different relationships with spiritual practice, each with its strengths and potential pitfalls.

tapasya's strength lies in its ability to marshal tremendous determination and focus. When specific spiritual attainment requires breaking through obstacles or making complex changes, its goal-oriented nature can provide the necessary motivation and structure.

The *sadhana* approach fosters contentment, reduces anxiety about achievement, and often leads to deeper insights precisely because attention isn't divided between present experience and future goals.

Integrating the Approaches: A Complete Spiritual Life

Both sets of distinctions we've explored (*shraddha*, *vishwas*, and *adhyatma*) and (*tapasya*, *sadhana*) represent complementary dimensions of spiritual life. One describes the depth of engagement with spiritual truth, while the other describes the style of approach to spiritual practice. These dimensions can interact in interesting ways:

- A person might have deep Faith (*shraddha*) and express it through goal-oriented *tapasya*, like undertaking a challenging pilgrimage or vow with devotional fervor.

- Another might engage in intellectual Belief (*vishwas*) through process-oriented *sadhana*, like regularly studying sacred texts with full presence and attention to the learning process.

- A third might pursue spiritual inquiry (*adhyatma*) through *tapasya* and *sadhana* at different times, sometimes engaging in intensive goal-oriented practices and other times in present-centered exploration.

The most balanced spiritual life often incorporates all of these elements:

- The Intellectual Foundation of Belief

- The Emotional Commitment of Faith

- The experiential depth of spiritual inquiry

- The focused determination of *tapasya*

- The present-centered awareness of *sadhana*

These aren't mutually exclusive but complementary aspects of a rich spiritual life that enhance and balance each other.

The Bhagavad Gita offers wisdom relevant to this integration when Krishna advises Arjuna to act with dedication but without attachment to results, suggesting a middle path that honors purposeful action and present awareness.

Your spiritual temperament may naturally incline you toward specific approaches. Some with goal-oriented personalities often resonate with *tapasya*'s clarity of purpose and intellectual clarity of Belief. Others with more contemplative natures may find *the present-centered approach of sadhana* and the devotional quality of Faith more conducive to inner peace.

Neither preference is wrong, but awareness of your natural inclination can help you recognize when you might benefit from incorporating elements of the complementary approaches. By doing so, you can create a more comprehensive spiritual practice.

Summary: The Dance of Spiritual Approaches

Let's recap what we've explored in this chapter:

- Belief (*vishwas*) is intellectually based, formed through learning, reading, and hearing about spiritual truths. It's a conclusion that something is true, even without direct experience.

- Faith (*shraddha*) elevates Belief to absolute truth or personal law. When directed toward divinity, it expresses itself through worship, which involves admiration, prayer, and emotional devotion.

- Spiritual inquiry (*adhyatma*) begins with Belief and Faith as starting points for deeper questioning and direct experience. Rather than stopping at acceptance, it continues to peel away layers of understanding to reach more profound truths.

- *tapasya* is acting with conviction toward a specific outcome, focusing on the goal to be achieved. It harnesses the power of determination and clear direction.

- *sadhana* is acting with awareness and mindfulness, finding fulfillment in the process rather than in future attainment. It cultivates presence and contentment.

- The fundamental distinction between *tapasya* and *sadhana* lies in where fulfillment is found—in achieving a future goal or the quality of the present experience.

Each approach has its virtues and limitations, serving different purposes at different times in your spiritual journey. A balanced spiritual life may incorporate elements of all approaches, allowing them to complement and enrich one another.

Understanding these distinctions is more than an academic exercise. It can transform how you approach spiritual teachings, practices, and experiences. By recognizing where you are in this progression and what style of practice might best serve you, you can cultivate the qualities needed for your current growth stage more consciously.

By being aware of all these approaches, you can develop a more nuanced spiritual life, one that honors both the power of aspiration and the wisdom of presence, intellectual understanding and emotional devotion, the value of the destination, and the sacredness of the journey.

Start Today: Your First Step

If there's one action I would encourage you to take right now, it's this: **Engage in Faith Practice (*shraddha*).** This practice will help you experience the transformative power of Faith and devotion, allowing you to move beyond intellectual understanding to an emotional connection with spiritual truth.

Here's how to begin:

Select a prayer, chant, devotional song, or ritual from a tradition that resonates with you. Set aside a few minutes in a quiet space where you won't be disturbed.

- Engage in this practice with full emotional investment, setting aside questioning or analysis.

- Focus on opening your heart, cultivating devotion, and surrendering to something greater than yourself.

- After your devotional session, reflect on how approaching spirituality through Faith and devotion feels to you. What strengths and limitations do you notice?

The power of this practice lies in its ability to engage your heart, not just your mind. By cultivating devotion and surrender, you establish a deeper connection with spiritual truths that transcends intellectual understanding to emotional certainty and commitment.

The faith-based devotional approach has sustained spiritual seekers throughout history, providing both the emotional nourishment and the unwavering certainty needed to navigate life's challenges. Even if faith practice doesn't feel natural to you initially, approaching it with sincerity and openness can reveal its unique gifts.

The heart-centered approach complements intellectual understanding and direct spiritual inquiry, creating a more balanced and integrated spiritual life.

REMEMBER, FAITH ISN'T ABOUT ABANDONING INTELLIGENCE BUT ABOUT ENGAGING A DIFFERENT KIND OF KNOWING—ONE THAT EMBRACES WITH THE HEART WHAT THE MIND HAS RECOGNIZED AS VALUABLE.

Sanatana Dharma

THE FLOWING RIVER OF SPIRITUAL EVOLUTION

sanatana dharma IS OFTEN TRANSLATED SIMPLY AS "ETERNAL RELIGION" or "eternal way." While this translation isn't wrong, it barely scratches the surface of what this profound concept truly represents. It's a bit like describing the Ganges or the Amazon River as "flowing water," technically accurate, but missing the magnificent ecosystem, the countless tributaries, the rich history, and the life-sustaining power it holds.

In this chapter, we'll explore *sanatana dharma* as a label for Hinduism and as a dynamic, ever-evolving spiritual ecosystem that has flowed through human history, adapting and absorbing various influences while maintaining its essential nature. We'll trace its journey from prehistoric spiritual expressions to modern manifestations, understanding how each stage of its evolution added new dimensions while preserving core elements from earlier periods.

Understanding *sanatana dharma* as a living, breathing phenomenon rather than a rigid set of beliefs provides us with insight into one of the world's oldest spiritual traditions and how spirituality evolves to meet human needs across different times and contexts. This perspective invites us to view our spiritual journey not as a fixed path, but as a personal contribution to the ever-flowing river of wisdom and practice.

Let's Dive Deeper

sanatana dharma originates from Sanskrit: *sanatana* means eternal or perpetual, and *dharma* refers to natural law, duty, or a righteous way of living. But these words don't convey the dynamic quality that makes this tradition resilient and relevant across millennia.

A better way to understand *sanatana dharma* is to consider it a mighty river. From a distance, a river appears to be a single entity with clear boundaries and a consistent identity. Look closer, however, and you'll see it's constantly changing. Every drop of water is in motion; tributaries join its flow, the riverbed shifts, and the relationship between the river and the surrounding landscape evolves continuously.

Yet despite this constant change, the river maintains its essential nature. The Ganges remains the Ganges despite its endless transformation. Similarly, *sanatana dharma* retains its core identity while continuously incorporating new elements and expressions.

With this metaphor in mind, let's trace the journey of this spiritual river through five major evolutionary phases that have shaped what we now call Hinduism, or *sanatana dharma*.

The Five Evolutionary Stages of *sanatana dharma*

1. Prehistoric Religion: The Wellspring of Gratitude

The journey begins with prehistoric religion, which includes the spiritual practices of early human communities living close to nature. While some might identify these as tribal or indigenous traditions, the essence of these traditions transcends cultural and ethnic boundaries.

The primary focus of these earliest spiritual expressions was gratitude, which involved a profound sense of thankfulness directed toward the immediate environment that sustained human life. People expressed reverence for trees, plants, and animals that provided food, shelter, and clothing. They honored their ancestors and elders, who had passed down vital knowledge for survival. Prehistoric religion wasn't abstract theology but practical spirituality emerging from daily life.

At this earliest stage, there was no concept of God or the divine as a cosmic principle. Instead, spirituality was rooted in tangible relationships with the visible world—the forest that provided food, the river that offered water, and the sun that gave warmth and light. When people looked at a majestic tree, they didn't just see wood; they recognized a living being worthy of respect and gratitude.

These prehistoric expressions formed the first springs of what would eventually become the mighty river of *sanatana dharma*. Nature-based gratitude remains a prominent aspect of Hindu practices today, evident in traditions such as offering the first portions of meals to deities or respectfully touching the earth before stepping on it in the morning.

2. Vedic Religion: Channeling Gratitude Through Ritual

As human communities developed more complex social structures and a deeper understanding of natural cycles, the spiritual current evolved into Vedic religion, named after the Vedas (ancient texts containing hymns, philosophical dialogues, and ritual guidance).

In this phase, the focal point remained gratitude, but it extended beyond the immediately visible world to embrace cosmic principles and forces. The eight elements we discussed in our exploration of divinity became objects of reverence and contemplation. These included earth, water, fire, air, space, mind, intellect, and ego.

An expanded awareness gave rise to *yajnas* (sacrifices) and ritual oblations offered to natural elements. People would perform ceremonies honoring *agni* (fire), *surya* (sun), *varuna* (water), and other personified forces of nature. These weren't mere superstitious acts but structured ways of acknowledging humanity's dependence on cosmic processes and expressing gratitude for them.

The Vedic texts themselves were far more than religious manuals. They contained astronomical observations, scientific principles, geographical knowledge, and cultural practices representing a comprehensive attempt to understand and harmonize with the world.

In this Vedic stream, gratitude becomes more systematic and cosmic in scope, creating channels for human consciousness to connect with universal principles. The Vedic current remains strong in contemporary Hindu rituals, where fire ceremonies and offerings to natural elements remain central practices.

3. Vedantic Religion: The Depths of Philosophical Inquiry

As the river of *sanatana dharma* continued to flow, it deepened through philosophical inquiry. The later portions of the Vedas, known as the Upanishads, and texts like the Bhagavad Gita introduced a profoundly reflective dimension to spiritual life. The third phase, which we refer to as Vedantic religion (from "Vedanta," meaning "end of the Vedas"), shifted its focus from ritual performance to knowledge and understanding.

The emphasis moved from what to do to why and how to do it. Spiritual practice wasn't just about performing correct rituals, but about comprehending the principles underlying the practices. Questions became as important as answers. Why do we exist? What is consciousness? How does the individual relate to the universal? These inquiries led to the development of sophisticated philosophical systems that addressed the nature of reality, consciousness, and human potential.

In the Vedantic current, gratitude wasn't abandoned but transformed through understanding. Rather than being a prescribed attitude, it emerged naturally from recognizing more profound truths. Rituals remained valuable but were understood as tools for awareness rather than ends in themselves.

This philosophical dimension represents the profound depths of the river, where contemplation, debate, and rational inquiry create space for intellectual engagement with spiritual questions. Such philosophical inquiry continues to flow through tradition through various philosophical schools, meditation practices, and texts that invite questioning rather than blind acceptance.

Philosophical inquiry is central to the foundation of our exploration, as it encourages a discriminative mindset that seeks truth through questioning rather than mere adherence to tradition. The emphasis on "how" and "why" rather than "what" reflects the essence of both the Upanishads and the Gita, which invite seekers to look beyond surface appearances to deeper principles.

4. Puranic Religion: The Widening Through Story

As the philosophical depths of Vedanta developed, another current emerged that would significantly widen the river's reach. The Puranic religion followed, centered on stories (*puranas*) that conveyed spiritual principles through narrative rather than abstract philosophy.

The Vedantic approach, while profound, required considerable intellectual effort and discipline. Not everyone had the time, inclination, or capacity for such philosophical inquiry. The Puranic tradition addressed this by translating complex ideas into accessible stories featuring gods, goddesses, heroes, and cosmic dramas.

These narratives weren't mere simplifications but powerful vehicles for transmitting values, cosmology, and spiritual practices to broader audiences. Stories about divine figures like *Krishna, Shiva, and Lakshmi* encoded philosophical principles in memorable forms, allowing them to be shared across social boundaries.

In this phase, storytelling (*katha*) and listening (*shravanam*) became central spiritual practices. Evening gatherings, known as *harikathas*, became common, where people would come together after work to hear stories that both entertained and enlightened them. These weren't just passive entertainments but invitations to reflection (*mananam*) on the principles embedded in the narratives.

The Puranic current significantly expanded participation in spiritual life, as stories could be shared across differences of education, occupation, and social standing. Narrative practices continue to flourish vibrantly in contemporary Hinduism, manifesting in regular *katha* events, dramatized versions of epics such as the Ramayana and Mahabharata, and a rich iconography that visually narrates sacred stories.

5. Classical Hinduism: The Convergence of Currents

The fifth evolutionary stage, which we might call Classical Hinduism, represents the convergence of all previous currents into a comprehensive tradition accessible to people across diverse circumstances and temperaments.

Classical Hinduism, which represents the most recognizable expression of what is now called Hinduism, drew upon elements from all previous phases: the nature reverence of prehistoric religion, the ritual structure of Vedic practices, the philosophical depth of Vedanta, and the narrative power of the Puranic tradition. It combined these into a multifaceted approach that could meet people wherever they were on their spiritual journey.

In this phase, *bhakti* (devotion) emerged as a prominent feature, offering a direct emotional connection to the divine through personal relationships with specific forms of God. The abstract principles discussed in Vedantic philosophy were now accessible through devotion to personified deities representing various aspects of the divine.

Divine personification created tangible focal points for spiritual practice by giving name and form (*nama-rupa*) to divine aspects. Each deity represented certain divine qualities, allowing practitioners to connect with specific aspects of divinity that resonated with their nature and needs.

The expression of devotion expanded through various modalities, including *bhajans* (devotional songs), *kirtans* (chanting), *satsang* (spiritual gatherings), and elaborate temple rituals. Music and dance became central spiritual practices, not mere cultural embellishments. These art forms created heightened awareness that could unite diverse participants in a shared experience.

Symbolism became increasingly important, with every element of ritual and art encoded with multiple layers of meaning. When a Hindu priest performs rituals today, the symbolic gestures toward natural elements connect contemporary practice to ancient Vedic reverence while adding layers of philosophical understanding developed through later phases.

This classical form significantly expanded participation in spiritual life across social boundaries. In particular, the *bhakti* (devotion) movement emphasized that divine connection was accessible to everyone, regardless of birth, education, or social status. The democratizing influence challenged rigid social hierarchies and opened spiritual practice to previously marginalized groups.

Temple construction flourished during this period, with various communities establishing sacred spaces dedicated to their chosen deities. These temples became centers for worship, education, the arts, and community gatherings, thereby further integrating spiritual practices into daily life.

Modern Hinduism: The Continuing Flow

We recognize modern Hinduism as this classical religion in its contemporary expression, which is still evolving, incorporating new currents while maintaining a connection with its ancient sources.

The adaptive nature of *sanatana dharma* is evident in how it continues to evolve in response to changing circumstances. Consider how digital technology has transformed religious practice in recent years. A decade ago, virtually performing rituals like *homa* (fire ceremony) would have seemed inappropriate or impossible to many practitioners. Today, it's increasingly common to participate in temple ceremonies via videoconferencing, sponsor rituals remotely, or access spiritual teachings through mobile apps.

These adaptations aren't compromises but expressions of the tradition's inherent flexibility. It has the capacity to maintain essential principles while embracing new forms of expression. What appears radical in one generation often becomes standard practice in the next, as the tradition continues to evolve while maintaining its essential nature.

We now come to the true meaning of *sanatana dharma*. Yes, it is eternal (*sanatana*), but its eternity isn't static. Instead, the perpetual flow of a living tradition remains relevant by continuously incorporating new tributaries while maintaining a connection with its source.

The eternity of *sanatana dharma* lies not in unchanging dogma, but in its capacity for endless renewal, the ability to absorb influences, adapt to changing conditions, and evolve to meet human needs across different eras while preserving core insights into the nature of consciousness, reality, and human potential.

As this evolution continues, the philosophical dimension becomes increasingly essential. In a world of rapid change and information overload, the Vedantic emphasis on how to think rather than what to think provides necessary guidance. The discriminative faculty celebrated in Vedanta helps practitioners distinguish between helpful innovations and distracting novelties, between adaptations that preserve essential principles and changes that might dilute them.

Summary: The River That Flows Eternally

Let's recap what we've explored about *sanatana dharma* and its evolutionary journey:

- Rather than a static set of beliefs, *sanatana dharma* is best understood as a dynamic, ever-evolving spiritual tradition, like a mighty river that maintains its identity while constantly changing.

- Its journey can be traced through five evolutionary stages, each contributing essential elements to the tradition we now call Hinduism:

  > Prehistoric religion centered on gratitude toward nature, ancestors, and elders

  > Vedic religion expanded this gratitude to cosmic principles through structured rituals

  > Vedantic religion introduced philosophical inquiry and an emphasis on understanding

  > Puranic religion made spiritual principles accessible through storytelling

  > Classical Hinduism integrated all previous elements with a focus on devotion and personal connection to the divine

- Modern Hinduism continues this evolution, adapting to contemporary circumstances while connecting with ancient sources of wisdom.

- The true meaning of *sanatana* (eternal) lies not in unchanging rigidity but in continuous flow—the tradition's capacity to evolve while preserving essential insights.

- As the tradition continues to adapt, the Vedantic emphasis on how to think rather than what to think becomes increasingly crucial for navigating change wisely.

The evolutionary understanding of *sanatana dharma* offers more than a historical perspective by providing a model for approaching spiritual life as a dynamic journey, rather than adhering to fixed rules. It invites us to participate consciously in the evolving river of wisdom, drawing from ancient sources while remaining responsive to present circumstances.

By recognizing ourselves as both inheritors and contributors to this flowing tradition, we can engage with spiritual practice more authentically, understanding that our innovations and adaptations may become tributary streams feeding the river for future generations.

Start Today: Your First Step

If there's one action I encourage you to take right now, it's this: **Explore the Five Currents in Your Life.**

The following practice invites you to examine how the five evolutionary stages of *sanatana dharma* manifest in your contemporary spiritual life. It will help you identify which currents are strongest for you and which might offer new dimensions for growth.

Here's how to begin:

Set aside quiet time. For each of the five currents we've explored, reflect on how it currently appears in your spiritual life:

- **Prehistoric (Gratitude):** How do you express gratitude toward nature, ancestors, and elders? What practices connect you with the natural world? You may offer thanks before meals, acknowledge the elements in your daily routine, or maintain family traditions honoring those who came before you.

- **Vedic (Ritual):** What rituals or ceremonies hold meaning for you? How do structured practices support your spiritual growth? These include daily prayer, fire ceremonies, worship at particular times of day, or other formalized observances that create sacred time and space.

- **Vedantic (Philosophy):** What fundamental questions drive your spiritual inquiry? How do you engage intellectually with spiritual concepts? Consider how you study texts, contemplate deep questions, or engage in philosophical discussions about the nature of reality and consciousness.

- **Puranic (Story):** What spiritual narratives have shaped your understanding? How do stories communicate truths that concepts alone cannot? Reflect on which myths, epics, or teaching stories resonate most deeply with you and how they inform your worldview.

- **Classical (Devotion):** What forms of devotional practice resonate with you? How do you establish a personal connection with the divine? Devotional practices might involve bhajans (devotional singing), *puja* (worship), pilgrimage, or cultivating loving relationships with specific manifestations of divinity.

For each current, note:

- One specific practice you currently engage in

- One practice you might explore further to deepen this dimension

- How strongly does this current flow in your spiritual life (is it a main channel or a small tributary?)

- Consider which current feels most natural to you and which feels most challenging. What might this reveal about your spiritual temperament and opportunities for growth?

- Reflect on how these different currents complement each other in a balanced spiritual practice. How might strength in one area support development in another?

The power of this exercise lies in recognizing the multidimensional nature of spiritual tradition and your relationship to it. By mapping how these five currents manifest in your life, you gain clarity about your natural inclinations and potential pitfalls. The gained awareness enables you to create a more balanced practice that honors your strengths while encouraging growth in areas that need development.

The prehistoric current connects us with nature and gratitude; the Vedic current provides structure and cosmic connection; the Vedantic current deepens understanding; the Puranic current nourishes imagination; and the Classical current cultivates devotional relationships.

By consciously engaging with all five currents, you participate more fully in the flowing river of *sanatana dharma*, drawing from its ancient sources while contributing to its continued evolution through your unique expression of timeless principles.

REMEMBER, A THRIVING SPIRITUAL LIFE TYPICALLY DRAWS FROM ALL FIVE CURRENTS, THOUGH THEIR PROPORTIONS MAY VARY BASED ON INDIVIDUAL TEMPERAMENT AND LIFE CIRCUMSTANCES.

PART TWO

Worship and Prayers

Worship

THE ART AND ESSENCE

WORSHIP IS ONE OF HUMANITY'S most profound and universal practices. Yet beyond the rituals and traditions lies a deeper essence, something that happens when we genuinely connect with something greater than ourselves. In this chapter, I aim to explore this essence with you, not as a distant academic concept, but as a living, breathing practice that can transform our everyday experiences.

You see, worship isn't just something that happens in temples or churches. It's not limited to specific times or places. At its core, worship is about connection to ourselves, others, and the divine energy that permeates everything around us. Whether you consider yourself deeply religious, casually spiritual, or simply curious about human traditions, understanding the true nature of worship can offer insights into how we navigate our lives.

Let's embark on this journey together, exploring the external practices and internal experiences that make up the rich tapestry of worship. Along the way, we'll discover how ancient wisdom from the Bhagavad Gita and Upanishads illuminates our modern understanding of connection, responsibility, and purpose.

Let's Dive Deeper

Understanding the true essence of worship offers us a path back to wholeness in a world that often feels disconnected and fragmented. It's about reconnecting with something timeless in our time-bound existence. So, let's roll up our sleeves and dive into what worship means beyond the surface-level understanding most of us have inherited. The insights we'll explore come from ancient wisdom traditions, but they speak directly to our modern lives, with all their complexity and challenges.

Worship, in its essence, can take two primary forms: external and internal. Both are pathways to the same destination, though they travel through different landscapes of experience. When we hear the word "worship," most people think of external worship. It's tangible and concrete in the form of the rituals we perform, the offerings we make, and the prayers we recite. There's something profoundly reassuring about external worship. When we bow before a deity carved in stone, brass, silver, or some other material, we give form to something formless, making the abstract concrete enough to grasp.

Why is this so comforting? Our minds naturally work with objects, names, and forms. That's our default thinking process. External worship meets us where we are, giving us something visible and tangible to focus on.

Internal worship, on the other hand, is subtle and formless. It happens in the quietness of our consciousness. Instead of interacting with an external representation of divinity, we contemplate and visualize the divine within our minds. We anchor ourselves in the image and the silence between our thoughts. Internal worship transcends the boundaries of time, place, and location, and you can slip into it whenever you need to, wherever you are.

Both forms of worship have their place and purpose. External worship is easier for most of us to practice consistently. There is a reason why religious traditions worldwide have developed elaborate rituals and ceremonies, as they help us focus, provide structure, and foster a sense of community. Internal worship, though often more challenging to maintain, can produce more profound and lasting effects because it dissolves the perceived separation between the worshipper and worshipped.

The True Meaning of Worship

But what is worship? Beyond the rituals and contemplations, what happens when we worship?

According to the wisdom of the Gita and Upanishads, true worship isn't about appeasing a distant deity or earning cosmic brownie points. It's about taking responsibility for your actions while recognizing that you're part of something larger than yourself. It's essential to understand that your actions and, yes, even your thoughts, set off ripple effects far beyond what you can see or control.

If you believe in a higher power, you might refer to the confluence of energies that shape these outcomes as "God" and give it a name and form. If you consider yourself more of a spiritual person, you might not worry as much about naming this energy. Instead, you acknowledge that your actions trigger cascading effects beyond your immediate vicinity or time constraints.

The fascinating thing is what happens next. When outcomes align with our wishes, believers often feel their faith strengthened. Some might question their beliefs when things don't go as planned, while others might interpret it as a test from a higher power. However, for true spiritualists, these judgments fall away. Good or bad, they're just outcomes. The spiritualist continues to perform thoughtful actions and move on with life.

In a nutshell, that's the entire message of the Bhagavad Gita! Isn't it remarkable that profound wisdom, when distilled, is straightforward yet transformative?

Worship as Hospitality: Treating the Divine as an Honored Guest

Let's shift our focus back to external worship for a moment because there's something beautiful about how many traditions, particularly Hinduism, approach it.

Have you ever considered that external worship mirrors how we treat an honored guest in our homes? Think about it. What do you do when someone you deeply respect and love visits your home? You prepare your space, offer refreshments, engage in meaningful conversation, share stories, and ensure their comfort.

Traditional external worship follows remarkably similar patterns. Consider these parallels:

- You might decorate your home with colorful flowers to welcome a beloved guest and create a pleasing, bright, and festive atmosphere. Flowers and garlands (*pushpam samarpayami*) are offered to the deity as part of worship.

- You'd light incense sticks to spread a sweet fragrance throughout your home. Similarly, in worship, incense (*dhoopam samarpayami*) is lit and circled three times to symbolize the deity's powers of manifestation, sustenance, and dissolution.

- As a hospitable host, you'd offer water to quench your guest's thirst. In worship, water (*jalam samarpayami*) is similarly provided to the deity.

- You might prepare a luxurious bath with special oils or fragrances for your guests. The deity is also bathed (*snanam samarpayami*) with water, sometimes enhanced with sandalwood paste, milk, yogurt, honey, or other substances. You'd provide clean clothes for your guest after their bath. In worship, cloth (*vastram samarpayami*) is used to wipe and dress the deity.

- You would ensure your guest is seated in a well-lit space. In worship, oil lamps (*deepam samarpayami*) are lit before the deity.

- You'd serve delicious food and fruits to your guests. Similarly, fruits (*phalam samarpayami*) and food offerings (*naivedyam samarpayami*) are presented to the deity.

- You might speak of your guest's excellent qualities during your time together. In worship, mantras and hymns highlight the deity's characteristics.

- Your family might gather to sing or celebrate with your guest. Devotional songs (*bhajans*) are chanted in worship, often with aarti ceremonies.

- You'd prepare a comfortable place for your guest to rest. Similarly, the deity is "put to bed" in a cushioned swing with melodious music (*laali*).

- Throughout the visit, you might share meaningful stories. In worship, philosophical and devotional stories (*pravachana*) are shared.

Isn't that fascinating? The rituals that might sometimes seem mysterious or arbitrary reflect the deeply human practice of hospitality. When we worship externally, we're treating the divine as an honored guest in our lives.

The Bridge Between External and Internal

While external and internal worship seem like separate practices, the goal is to create a bridge between them. External worship, with its tangible forms and rituals, provides structure and focus. But without an internal connection, it becomes an empty routine.

The key is to perform external worship with genuine love and commitment, allowing it to cultivate an internal connection. The external form becomes a gateway to the internal experience. As your practice deepens, the distinction between internal and external begins to blur. The deity outside and the divinity within are reflections of the same reality.

Given this understanding, we arrive at a crucial question: Do you have to go through elaborate processes with numerous offerings to worship properly? Not necessarily. As Krishna says in the Gita,

> *Offer with devotion a leaf, flower, fruit, or even just plain water. As the divinity in this universe, I will delightfully partake in that article offered with love*

The mindset matters, not the quantity or variety of offerings. Worship with love brings peace and bliss, whereas worship performed with indifference is merely a chore.

Summary: The Essence of True Worship

As we come to the end of our exploration, let's gather the essential insights about worship:

- Worship exists in both external and internal forms. External worship utilizes tangible objects, rituals, and offerings to focus our attention and create a structured experience. Internal worship happens in the realm of consciousness unbound by time, place, or form.

- The true meaning of worship isn't about appeasing a deity but taking responsibility for our actions while recognizing we're part of something greater. Our thoughts and actions create ripple effects beyond what we can see or control.

- External worship mirrors how we treat an honored guest, reflecting the human quality of hospitality. From offering flowers and fragrances to sharing food and stories, we create a space of reverence and connection.

- While elaborate rituals have their place and value, the essence of worship lies in our intention and emotional state. A simple offering with genuine love is more meaningful than elaborate rituals performed mechanically.

- The goal is to bridge external and internal worship, using tangible practices to cultivate intangible connections. When worship is performed with love rather than indifference, it brings peace and bliss rather than feeling like a chore.

These insights transcend specific religious traditions. Whether deeply religious, casually spiritual, or simply interested in human traditions, understanding the essence of worship can help you connect more deeply with yourself, others, and the divine energy that permeates everything.

Start Today: Your First Step

If there's one action I encourage you to take right now, it's this: **Create a simple personal worship ritual that bridges the external and internal.**

Here's how to begin:

- Choose something meaningful to you — a deity, a symbol, a natural element, or even an abstract concept like compassion or wisdom. Then, design a brief daily ritual that involves both external actions and internal contemplation.

- Perhaps you light a lamp or candle (external) and then sit in silence, visualizing the flame's light spreading through your consciousness (internal). You could place a flower before an image that inspires you (external) and then contemplate the qualities the image represents (internal).

The specifics matter less than the intention and consistency. Make it something you can practice daily, even for a few minutes. Approach it with genuine love rather than obligation.

As you continue this practice, notice how it affects your state of mind, relationships, and sense of connection to something larger than yourself. You will experience the timeless essence that worship has offered humanity across the centuries—a pathway to connection, meaning, and transformation.

REMEMBER, WHEN WORSHIP IS APPROACHED WITH GENUINE SINCERITY AND LOVE, THE BOUNDARY BETWEEN EXTERNAL RITUAL AND INTERNAL EXPERIENCE DISSOLVES, UNIFYING THE TWO INTO GENUINE DEVOTION.

Transforming Prayer

FROM TRANSACTION TO CONNECTION

I REMEMBER STANDING IN A BEAUTIFUL TEMPLE years ago, watching people around me pray intensely. Some whispered their requests, others closed their eyes in deep concentration, and a few I knew well even shared their promises: "Let my daughter get married, and I'll donate generously to the temple." I found myself wondering: Is this what prayer is supposed to be? A cosmic negotiation?

The question stayed with me for years, surfacing in quiet moments of reflection. Growing up, I was taught that prayer means asking for good grades, health, and fortune. There was a divine customer service line where we could submit our requests and hope for approval. But something about this approach never felt quite right to me.

Maybe you've felt the same way. Perhaps you've stood in your place of worship or the quiet sanctuary of nature and wondered if there's more to prayer than presenting a wish list to the universe.

Through years of studying the Bhagavad Gita and various spiritual philosophies, I discovered a profound transformation in my understanding of prayer. It wasn't just a different technique but an entirely different paradigm that shifted prayer from a transaction to a connection. And this shift didn't just change how I prayed—it changed my entire life.

Let's Dive Deeper

In this chapter, I aim to share what I've learned about the true purpose of prayer and how transforming your approach can bring about profound changes not only to your spiritual practice but to every aspect of your life. Let's explore together what happens when we stop treating prayer as a cosmic vending machine and start using it as a powerful tool for connection with the divine attributes that already exist within and around us.

Let's be honest about how most of us learned to pray. We typically approach the divine with a specific request in mind: "Please help me get this job," "Please heal my illness," and "Please help my team win this game." It's a transactional relationship! We ask for something and often promise something back in return.

I call this the "transactional prayer trap," and I fell into it for years. I can't count how often I've struck deals with the divine: "If you help me pass this exam, I'll circumambulate at the temple," or "If you help my loved one recover, I'll donate to charity." Sound familiar?

There's nothing inherently wrong with asking for help in times of need since it's a natural human impulse. However, when our entire relationship with the divine is based on transactions, when we only connect when we want something, we miss the true power and purpose of prayer.

Think about your closest human relationships for a moment. How would you feel if a friend only called you when they needed a favor? What if your child only spoke to you when they wanted money or permission for something? These relationships would feel hollow and one-sided, wouldn't they?

Yet this is precisely how many of us approach our relationship with the divine—as a one-way street where we ask God to give. And when our prayers aren't "answered" as we hoped, we often feel disappointed, abandoned, or even angry. We might think, "Why isn't God listening to me?" or "What did I do wrong?"

But what if we've misunderstood the very nature and purpose of prayer?

The Divine Is Not a Help Desk

As I deepened my spiritual studies, I came to a humbling and liberating realization: the divine is not a troubleshooting help desk. Let that sink in for a moment.

If you believe in a supreme being or divine energy that is truly omniscient and omnipotent, that is, all-knowing and all-powerful, then think about what that means. Such a being would, by definition, already know your needs, desires, and what's truly best for you. They would understand your situation more completely than you do yourself.

When we constantly remind God of what we want, aren't we implicitly suggesting that either:

The divine doesn't already know what we need

or

The divine knows but needs convincing to help us.

Both assumptions subtly undermine the omniscience and benevolence we attribute to the divine. As I contemplated this paradox, I realized that my transactional approach to prayer wasn't only ineffective, but also "an unpardonable sin." Strong words, I know, but consider what this means: when we pray only for outcomes, we insult the very power and wisdom of the Supreme Being we claim to worship.

The divine is not a vending machine where we insert prayers and extract blessings. It is not a genie bound to grant our wishes if we find the right words or perform the proper rituals. It is not a cosmic customer service representative handling our complaints and requests.

When we approach prayer with this transactional mindset, we diminish the divine and ourselves. We reduce an infinite, boundless source of wisdom and love to a mere wish-granter. And we reduce ourselves to mere consumers of divine favors rather than participants in a sacred relationship.

There must be a better way—and there is.

Purpose of Prayer: Connection, Not Transaction

If prayer isn't about asking for things, what is it for? Through my study of the Gita and other scriptures, I discovered a profound truth: we should pray not to receive something from the divine, but to connect with the divine attributes themselves.

Think about the qualities we often associate with the divine: wisdom, strength, compassion, peace, joy, love. These aren't just abstract concepts, but they're living energies, divine attributes that we can connect with and embody.

When we pray, intending to connect to these attributes, something remarkable happens. Instead of approaching the divine from a place of lack—"I don't have enough, please give me more"—we approach from a place of openness to receive what is already abundantly available.

It's like the difference between standing in a garden with a shopping list and demanding that the garden provide precisely what you want. Compare this to walking into that same garden with open hands and an open heart, ready to receive the bounty already there.

You aren't asking for anything when you pray to connect to the Supreme's character: strength, intelligence, and transcendental nature. You're aligning yourself with those qualities. You're opening yourself to embody those divine attributes in your own life. And this is where the magic happens. When you connect to divine attributes through prayer:

> You gain the strength and wisdom to exercise your
> free will judiciously

You naturally find yourself on the path of righteousness

You begin to attract people with similar characteristics

You start to experience life with greater bliss and fulfillment

The transformation from outcome-focused prayer to connection-centered prayer changes not just how you pray but how you live. When you pray for an outcome, you remain powerless, waiting for something outside yourself to change your circumstances. But when you pray for connection to divine attributes, you become empowered to change your circumstances through the wisdom and strength you receive.

Shifting Your Prayer Mindset

Now, let's get practical. How exactly do you make this shift from transactional to connectional prayer? It starts with changing the focus of your prayers.

Instead of praying for specific outcomes, pray for the divine attributes you need to navigate your circumstances. Move from outcome to attribute. Here's how this might look in practice:

Instead of: "Please cure my illness."

Try: "Let me connect to the divine attribute of wellness and vitality."

Instead of: "Help me get this job."

Try: "Let me personify the divine attributes of confidence, clarity, and purpose."

Instead of: "Make this relationship work."

Try: "Help me connect to the divine attributes of unconditional love, patience, and understanding."

Do you see the difference? In each case, you're shifting from asking for a specific result to connecting with the qualities you need to handle whatever comes your way. You're moving from a passive stance to an active one, from dependence to co-creation.

I'm not suggesting you abandon practical solutions to your challenges. If you're ill, by all means, see a doctor. If you're seeking employment, update your resume and expand your professional network. If you're struggling in a relationship, consider counseling. Divine connection doesn't replace practical action but enhances it by giving you the internal resources you need to take effective action.

A Simple Practice

If this seems overwhelming and if you're thinking, "Do I need to memorize a list of divine attributes from the Gita?" let me offer a more straightforward approach:

Focus on a personal form of divinity that resonates with you, whether Krishna or simply your conception of a loving universe.

With your gaze and attention fixed on this divine form, offer your gratitude with the words, "Thank you."

Remain in this grateful contemplation, connecting yourself to the divine presence.

The practice I've described, which is found in the Gita and Upanishads, enables you to connect with divine attributes without intellectualizing the process. Through sincere gratitude, you naturally invoke grace. *Gratitude, as we've discussed in previous chapters, is the doorway to divine connection.*

Remember the beautiful cycle:

Gratitude leads to grace, and grace leads to self and God-realization.

When that happens, your professional and personal life are transformcd.

The Power of Divine Connection

When you shift from transactional to connectional prayer, you'll begin to notice profound changes in your life:

1. Inner Strength

You'll find yourself responding to challenges with surprising strength. You'll still experience fear and uncertainty, but discover reserves of courage and resilience even within those challenging emotions.

2. Clearer Guidance

Decision-making becomes more intuitive. When connected to divine wisdom, you develop "discernment," which is the ability to see clearly what is right in each situation.

3. Authentic Relationships

You'll begin to attract people who resonate with the divine qualities you're embodying. Superficial connections may fall away, but deeper, more authentic relationships will take their place.

4. Greater Peace

The constant anxiety of wondering if your prayers will be "answered" dissolves. You realize that the divine is not withholding blessings until you say the right words or make the right offerings. Divine abundance is already available, and you're simply learning to align with it.

5. True Bliss

It is not the temporary happiness that comes from getting what you want but a more profound contentment that remains steady regardless of external circumstances.

One of the most powerful aspects of this approach to prayer is that it honors your free will. The divine has given you the freedom to make your own choices. Rather than asking the divine to override that freedom by forcing particular outcomes, you're asking for the wisdom and strength to exercise your free will judiciously.

That's what genuine empowerment looks like. With the divine on your side, or more accurately, with you aligned with the divine, there is no need to feel powerless in life's challenges.

Summary: The Transformation of Prayer

Let's recap the key insights we've explored about transforming our approach to prayer:

Traditional transactional prayer—asking the divine for specific outcomes can diminish our connection with the divine by:

- Implicitly questioning divine omniscience and benevolence

- Creating a one-sided relationship based on what we can get

- Keeping us in a state of powerlessness, waiting for external intervention

True prayer is about connection, not transaction. We pray not to get something from the divine but to connect with divine attributes such as:

- Wisdom and intelligence

- Strength and courage

- Love and compassion

- Peace and joy

When we make this shift, we:

- Honor the omnipotence of the divine and not insult

- Develop the inner resources to navigate life's challenges

- Attract people and circumstances that align with these divine qualities

- Experience greater bliss and fulfillment

The simplest way to practice connectional prayer is through gratitude by fixing our attention on the divine with appreciation and allowing grace to flow naturally into our lives. Connectional prayer doesn't replace practical action. It empowers. We still use our rational minds and take appropriate steps to address our challenges, but we do so with the added benefit of divine connection.

The outcome is a life in which prayer isn't a separate activity we do when we need something, but an ongoing state of connection that infuses everything we do with divine qualities. We transition from viewing prayer as a means to change God's mind about our circumstances to seeing it as a way to align our minds with divine wisdom.

Start Today: Your First Step

If there's one action I encourage you to take right now, it's this: **Transform a single prayer from transaction to a connection.**

Here's how to begin:

Think of something you've been praying about recently—a challenge you're facing, a decision you must make, or a situation you're concerned about.

Notice how you've been approaching this prayer. Have you been asking for a specific outcome? Have you been making deals or promises to the divine? There's no judgment here, just awareness. Now, reframe this prayer completely. Instead of asking for an outcome, identify what divine qualities or attributes would help you navigate this situation.

Find a quiet moment and bring your attention to the divine in whatever form resonates with you.

> Instead of saying, "Please give me [outcome]," say something like, "I commit to [attribute]."

> Instead of "Please solve this financial problem," try "I commit to managing my resources wisely and taking purposeful steps toward financial stability."

> Instead of "Please help me get this job," try "I commit to bringing my best self forward, embracing confidence, clarity, and purpose in this opportunity."

> Instead of "Please heal this relationship," try "I commit to practicing compassion and deepening my understanding of this relationship.

After expressing this connectional prayer, sit quietly and imagine yourself already embodying these divine qualities. How would you approach your situation differently if you had these attributes?

The essence of transforming your prayer life is such a simple shift, from asking for outcomes to connecting with divine attributes. By practicing just one prayer today, you begin to rewire patterns that may have been in place for years.

As you experience the difference this makes, you can gradually extend this approach to other areas of your life. Prayer becomes less about petitioning an external power and more about aligning yourself with the divine qualities already available.

Change the way you pray, and you change your life. Start with this one prayer today. With the divine on your side, there is no need to be powerless.

REMEMBER, THE DIVINE IS NOT A COSMIC VENDING MACHINE OR A TROUBLESHOOTING HELP DESK. WHEN YOU SHIFT YOUR PRAYER FROM REQUESTING TO CONNECTING, YOU HONOR THE OMNIPOTENCE OF THE SUPREME WHILE EMPOWERING YOURSELF TO PARTICIPATE ACTIVELY IN YOUR TRANSFORMATION.

The Four Devotees

HOW WE GROW IN SPIRITUAL AWARENESS

THE WAYS PEOPLE APPROACH SPIRITUALITY reveal fascinating patterns. Some pray only during times of crisis, while others perform regular rituals seeking material benefits. A third group pursues deep philosophical understanding, and a rare few seem to experience a divine presence in every moment of their lives. These different approaches aren't random variations; they reflect distinct spiritual personalities that have been recognized for thousands of years.

Before modern psychology developed personality assessments, the Bhagavad Gita provided a sophisticated framework for understanding the diverse spiritual temperaments. What's remarkable about Gita's approach is that it doesn't judge these personality types as good or bad but recognizes them as different starting points on the spiritual journey.

This chapter will explore the four spiritual personality types outlined in the Gita: the Distressed, the Acquirer, the Inquirer, and the Knower. Each represents a progressively deeper level of spiritual engagement. By understanding where you currently fit in this framework, you can recognize both your spiritual strengths and your opportunities for growth on the path toward fuller realization.

Let's Dive Deeper

The beauty of these four spiritual personalities is that they aren't static categories but points along a continuum of development. They represent the natural evolution of consciousness as we grow spiritually. Each type builds upon and includes elements of the previous ones while transcending their limitations.

Even more reassuring is that Krishna welcomes devotees of all four types. There's no harsh judgment for those who approach the divine primarily during times of need or for material gain. Instead, there is an understanding that these are natural starting points from which deeper connections can develop.

These four types are similar to how we learn any skill. We begin with a basic understanding and motivation, then gradually develop more sophisticated approaches as our experience and expertise grow. Just as we don't criticize a beginner violinist for not playing at a professional level, there's no judgment for being at an earlier stage of spiritual development.

Let's explore these spiritual personalities in detail, seeing how they relate to the divine and how they might evolve into the next level of awareness.

The Distressed: Spirituality Born from Crisis

The first spiritual personality type identified in the Gita is "the Distressed." Does this sound familiar? The person remembers the divine only during times of loss or difficulty. Perhaps their job is in jeopardy, they're facing financial troubles, they've received a concerning medical diagnosis, or they're dealing with a painful relationship breakdown. During these crises, they suddenly recall the powers of the divine and turn their attention toward seeking help.

For the Distressed, remembrance of the divine is transactional and transient and invariably linked to receiving some benefit. Their prayers often take the form of desperate pleas: "God, if you get me through this, I promise I'll..."

Once the hardship passes, however, the Distressed person typically returns to everyday life, and their spiritual connection fades into the background until the next crisis arrives, rekindling that momentary bond with the divine.

If we look for a parallel in ordinary human relationships, the approach of the Distressed resembles what we might call "selfish networking." Think of someone who only reaches out when they need something—a job referral, a favor, or some other form of assistance, but they disappear from your life once their need is fulfilled. The connection is point-to-point and momentary rather than an ongoing relationship.

Before judging this type too harshly, remember that many start here. When life is going well, it's easy to feel self-sufficient. It often takes a significant challenge to remind us that we're not in complete control. There may be forces beyond us that offer help or comfort. The Distressed may not have the most evolved spiritual outlook, but they've at least recognized the possibility of a higher power in times of need. That's the starting point.

The Acquirer: Spirituality as a Continuous Transaction

The second spiritual personality type is "the Acquirer." Unlike the Distressed, the Acquirer maintains a more consistent connection with the divine, but it's still primarily oriented around receiving benefits rather than giving or serving.

Acquirers pray to gain wealth, status, fame, or material comforts. Their prayers typically come with a wish list attached. Like the Distressed, they share the expectation of material benefit from their spiritual practices, but they're more proactive and consistent in their approach. They don't wait for a crisis to remember the divine. They regularly perform rituals, say prayers, or engage in spiritual practices to acquire more.

The Acquirer's relationship with the divine resembles a one-sided network or relationship, one that always takes but rarely gives back. They approach spirituality as a transaction: "I'll perform this ritual or say these prayers, and in return, I expect these benefits."

Krishna offers a fascinating perspective on the Acquirer. Rather than condemning this approach outright, he suggests that the Acquirer should at least become familiar with the source of all benefits. In other words, even if you primarily want to receive, it is essential to understand the origins of these gifts.

Specifically, Krishna advises the Acquirer to become knowledgeable about the source of all material abundance: the core gross elements (air, water, earth, space, and fire) and their characteristics, as well as the subtle elements (smell, taste, sight, touch, and sound). By directing the Acquirer's attention to these fundamental aspects of creation, Krishna encourages mindfulness, which in turn fosters a deeper appreciation for the source.

"Enjoy the sensory experience of smell and taste," Krishna advises. "Relish the visual appeal of sight. Feel the variability of touch. Experience the vibrations of sound." When the Acquirer gains this knowledge and appreciation, they thoroughly enjoy the creations of the material world rather than constantly grasping for more.

Krishna acknowledges that the Acquirer's innate nature is to accumulate, and in their quest to hoard more, they might resort to questionable practices. The divine doesn't prevent these activities, after all, each person has the intellect to make their own choices. But Krishna suggests that if the Acquirer develops awareness that divine energy underlies everything, this realization elevates them above the Distressed. There's hope that eventually, they might realize that life isn't all about getting, that giving is equally important.

The Inquirer: Spirituality as Exploration

The third spiritual personality type represents a significant leap in consciousness, and that is "the Inquirer." The great seer Vedanta Desikan described the Inquirer as someone on a journey to attain the supreme. Midway through this journey, the Inquirer pauses to rest, contemplating divinity and seeking direct experience before proceeding again.

What distinguishes the Inquirer from the previous types is the source of motivation. They're not primarily seeking relief from distress or material acquisition. Instead, they genuinely desire to understand. The Inquirer constantly asks, "Why?" They pursue spiritual bliss, seek to distinguish between the authentic self and the temporary body, and progress toward higher levels of spiritual development. The Inquirer plays in an entirely different league than the Acquirer. They adhere closely to the Gita's teachings, focusing on three key awareness practices:

- Meditating on the imperishable energy or soul that transcends the physical body

- Recognizing the material characteristics of the body, which temporarily houses this imperishable soul

- Understanding that actions ultimately determine one's life path

Like the Acquirer, the Inquirer begins by appreciating the material world through understanding its gross and subtle elements. But they go further, recognizing that human life begins at conception and that no one, not even the greatest saint, is free from karma (the law of action and consequence).

The Inquirer faces a profound challenge: experiencing the pure, imperishable soul while still embodied in physical form. During this exploratory process, they must remain detached from the outcomes of their actions. Their goal transcends action since they seek to experience the authentic self or soul directly. This pursuit might seem like a vicious maze, resolvable only through persistent inquiry.

The Inquirer represents a tremendous evolution beyond the previous types. They've moved from crisis-oriented transactional spirituality into genuinely exploring life's most profound questions. Their spiritual practice isn't about acquiring something, but about discovering the truth.

The Knower: Spirituality as Union

The fourth and most evolved spiritual personality type is "the Knower." The Knower is an Inquirer who, after pausing for realization, resumes the journey with even greater commitment and clarity.

For the Knower, the spiritual journey never ends. They understand that the destination transcends the limitations of space and time. Their goal isn't to achieve some exalted location or status, nor are they preoccupied with promises of liberation after death. Instead, the Knower possesses single-minded dedication, devotion, and commitment to knowing divinity directly.

The love a Knower experiences is not for any object or outcome, but it's pure longing for a merger with the divine source. Krishna makes a remarkable statement about such devotees in the Gita, saying that their overwhelming and limitless love consumes the divine itself. "The love I reciprocate," Krishna admits, "is no match for the love of the Knower."

Even more profoundly, Krishna declares, "The knower is always in my heart; in fact, the knower is myself." This revelation is significant, implying that existence depends on individuals like the Knower. Their very being participates in and sustains the divine reality.

The Knower's sole purpose is to love the divine unconditionally, never breaking the connection, always contemplating and rejoicing in divine glory. This devotee overwhelms the divine with love and cannot survive even a moment of separation. In return, Krishna says, the divine gives everything without limitation. When the giver is the sustainer of the universe with abundant riches, how could there be any limitation?

The Knower attains the distinguishing knowledge of the divine. The merger between Krishna and the Knower becomes complete and inseparable. Gita describes this moment of merger as a revelation of the ultimate truth, where the Knower can confidently declare, "Shri Krishna is everything."

This highest spiritual personality type represents the pinnacle of devotion, not as blind faith or desperate pleading, but as direct knowledge through loving union.

Krishna accepts all

One of the most beautiful aspects of the Gita's teaching is that Krishna regards all four personality types as sincere devotees—the Distressed, the Acquirer, the Inquirer, and the Knower. While the Inquirer and Knower receive the fullest measure of divine grace, Krishna acknowledges that even the Distressed and the Acquirer are developing spiritual inclinations through their prayers.

Krishna offers a touching perspective on this spectrum of devotion, saying, "All four personality types allow me to serve and be generous. Without my devotees, who would I serve?" This reveals a profound truth about the divine-human relationship. It's reciprocal. Even as devotees seek to serve the divine, the divine seeks opportunities to serve them in return.

This perspective encourages us to meet ourselves where we are. If you recognize yourself primarily as the Distressed or the Acquirer right now, there's no need for shame or self-judgment. These are valid starting points on the spiritual journey. What matters is the direction of movement, the gradual evolution from crisis-based or transactional spirituality toward the more profound explorations of the Inquirer and, ultimately, the unitive consciousness of the Knower.

Summary: The Journey Through Spiritual Personalities

As explored in this chapter, the Bhagavad Gita provides a remarkably nuanced understanding of the diverse spiritual temperaments among believers. Rather than presenting a one-size-fits-all approach to spirituality, it acknowledges that people connect with the divine in different ways, based on their current level of consciousness and motivation.

- The journey begins with the Distressed, who turn to the divine only in moments of crisis or need. Their spiritual connection is intermittent and primarily focused on receiving help during difficult times. While this represents an initial awakening to spiritual possibility, it remains limited by its crisis-driven nature.

- The Acquirer maintains a more consistent spiritual practice but still approaches the divine primarily as a source of material benefits. Their prayers and rituals aim to acquire wealth, status, health, or other advantages. Krishna advises these devotees to develop greater mindfulness about the source of all benefits and to appreciate what they already receive through the gross and subtle elements of creation.

- The Inquirer undergoes a significant evolution, moving beyond crisis management and acquisition to genuinely exploring life's more profound questions. The Inquirer seeks to understand the nature of reality, distinguishing between the temporary body and the eternal soul. Their spiritual practice centers on meditation, self-inquiry, and progressive detachment from outcomes.

- The journey culminates with the Knower, whose single-minded devotion transcends all limited motivations. The Knower loves the divine unconditionally, maintaining unbroken awareness of the divine presence and participating directly in divine reality. Krishna reveals that the Knower becomes inseparable from the divine: *"The knower is my own self."*

- The progressive framework reminds us that spiritual growth doesn't happen overnight. It unfolds gradually as our consciousness expands from self-centered concerns toward more universal awareness. Each stage builds upon the previous ones, incorporating their insights while transcending their limitations.

- Perhaps most importantly, Krishna's loving acceptance of devotees at all stages encourages us to be gentle with ourselves and others on the spiritual path. Whether you connect with the divine primarily through need, transactions, inquiry, or direct knowledge, your particular way of relating is honored as part of the greater journey toward full realization.

Start Today: Your First Step

If there's one action I encourage you to take right now, it's this: **Practice Intentional Elevation.** The practice involves three steps that can help you gradually move from your spiritual personality type to the next level of awareness.

Here's how to begin:

First, honestly identify your current primary type. Are you mostly the Distressed, connecting with the divine mainly during times of trouble? Are you primarily the Acquirer, consistently performing spiritual practices, but mainly focused on receiving benefits? Have you evolved to become the Inquirer, genuinely exploring more profound questions about reality? Or have you glimpsed the unitive consciousness of the Knower?

There's no judgment here, just honest self-recognition. Most of us contain elements of multiple types, but usually one predominates. Identify which one most characterizes your current relationship with life's divine or spiritual dimension.

Second, consciously acknowledge the value and limitations of your current approach. Each type represents a valid perspective and offers certain benefits. The Distressed experience relief during crises. The Acquirer receives material blessings. The Inquirer gains intellectual understanding and emotional detachment. The Knower experiences unity and boundless love. Whatever your type, appreciate what it offers you while acknowledging its limitations.

Third—and this is the key step—deliberately practice one quality of the following type on the spectrum for the next 21 days. Here's what that might look like:

- If you're currently Distressed, Practice remembering the divine during good times, not just crises. Set a daily reminder to express gratitude for something positive, consciously connecting this appreciation to the divine source.

- Suppose you're currently the Acquirer. Practice giving rather than just receiving. Each day, offer something—your time, resources, skills, or genuine attention—without expecting a return. Dedicate this giving to the divine.

- If you're the Inquirer: Practice moving beyond intellectual understanding to heartfelt devotion. Each day, spend time in silence, simply feeling a connection with the divine, allowing love to arise naturally without analysis or questioning.

- Suppose you're already experiencing qualities of the Knower. Practice seeing the divine in every person you encounter. Each day, consciously recognize at least three people as embodiments of divinity, treating them with the reverence you would offer to the divine directly.

Intentional elevation doesn't ask you to abandon your spiritual personality or force yourself into a type that doesn't yet feel authentic. Instead, it invites you to gently expand your awareness by incorporating one element of the next elevated type. Over time, this expansion can facilitate a natural shift from crisis-driven spirituality toward more continuous, inquiry-based, and ultimately unitive approaches, as described in the Gita. Intentional elevation supports the natural unfolding, helping you recognize and nurture the seeds of greater awareness that are already present within you.

REMEMBER KRISHNA'S LOVING PERSPECTIVE: ALL FOUR TYPES ARE DEVOTEES. YOUR SPIRITUAL JOURNEY UNFOLDS AT ITS OWN PACE, FOLLOWING ITS ORGANIC DEVELOPMENT PATTERN.

The Other Side of Faith

UNDERSTANDING FOUR NON-BELIEVERS

THE JOURNEY OF SPIRITUAL UNDERSTANDING doesn't divide neatly into believers and non-believers. Even those who don't identify with traditional faith possess distinctive spiritual personalities that shape how they approach life's fundamental questions. The Bhagavad Gita, with its profound psychological insights, acknowledges this reality and provides a sophisticated framework for understanding various types of what it terms "agnostic" perspectives.

What makes this framework so fascinating is its fluidity. These aren't rigid categories but rather states of consciousness that we might all move between, depending on circumstances, moods, or phases of life. Even if you consider yourself a devoted believer, you may occasionally think from an agnostic perspective in certain situations or contexts.

Before we explore these four personality types, let's clarify what distinguishes a believer from an agnostic, as defined in the Gita. The core difference lies in where one places one's faith. Both believers and agnostics have faith, but they point in different directions. An agnostic primarily believes in their existence and capabilities, whereas a believer acknowledges both their existence and the existence of a divine reality that transcends the material world.

Rather than creating a hierarchy of better or worse approaches, we're simply mapping different ways people orient themselves toward life's more profound questions. With that understanding in place, let's explore the four personality types of agnostics that Krishna describes in the Gita.

Let's Dive Deeper

These four agnostic personality types complement the believer types we explored in the previous chapter. Together, they create a comprehensive map of how humans relate to questions of meaning, purpose, and transcendence. What makes this framework valuable isn't its ability to label or judge others but the mirror it holds up to our patterns of thinking and living.

Most of us will recognize aspects of multiple personality types within ourselves, perhaps predominantly one type, but with elements of others appearing in different contexts or periods of our lives. Even dedicated believers may find themselves operating from an agnostic perspective at times, just as committed agnostics might occasionally experience moments of spiritual openness.

Gita's wisdom reminds us that spiritual growth isn't about forcing ourselves into new beliefs or practices but about becoming increasingly aware of our current patterns with honesty and compassion. From this awareness, natural evolution becomes possible, not through external pressure but through internal realization.

The Grossly Foolish: Living Without Purpose

The first type of agnostic personality the Gita describes might sound harsh to modern ears: "the grossly foolish." But before we react to the label, let's understand what it means in this context.

These individuals aren't lacking in intelligence or effort. In fact, they often work extremely hard. What characterizes this type is that they work hard but not smart, in the most profound sense of the word. They go through life without making even the slightest effort to understand their purpose or the true nature of existence. Worries and the pursuit of petty gains fill their days, caught in what we might call a "rat race" with little time for deeper reflection. We all know people resembling the grossly foolish type, and perhaps we are like them at times. The alarm goes off, we rush through breakfast (if we eat it at all), commute to work, tackle one urgent task after another, come home exhausted, distract ourselves with entertainment, fall asleep, and repeat the whole cycle the next day. Weeks turn into months, months into years, and one day, we may wonder where all the time has gone.

What makes this approach "foolish" in the Gita's view isn't a lack of effort or ability but a lack of reflection. These individuals never pause to ask the bigger questions: Why am I here? What gives my life meaning? What am I truly seeking? What is the nature of reality beyond what I can immediately perceive? They fail to clarify their priorities or determine what truly matters to them beyond social conditioning.

For this personality type, spiritual growth and the pursuit of more profound knowledge remain alien concepts. Life drifts by without clear direction or purpose, not because they don't care, but because they're too caught up in the daily grind to step back and gain perspective.

Academic credentials or career achievements offer no immunity here—the most capable individuals can still find themselves caught in this pattern when they avoid reflecting on existence's fundamental questions. The busyness of modern life makes this personality type perhaps more common now than ever before.

Superficially Knowledgeable: Ritual Without Understanding

What's unexpected about this group is that they genuinely see themselves as believers in divinity. These are individuals who appear knowledgeable and think they possess a discriminating understanding of divinity. Still, their knowledge is only superficial. They lack a deeper understanding of the inner meaning behind spiritual concepts and practices.

You may recognize this type in individuals who follow scriptures and philosophies or perform religious rituals without understanding their deeper purpose and intent. They go through the motions of spiritual practice but miss the transformative essence for which those practices were designed to facilitate.

The paradox here is that while these people consider themselves faithful believers, their actual engagement remains with religious structures and customs rather than the divine essence of those forms. They confuse tradition and religion with spirituality or God-realization, mixing these distinct dimensions without discernment.

Often, these individuals are operating from conditioning they received in childhood, following familiar patterns without ever stepping back to analyze them objectively. Fear frequently overshadows their decision-making—fear of breaking tradition, fear of divine punishment, fear of social disapproval, or simply fear of the unknown territory that lies beyond their comfortable routines.

The Gita doesn't suggest abandoning tradition or religious practices, as these have their proper place and value. The issue is failing to recognize that tradition, religion, and spiritual realization are not identical, though they can complement each other when properly understood. Each has a role to play in a well-examined life, but that role needs to be identified and engaged consciously rather than automatically.

As the Gita points out, even a simple prayer offered with genuine devotion is more spiritually effective than elaborate rituals performed without understanding or heartfelt connection. It's not external action but the internal state that determines whether a practice leads to deeper spiritual awareness or merely reinforces superficial patterns.

Confused Seeker: Misled by Company

The confused seeker represents an evolution from superficial knowledge. These individuals have invested considerable time and effort in learning spiritual teachings. They might know scriptures thoroughly and consider themselves serious spiritual practitioners. However, they become confused and misled through association with others who misinterpret or misapply these teachings.

Here, we see how profoundly our spiritual communities can shape, and sometimes distort, our understanding of truth. When surrounded by people with distorted views, even someone with access to profound teachings can become confused about their meaning and application. These individuals often follow a particular path simply because the majority around them are doing so, assuming that common practice must equal spiritual truth.

We observe similar dynamics in spiritual circles, where collective consensus often overrides personal investigation and inner knowing. The confused seeker falls into the trap of believing that following established patterns will provide a spiritual "safety net"—they've checked all the required boxes, so surely they must be on the right path.

What's particularly tragic about this personality type is that they're often sincere seekers who genuinely want to understand truth and connect with divinity. However, their engagement with others muddies their understanding, distorting their reasoning and leading them into faulty logic. A clear perception of divinity becomes obscured by layers of misinterpretation.

We frequently observe this phenomenon in religious contexts, where the teaching of scriptures with misleading interpretations serves particular agendas rather than promoting spiritual liberation. These distorted teachings ultimately cause more harm than good, leading sincere seekers further from authentic understanding rather than closer to it.

We learn from the confused seeker that spiritual progress requires the ability to distinguish authentic wisdom from well-meaning but misguided interpretations.

Rational Denier: Science Without Spirit

The rational denier encompasses individuals who consider themselves champions of logic, science, and intellectual sophistication. Unlike the previous types, who might maintain some form of religious practice, these individuals explicitly reject the existence of divinity, often considering themselves "above" such beliefs.

While genuine scientific inquiry and rational thinking are invaluable tools for understanding reality, rational deniers often employ scientific rhetoric strategically, using it to confirm their preconceptions rather than pursue genuine inquiry. Instead of approaching the question of divinity with open-minded inquiry, they use certain aspects of religious tradition or practice as straw-man arguments to dismiss spiritual reality altogether.

What characterizes this group is not their commitment to reason, which is admirable, but their failure to distinguish between cultural and religious traditions (which may indeed contain elements that don't stand up to rational scrutiny) and the possibility of a transcendent dimension to existence (which remains open to inquiry). Like the second and third personality types, they confuse religion, tradition, and divinity and reject the entire package.

These individuals often claim the supremacy of human reason and the material world, seeing no need for a divine dimension to explain the universe's existence. Yet, according to the Gita, they fail to recognize that their very capacity for rational thought depends on consciousness itself—the fundamental awareness that underlies all experience and makes scientific observation and reasoning possible in the first place.

The rational denier doesn't realize that their existence itself relies on what the Gita calls the "fundamental aspects of pervasive consciousness," the gross and subtle elements that constitute the universe. In modern terms, we might say they take for granted the astonishing fact that the universe exists at all, that it operates according to intelligible laws, and that human minds have evolved the capacity to comprehend these laws—all remarkable circumstances that at least warrant philosophical wonder, even if one doesn't arrive at theistic conclusions.

Instead of using their intellectual capacities to promote understanding and inclusion, some in this category, unfortunately, use their rational stance to drive divisions. They set up an opposition between science and spirituality that isn't necessary, missing the possibility that these could be complementary approaches to understanding different dimensions of reality.

Finding Ourselves in These Patterns

As Krishna observes in the Gita, it's generally futile to try to change agnostics through argument or persuasion. Genuine transformation comes from within, triggered by personal realization rather than external pressure. The same principle holds for believers—genuine transformation emerges from personal revelation rather than external persuasion.

Looking at all eight personality types covered across these two chapters—the four believer types (Distressed, Acquirer, Inquirer, and Knower) and the four agnostic types we've just explored, you might recognize that you align with different types in different contexts or phases of life.

You could approach work from the perspective of the Grossly Foolish, focusing entirely on productivity without more profound reflection. Perhaps you engage in specific spiritual or religious traditions, such as the Superficially Knowledgeable, who go through the motions without connecting to their deeper meaning. In intellectual discussions, you might adopt the stance of the Rational Denier. At the same time, in times of crisis, you might suddenly find yourself in the position of the Distressed Believer, reaching out for divine help.

Rather than viewing these shifts as character flaws or contradictions, we can recognize them as natural expressions of our multifaceted inner lives. By recognizing our current patterns with honesty and compassion, we create the possibility for growth, not through forced change but through the natural evolution of consciousness as we become more aware of our habitual ways of thinking and being.

Summary: The Journey Beyond Labels

As we've explored in this chapter, the Bhagavad Gita offers a sophisticated framework for understanding different ways people relate to the concept of divinity, including those who don't consider themselves believers in the traditional sense.

- These four agnostic personality types—the Grossly Foolish, the Superficially Knowledgeable, the Confused Seeker, and the Rational Denier—represent different ways people might live without a conscious connection to spiritual reality.

- The Grossly Foolish work hard but without reflecting on a deeper purpose, caught in the daily grind without ever examining what gives life meaning beyond immediate concerns.

- The Superficially Knowledgeable follow spiritual forms and traditions without understanding their inner significance, mistaking ritual for realization.

- The Confused Seeker studies spiritual teachings but becomes misled through association with others who distort their meaning.

- The Rational Denier employs selective reasoning to dismiss the spiritual dimensions of existence entirely, unable to distinguish between religious traditions and the possibility of a transcendent reality.

- What makes this framework so valuable isn't its ability to categorize or judge others but the mirror it holds up to our patterns of thinking and living. Most of us will recognize aspects of multiple personality types within ourselves, perhaps predominantly one type, but with elements of others appearing in different contexts or periods of our lives.

- Even dedicated believers may find themselves operating from an agnostic perspective at times, just as committed agnostics might occasionally experience moments of spiritual openness.

- Gita's wisdom reminds us that spiritual growth isn't about forcing ourselves into new beliefs or practices but about becoming increasingly aware of our current patterns with honesty and compassion. From this awareness, natural evolution becomes possible—not through external pressure but through internal realization.

- Ultimately, these personality types aren't permanent identities but stages in an ongoing journey of consciousness. Whether we currently identify more with believer or agnostic perspectives, the invitation is the same: to examine our assumptions, deepen our understanding, and remain open to dimensions of reality that might extend beyond our current comprehension.

The most profound spiritual growth often occurs not when we rigidly adhere to a particular identity—whether "believer" or "non-believer"—but when we hold our current understanding lightly, remaining receptive to new insights that might transform our perspective in unexpected ways. In this willingness to question and stay curious, wisdom finds its fertile ground.

Start Here: Your First Step

If there's one action I encourage you to take right now, it's this: **Practice what I call "compassionate self-observation" for the next week.** You'll cultivate a friendly awareness of how you relate to questions of meaning and transcendence in ordinary moments. Rather than trying to change your current perspective or force yourself into a different personality type, notice how you're relating to questions of meaning, purpose, and transcendence in various situations.

Here's how to begin:

Each morning, set an intention for the day. You might say to yourself: "Today, I'll notice my spiritual patterns without trying to change them." During the day, pay particular attention to moments when:

You feel caught in busyness without reflection (Grossly Foolish pattern)

You perform habitual practices without connecting to their deeper meaning (Superficially Knowledgeable pattern)

You accept others' interpretations without questioning their validity (Confused Seeker pattern)

You dismiss spiritual dimensions entirely based on intellectual arguments (Rational Denier pattern)

You reach out for help during difficulties (Distressed pattern)

You seek specific benefits through spiritual practices (Acquirer pattern)

You investigate more profound questions about reality (Inquirer pattern)

You experience moments of unity or boundless love (Knower pattern)

When you notice one of these patterns emerging, refrain from judging or trying to change it. Acknowledge: "I'm experiencing the [pattern name] perspective right now." Notice how it feels in your body, what thoughts accompany it, and what triggered this particular way of relating to reality. At the end of each day, take a few minutes to reflect on what you observed. Which patterns appeared most frequently? Were there situations that consistently triggered particular perspectives? Did you notice any patterns you weren't previously aware of? Instead of pushing for change, the breathing room between consciousness and conditioning lets authentic development emerge at its own pace.

After a week of this practice, you'll likely have a clearer sense of which spiritual personality types currently predominate in your life. The insight you gain becomes precious, not for creating self-criticism, but for grounding genuine development in truthful self-understanding. By approaching self-discovery with kindness and patience, you honor both your present reality and the timeless insights shaped by the Gita's sophisticated view of spiritual psychology.

REMEMBER, THE GOAL ISN'T TO FORCE YOURSELF INTO WHAT YOU IMAGINE TO BE A "BETTER" OR "MORE ADVANCED" SPIRITUAL PERSONALITY TYPE. IT'S TO DEVELOP GREATER AWARENESS OF YOUR CURRENT PATTERNS SO THAT YOUR NATURAL EVOLUTION CAN UNFOLD FROM A PLACE OF TRUTH RATHER THAN PRETENSE.

Temple Worship

HERE'S A PROVOCATIVE QUESTION: "Why should I even bother going to a temple?" It's not an offensive question at all. It's a perfectly rational one, especially for the inquiring minds of today's youth and adults alike. If divinity is everywhere and God exists in everything around us, why do we need a specially constructed place to connect with the divine? Why make an effort to visit a physical building when the spiritual essence we seek is supposedly all around us?

These are precisely the questions we'll unpack together as we move forward. And trust me, the ancient wisdom of the Gita and the Upanishads has some fascinating insights on this very question.

Let's Dive Deeper

Before we trace the historical evolution of temples, let's pause to consider this question a bit longer. It's a question I've heard countless times from teenagers, college students, and even adults who are reconnecting with their spiritual roots.

The question comes from a place of genuine curiosity and, sometimes, practical concern. If I'm busy with work, family, and numerous other responsibilities, why should I make time to visit a temple? If I can meditate at home, read spiritual texts on my phone, or feel connected to nature during a morning walk, what unique value does a temple visit offer?

Our current way of thinking sometimes bypasses a key insight here. We tend to approach spirituality as an individual pursuit—something between me and the divine. However, traditional spiritual practices, prevalent across nearly all cultures, have long recognized the power of community, shared spaces, and concentrated energy.

You can work out at home with minimal equipment. But many people still join gyms. Why? Because there's something about a dedicated space filled with others on the same journey that helps focus our energy and intention. The environment itself becomes a catalyst for the activity.

Similarly, while divinity exists everywhere, temples were designed to be catalysts for spiritual connection, not because God is only there, but because that space is designed to help us connect with the divine more effectively.

As we explore the evolution and purpose of temples, consider this modern analogy. The temple isn't the only place to connect with divinity, just as a gym isn't the only place to exercise. However, there are specific advantages to dedicated spaces that have been cultivated for a particular purpose over generations.

The Evolution of Temple Worship

From Natural Elements to Sacred Spaces

When we examine the ancient Vedantic perspective, as discussed in the chapter on the true meaning of *sanatana dharma*, worship was initially directed toward the natural elements. The Gita describes these fundamental substances, and Krishna outlines the eight divisions of nature: earth, water, fire, wind, space, mind, intellect, and the sense of self.

Among these elements, fire held a special significance. Why? Fire represented the most visible form of divinity through its connection to the sun and the light it emitted. Fire's special significance explains why offering oblations to it became the heart of Vedic practices.

Interestingly, the concept of a temple as we know it today wasn't part of early Vedantic traditions. Households were self-contained spiritual centers with three types of sacred fires for worship. Fire also symbolizes that nothing in this world is permanent and follows a cycle of birth, growth, and destruction.

> The *gaarhapatya*, or householder fire, was always kept burning as a constant source of energy for the home.

> The *ahavaniya* fire was used for offering sacrifices and invoking the power of deities, creating a direct channel of communication with the divine.

> The *dakshinagni* fire in the south served as a protective and spiritual fire used for ancestral crematory rites, maintaining the connection between the living and those who had passed away.

As communities expanded and grew, maintaining the three sacred fires in each household became impractical, and worship transitioned from being a mental practice to an external action. It was only later, during the *puranic* period, that the concept of the temple evolved into what we recognize today as part of modern Hinduism.

Why Temples Emerged: Five Key Purposes

Temples didn't emerge by accident. They served specific social and economic functions, bringing stability to communities. Let me share the five main reasons temples became central to community life:

Community Epicenter:

Temples were constructed at the heart of villages and towns, creating a central gathering place. Even today, if you visit villages in India, you'll notice temples often occupy the central location.

Community Betterment:

Under the watchful eyes of the deity, people would make essential decisions and undertake programs for the welfare of the community.

Strategic Shelter:

Many ancient temples were constructed on hills, offering refuge during floods or heavy rainfall. Their architecture made them natural shelters where everyone could find safety and be served food during emergencies.

Charity Center:

Temples became places for sharing and giving—clothing, food, money—making them hubs of charitable activities.

Education Hub:

Temples were places of higher learning, a tradition that later transitioned to specialized schools or gurukuls, though temples never entirely lost their educational significance. They served as places for delivering education to a captive audience. The above necessities gave rise to the temple movement, addressing all five aspects mentioned above.

The Science of Sacred Spaces

As devotion to personal forms of the divine grew and the bhakti movement spread, the number of temples increased. As temples multiplied, the need for consistent standards arose, leading to the creation of the *agama* scriptures.

These *agamas* prescribed detailed standards: the height of a deity, the dimensions of a temple, the shape of the structure, and the specifications for the sanctum where the main deity would be consecrated.

They were created with a scientific approach in mind. For example, the temple bell's shape was designed to create specific vibrations. The height at which the main deity was placed was calculated so that vibrations would return in a particular way. Science was infused into these sacred architectural guidelines, transforming temples into places where energies could converge.

It's like having air all around you, but turning on a ceiling fan creates a concentrated force of air. Similarly, while divinity exists everywhere, the temple channels that energy in a focused way.

The Personal Connection to Temples

But why do we connect with some temples and not others? Your spiritual frequency becomes the determining factor in this case.

When a temple adheres to ethical practices and focuses on cultivating peaceful, righteous minds, you may find yourself in alignment with its principles. Out of twenty temples in your area, you might feel drawn to just two of them. The heart-level bond forms during your actual temple experience.

Perhaps it's the deity or how they dress and decorate it. It could be the way the temple vibrates with energy or how sounds resonate within its walls. All these factors trigger emotional responses, and when they give you a pleasant feeling, you naturally feel more connected and want to return.

Temples also become sources of energy in another powerful way. When no one is around, the silence itself provides a space for contemplation and reflection—what I like to call "connection." Just knowing that many like-minded people gather there creates a special atmosphere. When they come together, there's a rush of energy; when they disperse, there's absolute silence, and it's a silence in which you can find peace and self-reflection.

The Practical Benefits of Temple Visits

- The routine of temple visit brings discipline into your life.

- You're taking time away from your regular activities to visit a place of contemplation and reflection.

- You also develop social connections and community support. Even in today's fast-paced world, visiting a temple allows you to meet people and become part of a supportive community.

- When you support a temple through volunteer work, service, or financial contributions, you help create a place where people cultivate practices of service, charity, and discipline, ultimately becoming better spiritual beings.

Summary: The Value of Temple Visits

Throughout this chapter, we've explored the fundamental question that many people ask: "Why should I even bother going to a temple?"

- Temples function more than just buildings. They serve as spiritual infrastructure in our communities, offering tangible benefits that extend far beyond religious obligation.

- Divine may be omnipresent, but temples provide focused points of spiritual energy that make connection more accessible in our distraction-filled world. Rather than being outdated relics, temples emerge as relevant tools for modern spiritual seekers who need structure, community, and dedicated space for inner growth.

- Temples offer multifaceted value in contemporary life, serving both individual spiritual development and broader community needs.

- Temples serve as focused points of spiritual energy in a world where divinity is everywhere but often challenging to connect with.

- The value of a temple lies not just in the deity consecrated there but in the convergence of energies, the community it fosters, and the personal spiritual practices it nurtures. A temple is a powerful tool for your spiritual journey.

Start Today: Your First Step

If there's one action I encourage you to take right now, it's this: **visit a temple with a fresh perspective.** Don't go with preconceived notions or to follow tradition; instead, go with mindfulness and awareness.

Here's how to begin:

Observe how you feel when you enter. Notice the energy of the space, the silence between ceremonies, the architecture, and the vibrations of sounds. Pay attention to your emotional responses. Then, sit quietly in a corner and be present. Allow yourself to experience the convergence of energies without expectation.

After your visit, take a few minutes to reflect on your experience. What resonated with you? What didn't? Approaching temple visits with such awareness may transform your perception of these ancient spaces and their value in today's world.

REMEMBER, THE GOAL ISN'T TO EMBRACE ANY SPECIFIC FAITH SYSTEM—IT'S TO ENCOUNTER WHAT TEMPLES OFFER AT THEIR CORE: CONCENTRATED SPACES FOR DIVINE CONNECTION, COMMUNITY BONDS, AND SELF-REFLECTION.

PART THREE

The Seeker's Path

Finding Your Path

ROLE OF ACHARYAS, GURUS, AND TEACHERS

LET'S DISCUSS SOMETHING that many of us experience on our spiritual journey. Do you know that feeling when you've read all the books, attended the workshops, and tried various practices, yet something still feels missing? I've been there too. In my journey, I've discovered a significant gap between understanding and embodying spiritual principles. That's precisely where guidance becomes essential and transformative in our lives.

To fully absorb and apply the message of texts like the Gita and live a Spiritual life of purpose in this contemporary world, most of us need guidance from someone special who can illuminate the path for us. But who exactly are these guides, and how do they differ from one another?

Let's Dive Deeper

This chapter will explore three distinct types of spiritual guides: the Acharya, the Guru, and the Teacher. Though we often use these terms interchangeably, they represent unique roles that serve different aspects of our development. Understanding these differences helps you recognize the type of guidance you need at various stages of your journey and how to effectively seek it out.

Let's embark on this exploration together, unpacking the wisdom of ancient traditions to find theoretical and practical guidance for our modern lives.

The Acharya: Architect of the Spiritual Path

Imagine standing at the foot of a vast mountain range, uncertain of which peak to climb or which path might safely lead you to the summit. An Acharya is like the master navigator who has not only mapped the entire range but has personally scaled its heights and returned to share what they've discovered.

An Acharya is a spiritual master in the truest sense—a practitioner blessed with divine grace who absorbs the tenets and teachings of sacred texts such as the Gita. Based on that profound knowledge, the Acharya defines the spiritual path that leads to the ultimate destination: connection and union with the divine.

The path laid down by an Acharya becomes the foundation for spiritual development, creating a framework that other teachers can follow and emulate. Their contribution isn't merely philosophical but practical, providing a roadmap for those who come after them.

In Hindu philosophy, we're fortunate to have had three great Acharyas who walked this earth: Shri Sankara (8th century), Bhagavad Ramanuja (11th century), and Acharya Madhwa (13th century). Each brought unique philosophical insights and far-reaching visions to their interpretation of ancient wisdom. Their teachings, expositions, and translations of ancient scriptures, such as the Gita, remain valuable for seekers today.

Each of these three Acharyas saw reality from different planes of consciousness, giving us complementary perspectives on our relationship with the divine:

Sankara: The Vision of Non-Duality

Sankara lived in the 8th century and possessed the vision and divine insight to perceive a state of consciousness where the entire universe merges into a unified whole. In this vision, all that remains is a single, undivided, non-dualistic eternal cosmic entity called *brahman*.

The cosmic entity, an impersonal form best visualized as an energy grid pervading the entire universe, is also referred to as the Supreme. In the Gita, Sankara identifies this Supreme as Krishna.

In Sankara's view, *brahman* is a holistic and complete entity with no lack. Everything else in the universe is simply a projection of *brahman*. Our perception of separation and difference is driven by ignorance, known as *maya*. Only through reasoning and the logic of discrimination can we identify our true selves and merge with the whole cosmic entity.

According to Sankara's philosophy, which he views as a core tenet of the Gita's message, the purpose of life is self-inquiry, the practice of looking beyond appearances to recognize the one reality underlying all diversity.

You might experience Sankara's non-duality when you look beyond the names and forms that appear before you and recognize the same spirit or energy behind them all.

Ramanuja: The Vision of Qualified Non-Duality

Bhagavad Ramanuja lived in the 11th century, and his philosophy aligns with a plane of consciousness where reality, in all its diversity, reigns supreme. Unlike Sankara, Ramanuja doesn't attribute the multiplicity of existence to ignorance but accepts it as real.

Ramanuja proposed a three-pronged realistic approach that acknowledges the following:

- The individual soul

- The surrounding nature serves as a platform for the body

- The supreme soul or divine, which is the efficient cause of individual souls and nature

According to Ramanuja, the purpose of life is the merger of the individual soul with the supreme soul through complete surrender to divinity, which is a core teaching of the Gita. Through this surrender, the individual soul acquires the divine characteristics of the Supreme while retaining its distinct identity. Ramanuja referred to such a state as "liberation."

Ramanuja's approach blended theism and philosophy, translating abstract impersonal concepts into lived reality. You may experience Ramanuja's qualified non-duality when you recognize the distinctions between individuals around you and yet understand that they're all integrated with a common source, which means they can never have a truly separate existence.

Madhwa: The Vision of Duality

At the level of consciousness we experience routinely in daily life, we perceive duality through the separation between ourselves and others, between the individual soul and the divine.

Acharya Madhwa, through his philosophy of duality, clearly articulated this distinction by describing the individual soul as an image of the supreme soul. The individual possesses qualities such as kindness, compassion, righteousness, and many others that represent the characteristics of the supreme soul.

According to Madhwa, since we are merely an image of the supreme, we cannot truly become one with it. For Madhwa, the purpose of life is to engage in eternal devotion to the Supreme, and only through utmost grace can we even aspire to become one with the divine. Through this focus on devotion, Madhwa also integrated theism and philosophy.

You may experience Madhwa's duality when you perceive each person as distinct, while recognizing that devotion helps bridge the gap between yourself and divinity, as well as between yourself and the rest of the universe.

Beyond Philosophical Debate

There will always be debate about which of these three perspectives is most accurate, but here's a liberating truth: each theory applies to a different state of consciousness in our minds. They're not mutually exclusive but complementary, revealing different facets of our relationship with ultimate reality.

Follow any of these three Acharyas, and you'll be light-years ahead in your spiritual development. Their collective wisdom provides a comprehensive understanding of our relationship with the divine, from complete unity to loving duality.

The Guru and the Teacher: Complementary Guides

While an Acharya creates the spiritual map, we still need guides to help us navigate that map in our lives. Gurus and Teachers fulfill this navigational role. Though we often use these terms interchangeably, they represent distinct roles with different approaches to guidance.

The Guru: Mirror of Truth

A Guru is a mentor who illuminates the path laid out by the Acharya. The word "Guru" comes from two Sanskrit roots: "*gu*," meaning darkness, and "*ru*," meaning dispeller—a Guru dispels the darkness of ignorance.

The veil of ignorance gradually lifts as we walk the spiritual path with a Guru's guidance. The unveiling of ignorance occurs not through instruction but through reflection, and a Guru is that mirror, showing us our true nature without distortion. A Guru must help you uncover yourself, revealing what's already there rather than adding something new.

The Teacher: Provider of Knowledge

A teacher, by contrast, instructs. There is effort involved in teaching, which involves breaking down complex ideas, presenting them systematically, and ensuring they're understood. Such instructional effort puts a particular strain on the Teacher that isn't present in the Guru's reflective approach.

While a Guru is about learning through self-discovery, a teacher is about instruction. They focus on the deliberate imparting of knowledge and skills. Learning from a teacher is often specific to a particular domain, while learning from a Guru has universal applicability.

Fundamental Differences

Let me share some fundamental differences that might help you recognize these distinct roles in your own life:

- A Teacher answers your questions; a Guru questions your answers.

- A Teacher teaches you the components of the path of progress; a Guru illuminates the way and leaves it to you to walk that path.

- A Teacher focuses on preparedness and helps you build your comfort zone; a Guru focuses on taking you out of your comfort zone.

- A Teacher measures your learning and reports progress; a Guru is a mirror in which you discover and see for yourself.

- A Teacher helps you acquire what you need to know; a Guru lets you let go of what you think you know.

- When you finish with a Teacher, you celebrate; when a Guru finishes with you, life celebrates.

In our journey, we need both Teachers and Gurus. Teachers give us the components and frameworks for understanding life and its challenges. As we progress in age, career, and spiritual development, we need Gurus—unbiased mirrors who fearlessly question our feelings, answers, and approaches.

A Guru takes us out of our comfort zone, helps us let go of attachments to outcomes, and keeps us focused on our actions.

With a Guru's guidance, we recognize the obstacles that block our path and stay on course. A qualified Guru helps us get unstuck in the maze of life, where we often see only the trees or only the forest, but never both simultaneously.

It's worth noting that an individual can embody both roles, being a Teacher in some contexts and a Guru in others. Some rare individuals serve as Acharya, Guru, and Teacher all at once, though such complete guides are precious and rare.

The Example of Arjuna and Krishna

The relationship between Arjuna and Krishna in the Bhagavad Gita exemplifies the necessity of guidance in our spiritual journey.

Although an individual of superior intellect and skill, Arjuna found himself paralyzed by confusion on the battlefield. Out of kindness and compassion, he was grief-stricken at the prospect of fighting his family members. He pleaded with Krishna and was willing to forsake all material wealth gained through war.

Arjuna missed the crucial point due to his emotional state, confusing righteous action with its outcomes. How often do we make the same mistake? We become so focused on the events unfolding before us that our judgment becomes clouded, and we fail to see the more profound truth.

That's precisely why we all need Teachers and Gurus. Like Arjuna, we sometimes reach a point where we're confused, dejected, and unable to move forward. It's at these moments of surrender that transformation becomes possible.

The magic began when Arjuna finally became silent, surrendering himself mentally and physically to the divine for guidance. Krishna, serving as both Teacher and Guru, delivered a mystical experience. His message included the entire gamut of manifestation, sustenance, purposeful living, and much more — the wisdom that continues to guide millions of seekers today.

Summary: The Guidance We Need

As we've explored in this chapter, spiritual guidance comes in several forms, each serving a different aspect of our development. Regardless of where you are in your journey, there's a form of guidance that's right for you.

- Acharyas are the master architects who lay down the spiritual path based on their profound realization and understanding of sacred texts. In the Hindu tradition, Sankara, Ramanuja, and Madhwa represent three complementary perspectives on our relationship with the divine, ranging from complete non-duality to loving duality.

- Gurus are mirrors that reflect our true nature, dispelling ignorance and helping us uncover what is already within. They question our answers, take us out of our comfort zones, and help us let go of what we think we know.

- Teachers are instructors who impart specific knowledge and skills, helping us build our understanding component by component. They answer our questions, help us develop competence, and measure our progress.

- In different stages of life, we may need different types of guidance. Sometimes, we need the systematic instruction of a Teacher to master new concepts or skills. Other times, we need the reflective presence of a Guru to question our assumptions and help us break through barriers. We always benefit from the wisdom of Acharyas, who have mapped the territory of spiritual development through their profound realizations.

The beauty of such understanding is that it enables us to recognize the type of guidance we need at any given moment and seek it accordingly. It also reminds us that no single perspective has a monopoly on truth — different approaches serve different states of consciousness, complementing rather than contradicting each other.

Start Today: Your First Step

If there's one action I encourage you to take after reading this chapter, it's this: **Identify the type of guidance you need right now.**

Here's how to begin:

Take some quiet time to reflect on your current stage in the journey. Are you seeking foundational knowledge that requires a Teacher's systematic instruction? Are you stuck in patterns that might benefit from a Guru's reflective questioning? Or are you trying to understand the bigger picture of spiritual development, which might be illuminated by studying the teachings of great Acharyas?

Once you've identified the type of guidance that would serve you best, commit to finding a formal Teacher in a specific tradition, connecting with a mentor who can serve as a Guru in your life, or dedicating time to study the writings of great Acharyas. The key is to recognize the kind of guidance you need and remain receptive to it in any form it appears.

REMEMBER THAT GUIDANCE DOESN'T ALWAYS COME IN EXPECTED FORMS. SOMETIMES, A BOOK, A CONVERSATION WITH A FRIEND, OR EVEN A CHALLENGING LIFE EXPERIENCE CAN SERVE AS A TEACHER OR A GURU IF WE APPROACH IT OPENLY AND HUMBLY.

Really Need a Guru?

ACHARYAS, GURUS, AND TEACHERS play distinct roles in our spiritual development. In the previous chapter, we saw how each serves a unique function—from the Acharya, who maps the spiritual territory, to the Guru, who mirrors our true nature, and the Teacher, who imparts specific knowledge. Now, let's delve deeper by examining a question that naturally arises: Is having a formal Guru necessary for spiritual progress? The answer deserves more nuanced consideration.

"You need a guru on your spiritual path."

"Finding your true guru is crucial for spiritual growth."

"Without a guru, spiritual progress is nearly impossible."

If you've spent any time exploring spiritual traditions, particularly those with roots in India, you've probably heard statements like these. The idea that a guru is necessary for spiritual advancement is so deeply ingrained that questioning it can feel like defying tradition and crossing forbidden lines.

But what if we did question it? What if we approached this topic not with blind acceptance or stubborn rejection but with thoughtful inquiry? After all, isn't deep inquiry itself a spiritual practice?

I remember my struggle with this question. Growing up in a traditional household, I was taught that finding a guru was an essential milestone on the spiritual path. However, my observations revealed a more complex reality: many guru followers didn't seem to develop genuine wisdom, while some who walked more independent paths embodied profound spiritual understanding.

The contradiction between formal teaching and my observations troubled me until I studied the Bhagavad Gita more deeply. What I discovered was far more nuanced than the simplistic "you must have a guru" narrative. Krishna's teachings to Arjuna offer insights that can help us approach this question with respect for tradition and intellectual honesty.

Let's Dive Deeper

This chapter will explore the Gita's teachings about spiritual guidance, dispelling ignorance, and recognizing genuine spiritual mastery. Rather than providing a definitive answer, I aim to offer a framework for making this decision in alignment with your unique spiritual journey.

Let's begin with a fundamental question: What exactly do we mean by "guru," and what role is this person supposed to play in our spiritual lives?

The word "guru" has been so frequently used in popular culture that its original meaning has become somewhat diluted. We hear about "fitness gurus," "tech gurus," and "fashion gurus," anyone with expertise in a particular field.

However, in the traditional spiritual sense, the word "guru" has a specific meaning: to dispel ignorance. The Bhagavad Gita exemplifies this concept. Krishna serves as Arjuna's Guru, helping him overcome his confusion and moral dilemma on the battlefield. By the end of their dialogue, Arjuna declares in chapter 18, verse 73:

Listening to you, I've overcome ignorance and gained wisdom

But notice something important here: Krishna doesn't magically transfer wisdom to Arjuna or take responsibility for Arjuna's enlightenment. He provides guidance, answers questions, challenges assumptions, and offers a framework for understanding. But ultimately, Arjuna must think, process, and integrate these teachings. The responsibility for dispelling ignorance remains with the student, not the Teacher.

A crucial distinction often overlooked in discussions about gurus is that spiritual growth remains your responsibility. A true guru doesn't take away your responsibility for your spiritual growth but helps you fulfill that responsibility more effectively.

What Does the Gita Say About Gurus?

It might surprise you that the Bhagavad Gita doesn't emphasize "*guru*" as many contemporary spiritual traditions do. The Gita doesn't mandate the guru-disciple relationship in a rigid, formalized religious way. Krishna demonstrates the qualities of an ideal guru through his actions and teachings, as acknowledged in chapter 11, verse 43.

The Gita emphasizes the importance of a spiritual guide or master, namely someone with wisdom who can help us navigate the complexities of spiritual life. Gita advises that one shouldn't hesitate to seek guidance from a spiritual master to gain clarity.

But who qualifies as a spiritual master? According to the Gita, a spiritual master is someone who spreads and lives the message of spiritual learning. They practice *achara* (disciplined living) and *vichara* (intellectual inquiry and understanding). Such individuals might be referred to as Acharyas—teachers who lead by example.

A vital point emerges: the Gita seems less concerned with formally designating someone as your "guru" and more focused on the quality of guidance you receive and your relationship to that guidance. What matters is having access to wisdom that helps dispel your ignorance, not necessarily the label you give to the source of that wisdom.

What Kind of Ignorance Does a Guru Help Dispel?

When we talk about dispelling ignorance, what exactly are we referring to? It's not about becoming a walking encyclopedia or memorizing complex philosophical concepts. Spiritual ignorance is much more fundamental and relates to our understanding of ourselves and our place in the universe.

Based on the teachings of the Gita, let's explore five key dimensions of ignorance that a spiritual master helps us overcome:

1. The Body-Soul Distinction

Perhaps the most fundamental ignorance is the misidentification of ourselves with our physical bodies alone. A spiritual master helps us understand that there is an energy, the soul, atma, or life energy, common to all beings and utterly independent of the physical form.

Far from being merely an abstract concept, when you truly recognize yourself as more than your body, you transform how you relate to pleasure and pain, success and failure, and even life and death. This is the foundation for equanimity in all circumstances.

2. The Complexity of Causation

Another form of ignorance is believing we have complete control over the outcomes of our actions. The reality, as the Gita teaches, is far more complex. Any result is the culmination of countless interrelated causes and effects, which is a "spaghetti" of actions performed by you and innumerable others, both living and non-living.

Some of these causes may have occurred in the distant past, while others are yet to unfold in the future. The web of causation is so intricate that it's beyond anyone's complete comprehension, so we might ultimately say an outcome is "God's wish." Understanding this complexity helps us act with both determination and detachment.

3. Methods of Contemplation and Learning

Spiritual growth isn't random; it involves specific practices and approaches that have been refined over thousands of years. A spiritual master helps us understand this contemplation, meditation, and learning methods, saving us from wasting time on ineffective approaches or getting lost in practices that might even be counterproductive.

These aren't one-size-fits-all prescriptions but frameworks adapted to individual temperaments and circumstances, another area where guidance proves invaluable.

4. The Three Modes of Material Nature

The Gita teaches that all actions and tendencies fall into three categories or "modes" of material nature: *sattva* (goodness, purity), *rajas* (passion, activity), and *tamas* (ignorance, inertia). We all operate within a mixture of these three modes, but spiritual progress involves gradually increasing sattva while decreasing rajas and tamas.

A spiritual master helps us recognize which mode drives our thoughts and actions and directs even our passionate or lethargic tendencies toward righteous action. Such discernment isn't easy to develop independently, as we're often blind to our patterns.

5. Self-Control, Compassion, and Charity

Ultimately, a spiritual master guides us in cultivating the balanced trinity of *dama* (self-control), *daya* (compassion), and *dana* (charity or generosity). These qualities lay the foundation for personal peace and have a positive impact on the world.

Self-control without compassion can become rigid and judgmental, while compassion without self-control can lead to enabling harmful behaviors. Charity alone can be misguided or ineffective. A spiritual master helps us develop all three in harmony.

For someone to truly be called a guru, their guidance should address these dimensions of ignorance. They should help us see more clearly, rather than making us more dependent on their vision.

How Do You Know You're Making Progress?

With or without a formal guru, how can you tell if you're dispelling ignorance and making spiritual progress? The Gita offers two clear markers:

1. Steady Wisdom Amid Challenges and Pleasures

In chapter 2, verse 56, Krishna describes the person of steady wisdom as maintaining calm and composure in the face of challenges and pleasures. The equanimity described here isn't about suppressing emotions but developing a perspective that isn't entirely swayed by external circumstances.

Such equanimity occurs naturally when you detach from outcomes and focus on the actions themselves. However, such a state is impossible to maintain if you're still deeply identified with your body and its experiences alone. In this book, I will guide you through multiple approaches to detach from outcomes.

2. Service Over Personal Attainment

Chapter 6, verses 21 and 22, describes another sign of progress: this happens when your communion with divinity leads you to perform righteous actions according to your role in life, and in doing so, service to humanity takes priority over personal attainment.

The orientation toward service creates unshakability—the Gita says you become *"rock solid even in the greatest calamity."* Not because you don't feel the calamity, but because your sense of purpose transcends personal comfort or success. Your life transitions toward *seva*, making service your life's purpose.

These markers help us evaluate our progress more objectively than vague feelings or mystical experiences that might be misleading. They ground spiritual growth in our daily lives and responses to life's circumstances, providing a more reliable basis for understanding.

Pathways to Spiritual Learning

So, how do you begin this process of dispelling ignorance, whether with a formal guru or not? Gita suggests two complementary approaches:

1. Humble Inquiry to a Spiritual Master

Chapter 4, verse 34 advises approaching a spiritual master with humility (*pranipaatena*) and an open mind. An attitude of receptivity is crucial. If we approach spiritual learning with arrogance or a closed mind that's already in a mode of confirmation bias, then we block our progress.

The emphasis here is not on finding a perfect guru, but on cultivating the right attitude as a student — humility, sincerity, and openness to growth.

2. Listening with Faith and Understanding

Chapter 18, verse 71, emphasizes the importance of listening with faith, practicing what you learn, and intellectually understanding it. The faith referred to isn't blind faith, but a working faith, a willingness to test teachings in the laboratory of your own life and see their effects.

Notice that the Gita doesn't separate intellectual understanding from practice—the two go hand in hand. Theory without application remains abstract, while practice without understanding can become mechanistic.

The Many Forms a Spiritual Master Can Take

One of Gita's most liberating teachings on spiritual guidance is the recognition that it can take many forms. A spiritual master doesn't have to be a bearded sage in orange robes (though they certainly can be); they can also be a person of any age, gender, or background.

The Gita emphasizes the importance of being associated with spiritual wisdom and those who embody it. Such associations can take various forms:

- It might be someone alive now who guides you either in person or virtually

- It could be a sacred text like the Gita itself, with someone helping you understand its authentic meaning

- It might be someone in the broader society whom you've never met personally, but who serves as a role model

- Or it could even be society itself, from which you learn through your inquiry and self-reflection

What matters is not the form, but the substance, and questioning whether this source of guidance helps you dispel ignorance in the five dimensions we discussed earlier.

However, there is one fundamental characteristic to look for: a genuine spiritual master will always encourage *achara* (disciplined living) and *vichara* (intellectual inquiry). They will never ask you to proceed based solely on unquestioning belief. If someone discourages questioning or demands unquestioning obedience, that's a red flag, not a sign of spiritual authority.

The Ultimate Goal of Spiritual Guidance

Something remarkable happens to those who successfully dispel ignorance with the help of spiritual guidance. In chapter 7, verse 18, the Gita explains that their intellect gradually merges with the universal or divine intellect. They've attained the supreme goal of a liberated life in this state.

Attaining this state doesn't mean they lose their individuality or ability to function. Instead, their perspective expands beyond personal limitations to embrace a universal understanding. Their actions become increasingly aligned with *dharma* (cosmic order and righteousness) rather than driven by egocentric desires.

This brings us back to our original question: Do you need a guru? Perhaps the most balanced answer from Gita's perspective would be this: More important than having someone you formally designate as your Guru is having an intent of inquiry and spiritual learning. When you cultivate this intent sincerely, appropriate guidance tends to appear in your life — sometimes in the form of a traditional guru, but often in less conventional forms.

As the Gita suggests, when the student is ready, the spiritual master shows up, but it is not always in the package we might expect.

Summary: Beyond the Guru Question

Let's bring together the key insights we've explored about spiritual guidance:

- Spiritual guidance can take many forms, from traditional teachers to books, role models, or even one's reflections on life experiences.

- A genuine spiritual master always encourages disciplined living and intellectual inquiry, never demanding naive belief.

- In the traditional sense, a guru is someone who helps dispel ignorance, rather than taking responsibility for one's spiritual growth or demanding unquestioning obedience.

- The ignorance a spiritual master helps dispel includes misidentification with the body, misunderstanding causation, lack of knowledge about spiritual practices, confusion about the modes of nature, and imbalance in self-control, compassion, and charity.

- The Bhagavad Gita emphasizes the importance of spiritual guidance but doesn't mandate a formal guru-disciple relationship as understood in contemporary spiritual circles.

- Signs of genuine spiritual progress include equanimity in the face of life's ups and downs and an orientation toward service rather than personal gain.

- Pathways to spiritual learning include approaching wisdom with humility, open-minded inquiry, and listening with a working faith that combines practice with intellectual understanding.

- The ultimate goal is a state where your intellect aligns with universal wisdom, leading to a liberated life.

Perhaps the most important takeaway is this: Rather than feeling pressured to find "the one true guru," focus on cultivating an attitude of sincere inquiry and openness to spiritual wisdom. With this orientation, appropriate guidance appears in your life at the right time and in the proper form for your unique journey.

The balanced approach outlined in the Gita respects tradition without being bound by its external forms. It encourages us to be both discerning about the guidance we receive and humble about our need for it.

Start Today: Your First Step

If there's one action I encourage you to take after reading this chapter, it would be this: Conduct what I call a "**Guidance Audit**," a thoughtful assessment of the sources of spiritual guidance in your life right now.

Here's how to begin:

Begin by listing all the current sources of spiritual guidance in your life. These might include:

- Formal teachers or mentors

- Books or sacred texts

- Friends or family members who offer wisdom

- Communities you belong to

- Role models you admire but may not know personally

- Podcasts, videos, or other media that inspire spiritual reflection

- Nature or other environments that spark insight

For each source of guidance, reflect on these questions:

- Does this source help me distinguish between my true self and physical identity?

- Docs it hclp me recognize and work with the different modes (*sattva, rajas, tamas*) operating in my life?

- Does it foster the development of self-control, compassion, and generosity?

- Does it encourage both disciplined living and intellectual inquiry?

- Do I notice greater equanimity and service orientation due to this guidance?

Based on your reflections, identify:

- Sources of guidance that are genuinely helping dispel ignorance

- Potential gaps in your current guidance

- Sources that might be creating more confusion or dependency

Consider one specific action you can take to strengthen the quality of spiritual guidance based on what you've discovered. These might be:

- Deepening your engagement with a particularly valuable source

- Seeking new guidance in an area where you feel a gap

- Creating more space for your reflective practices

- Gracefully distancing yourself from sources that foster dependency rather than clarity

The guidance audit isn't about judging your spiritual path or forcing yourself to find a traditional guru if that doesn't resonate with you. It's about becoming more conscious of how wisdom flows into your life and taking responsibility for creating conditions where genuine guidance can flourish. This audit clarifies and strengthens that intent, creating fertile ground for wisdom to grow in your life.

REMEMBER WHAT THE GITA TEACHES: WHEN YOU HAVE A SINCERE INTENT OF INQUIRY AND SPIRITUAL LEARNING, THE GUIDANCE YOU NEED TENDS TO APPEAR.

The End of Suffering

SUFFERING IS SOMETHING WE ALL EXPERIENCE but rarely fully understand. It's a topic that touches everyone, regardless of who you are, where you live, or what you've accomplished in life. If I were to ask you a simple question, "Who doesn't suffer?" you might struggle to name a single person, including yourself.

What I'm about to share isn't just theoretical knowledge I've picked up from books or seminars. I've drawn these insights from the wisdom of the Gita and Upanishads and put them into practice in my own life. I've tested these approaches, lived with them, refined them through experience, and seen their transformative power firsthand.

I'm not offering you untested theories when discussing the end of suffering. I'm sharing a pathway that I continue to walk myself. When it comes to something as crucial as alleviating our pain, preaching isn't enough. We need practices that work in real-life messiness.

Let's Dive Deeper

Before we can discuss ending suffering, we need to understand what it is. At its core, suffering is an experience of pain and distress. I want you to notice that I emphasized the word "experience" because without experience, there is no suffering. When you're under anesthesia during surgery, you don't experience the cutting and stitching of your body. Although the actions are occurring, you're not aware of them because you're unconscious. Yet when you're fully awake, even something as tiny as a mosquito bite can cause noticeable suffering.

The ancient texts inform us that we're all in a state of *samsara*, wandering through cycles of birth and death, riding this rollercoaster of experiences as part of our existence. Yes, we experience pleasure and relief, but those moments often seem fleeting. The pain and distress tend to leave lasting impressions, shaping our memories and influencing our future choices.

The Two Components of Suffering

Suffering has two distinct components; understanding both is crucial for finding your way out.

The first component is what I refer to as external suffering. It's what happens "to us." These are the forces outside us that we typically blame for our pain: a health crisis, being passed over for a promotion, a car accident caused by another driver, natural disasters that damage our homes, or witnessing the suffering of people we love.

When most people think about suffering, this external component comes first. Some attribute it to *karma*, describing it as a debt we must pay in this lifetime. The reality is that no one escapes these external causes. They are simply part of being human.

However, there's a second, deeper component that's often overlooked: internal suffering. This suffering occurs entirely within us, and here lies the crucial insight that external causes have no impact whatsoever unless we acknowledge and respond to them internally.

Remember the anesthesia example? External conditions may be harrowing, but without conscious awareness, there's no suffering. As the Gita and Upanishads teach, suffering only occurs when there is internal acknowledgment and response.

How you respond to external causes defines your internal suffering. React emotionally and instinctively, and your suffering intensifies. Responding thoughtfully and with awareness can significantly reduce it, possibly even eliminate it.

Managing External Suffering

Though we can't eliminate external causes of suffering, we can certainly manage them. There are two primary approaches:

The first is money, the most apparent and standard method. We utilize financial resources to mitigate the impact of external hardships. We seek the best medical treatments, buy comfortable homes and cars, pay for insurance, and save for retirement. Money helps us minimize pain and distress, and there's wisdom in financial preparation.

But as we all know, money can't solve everything. Even with the finest material comforts, suffering can persist, and this is where the second approach becomes essential.

The ancient texts prescribe something called "*satsang*," being in the company of the pure, pious, like-minded, and compassionate. The word itself breaks down to *sat*, meaning purity, and *sang*, meaning company. True *satsang* softens the blow of external suffering by providing social, moral, physical, financial, and operational support.

People gather in temples and other sacred spaces for this reason, not because that's the only place to find divinity, but because these environments facilitate *satsang*. When you participate in a community with shared values, focusing on service rather than taking, you naturally lessen the impact of external suffering while helping others do the same.

The Upanishads refer to the three Ds—*daya* (compassion), *daana* (charity), and *dama* (self-restraint). Imagine starting each day by saying, "Lord, put me to good use today for the *satsang*." The constant practice (*abhyasa*) of these principles helps manage and minimize external suffering.

Ending Internal Suffering

Now, let's address the heart of suffering, which is the internal component. Without your awareness and acknowledgment, suffering doesn't exist. Gita offers three powerful approaches to managing and ultimately ending this internal suffering:

First, adopt a mindset of responsibility and duty in every action. See yourself responsible for maintaining a healthy body, training your mind to respond rather than react, and fulfilling your duties to your family and loved ones. Adopting this duty-oriented approach transforms potential suffering into purposeful action.

Second, don't let selfish love overshadow responsibility and duty. The Gita offers the perfect example in Arjuna, who initially allowed his attachments to close his eyes to his larger responsibilities. Similarly, his opponent's fatherly love prevented him from seeing his son's deceitfulness, ultimately leading to devastating consequences. When we elevate personal attachments above our deeper responsibilities, we create conditions for profound suffering.

Third, move from fear to faith. This transition from fear to faith occurs naturally as you begin questioning unquestioning beliefs and develop genuine inquiry. Faith emerges when you cultivate respect for what you have, even if it seems minimal, and for everything around you. Cultivating faith isn't about religious dogma, but rather about developing trust in life's inherent wisdom and understanding.

The *satsang* I described earlier provides an ideal environment for developing these practices, offering the support and guidance needed to transform your relationship with internal suffering. Regular participation in such a community allows you to grow spiritually and cultivate a discipline that extends throughout all aspects of your life.

The Practice of Ending Suffering

Ending suffering is not a one-time achievement but an ongoing practice. The Sanskrit word "*abhyasa*" refers to constant, dedicated repetition, and that's precisely what's required. You must consistently apply these principles, observing your reactions, adjusting your responses, and deepening your understanding.

The consistent application of these principles transforms one's experience of life's inevitable challenges. Rather than being overwhelmed by external events or trapped in one's internal reactions, one develops the ability to respond with clarity, compassion, and wisdom. The roller coaster of *samsara* doesn't stop, but one learns to enjoy the ride instead of being terrified by it.

This approach is powerful because it works regardless of your circumstances. The same principles apply when facing significant life challenges or everyday irritations. You create a foundation that can withstand any storm by focusing on responsibility rather than victimhood, duty rather than selfish attachment, and faith rather than fear.

Summary: Journey to End Suffering

The journey to end suffering begins with understanding its true nature. Suffering isn't just what happens to us externally, but how we process those experiences internally. While we can't control all external events, we have tremendous power over our internal responses.

- Managing external suffering involves practical preparation, such as financial security, and cultivating a supportive community, like *satsang*. These elements don't eliminate external challenges but cushion their impact, creating conditions for more profound transformation.

- The fundamental transformation occurs when we address internal suffering by embracing responsibility and duty, moving beyond selfish attachments, and cultivating faith rather than fear. We fundamentally change our relationship with challenging experiences. These aren't separate techniques but interconnected aspects of a unified approach to living.

- The *satsang* provides the ideal environment for this transformation, offering practical support and spiritual guidance. Within this supportive community, we practice the discipline to respond to life's challenges with awareness rather than reactivity. We develop the capacity to quench the fires of suffering before they consume us.

- The approach isn't about reaching a perfect state where challenges never arise. It's about developing the wisdom to navigate life's ups and downs with grace and clarity. The roller coaster of *samsara* continues, but rather than being at its mercy, we learn to enjoy the ride, finding peace amid movement and stillness within the ever-changing world.

Remember that this path requires continuous practice (*abhyasa*). Each day presents new opportunities to apply these principles, and with consistent effort, what begins as a conscious technique gradually becomes natural wisdom. The peace you seek is not in escaping life's challenges but in transforming your relationship with them.

Start Today: Your First Step

If there's one action I encourage you to take right now, it's this: **Find your *satsang*.**

Here's how to begin:

Look for a community of like-minded individuals committed to spiritual growth, mutual support, and service to others, such as a formal religious organization, a volunteer organization, or a circle of friends who share your values and aspirations.

Start where you are with what's available to you. You might begin with just one or two people who share your commitment to personal growth and service. Once you've identified your potential *satsang*, commit to regular participation. Show up not to receive but with the question, "How can I serve?" Asking "How can I serve?" immediately transforms your relationship with suffering.

Each morning, before you begin your day, take a moment to say, "Lord, put me to good use today for the *satsang*." Your daily intention sets the tone for everything that follows, orienting you toward service rather than self-concern. By committing to your *satsang* with an attitude of service, you take the most direct and consequential step toward ending suffering.

REMEMBER, THE COMMITMENT TO COMMUNITY ISN'T JUST ABOUT FINDING SUPPORT FOR YOURSELF (THOUGH THAT WILL NATURALLY HAPPEN). IT'S ABOUT CREATING A CONTAINER WHERE GENUINE TRANSFORMATION BECOMES POSSIBLE—FOR YOURSELF AND OTHERS.

Gratitude

THE TRANSFORMATIVE POWER

SOMEONE TELLS YOU TO BE MORE GRATEFUL, and immediately, you feel that slight resistance. I used to find myself inwardly rolling my eyes. "Yes, I know gratitude is important," as though I already understood it! It wasn't until a later period in my life that I began to realize that gratitude isn't just a nice sentiment or a spiritual checkbox to tick. It's a profound practice that transforms our relationship with everything around us. What I once saw as a simple concept —being thankful for what I have — revealed itself as a powerful bridge connecting my inner spiritual journey with the world around me.

Let me share what I've learned about why gratitude matters so deeply and how it might be the missing piece in your spiritual practice, even if you thought you already had it covered, as I did.

Let's Dive Deeper

Have you ever noticed how many spiritual practices are essentially solitary experiences? Consider meditation, prayer, and studying texts like the Bhagavad Gita. These are activities we typically engage in on our own. The transformation happens internally, within the privacy of our consciousness.

Our most profound spiritual insights need a bridge to connect them with our lived human experience and those around us.

Spirituality can become abstract, theoretical, or detached from life without this bridge. That bridge is gratitude.

As Krishna teaches in the Gita, gratitude leads to ultimate peace. This teaching reveals a practical pathway for integrating spiritual understanding into everyday life. But what exactly does gratitude mean in practice? What makes it so powerful? To understand this, we must look beyond the surface-level "thank you" and explore the deeper dimensions of grateful living.

When someone says, "I'm grateful," the conversation often stops there. We don't dig deeper to understand: what exactly are we grateful for? Grateful to whom? What does gratitude mean in practice?

Through my journey and study of the Gita's teachings, I have come to see gratitude as fundamentally about connection. It's about recognizing and appreciating the intricate web of relationships that sustain our existence at every moment. There are three essential connections that genuine gratitude acknowledges:

1. Connection to Divinity Within and Around Us

The first dimension of gratitude begins with recognizing the divine spark within yourself. We are not referring to spiritual pride, but it's about acknowledging the miracle of your existence.

Think about something as simple as waking up each morning. We take it for granted, don't we? But that life force that the Gita refers to as *prana* flowing through your body is a divine action. The fact that your heart beats without you having to remember to tell it to, that your lungs know how to breathe while you sleep—these are everyday miracles deserving recognition.

I remember a period when life felt like a constant struggle. One evening, I went to bed feeling utterly hopeless. The next morning, I awoke to the unexpected, good news that shifted my perspective entirely. That dramatic change in my internal weather, from despair to hope in a night's sleep, reminded me that we're connected to something larger than our momentary thoughts and feelings. Being grateful for these shifts connects us to the divine flow of life.

Our link to the divine naturally extends outward, embracing all we encounter in our journey. When was the last time you appreciated someone's presence in your life, not for what they did for you, but simply for who they are? When you invite others to share in your celebrations and appreciate their presence despite past differences, you're practicing gratitude for the divine as it manifests in human form.

In scriptural terms, this is devotion to the *bhaagavatha*—the divine as it appears. It's seeing God not as distant and separate but as present in everything and everyone around you.

2. Connection to the Supreme Power

The second dimension involves acknowledging a supreme power that sustains the universe. The concept can be challenging to grasp because, by definition, the supreme is boundless. How can our limited minds comprehend the unlimited?

None of us has truly seen this power directly. If someone claims they have, they're likely confining the limitless to their limited human perception. Instead, we experience the supreme through its characteristics: the love we feel for others, the compassion we witness in difficult times, and our capacity for devotion and surrender.

As Krishna says in chapter 18, verse 62 of the Gita, *"Surrender with a grateful heart."* Gratitude in this dimension means appreciating these divine qualities wherever we encounter them. You can give this supreme power a name or associate it with specific attributes, which is fine. That's why every prayer or mantra about a deity highlights particular characteristics. We express gratitude by connecting with these qualities.

I witnessed the importance of this connection during a family ceremony years ago. The priest conducting our puja was distracted, checking his phone between mantras. I remember gently asking him to be fully present. For those sacred moments, his complete attention was essential. He was expressing gratitude to the supreme on our behalf, a profound responsibility that demanded complete presence.

A grateful acknowledgment of the supreme reminds us that we can honor and connect with divine qualities in our experiences, despite our limited ability to fully grasp the infinite reality.

3. Connection to a Supportive Foundation

For gratitude to flourish, we need a foundation. We need an environment that nurtures our spiritual growth. Without this support, how can we truly develop and express gratitude?

Some people are fortunate to find this foundation at home through parents or mentors who guide their spiritual development from an early age. Others seem to arrive with innate spiritual tendencies, which some traditions call vasanas — the tendencies carried over from previous experiences. This is why some children absorb spiritual teachings remarkably easily, as if they are remembering rather than learning. But what about those without these advantages? Where can they learn to develop gratitude?

Temples, ashrams, spiritual communities, and teachers are vital for those seeking to develop gratitude without the benefit of early learning. These institutions and individuals provide the foundation, the *dravya,* where our latent qualities can emerge and grow. They're like gardeners watering seeds that were already within us, helping them sprout and flourish.

My journey reflects this. Thirty years ago, I knew little about spirituality beyond basic religious practices. Standing on the foundation provided by teachers and traditions allowed me to begin and continue this journey of gratitude.

Even with support, the spiritual path unfolds differently for each person. That's perfectly normal and to be expected. If you have the physical ability and opportunity to practice gratitude, consider it essential, not optional.

It's like having daylight to clean your house. When you possess strength and capability, utilize them to cultivate gratitude. You're fulfilling your purpose by cultivating grateful awareness and helping others do the same, just as a river flows without questioning its nature.

Living with Gratitude: Practical Applications

Understanding gratitude intellectually is one thing; living it is another. How do we translate these three dimensions of connection into daily practice?

I've found that intention is the starting point. Each morning, try waking with this simple thought: "Krishna, put me to use today." Such a morning intention harmonizes your actions with divine purpose, unveiling countless moments for significant connection in the hours ahead.

Notice how this shifts your perspective from "What can I get today?" to "How can I serve today?" Moving from "getting" to "giving" fundamentally alters your relationship with each person you encounter throughout the day. Suddenly, the cashier at the grocery store, your colleague at work, or your child asking for help with homework are no longer interruptions in your day, but opportunities to express gratitude through presence and service.

Another helpful practice I've found is "gratitude pauses." Several times throughout the day, particularly during transitions like entering a meeting, starting your car, or beginning a meal, take a moment to recall one thing you're grateful for in that moment. These brief pauses rewire your nervous system over time, training your mind to notice what supports you rather than what lacks.

Gratitude also transforms our perspective on challenges. When difficulties arise, and they inevitably will, the practice of gratitude doesn't mean denying reality or forcing oneself to think positively. Instead, it invites us to ask: "What might this situation teach me? How might this challenge be serving my growth?" Often, our most significant difficulties become, in retrospect, our most excellent teachers. Living gratefully means embracing challenges with trust in their hidden purpose rather than forcing artificial positivity.

Summary: Gratitude is the best Attitude

As explored in this chapter, gratitude isn't just a simple emotion or social nicety. It's a profound practice that transforms our relationship with ourselves, others, and the world around us. Through the three dimensions of connection — our connection to the divine within and around us, to the supreme power, and to our supportive foundation — gratitude becomes a bridge between our internal spiritual journey and our lived human experience.

When we cultivate grateful awareness, several transformations naturally occur:

- We shift from scarcity to abundance. Rather than focusing on what's missing, we notice the countless supports that make our lives possible in each moment.

- We move from isolation to connection. Gratitude reminds us that we are never truly alone but part of an intricate web of relationships, both seen and unseen.

- We transition from meaninglessness to purpose. By recognizing the gift of our existence, we naturally seek to offer our unique gifts in return.

- We bridge the gap between abstract spirituality and concrete experience. Through the practice of gratitude, concepts that might otherwise remain theoretical become lived realities.

- Gratitude truly is the most transformative attitude we can adopt. It doesn't require exceptional circumstances as it's available to us regardless of our external conditions.

- Even in our most difficult moments, there remains the miracle of breath, consciousness, and the opportunity to grow through challenge.

The beauty of gratitude is that you don't need to wait to master complex techniques or accumulate vast knowledge before beginning. You can start right now, in this moment, by simply noticing and acknowledging what's supporting you.

The practice of gratitude is both the beginning and the fulfillment of the spiritual journey. It's both the seed and the fruit. By cultivating grateful awareness, we not only transform our own experience but also contribute to healing our divided world.

Start Today: Your First Step

If there's one action I encourage you to take right now, it's this: **Practice the Three-Connection Gratitude.**

Here's how to begin:

- **Connect with the divinity in yourself and others:** Place your hand on your heart and acknowledge one aspect of your being that you're grateful for today. Consider appreciating your body's resilience, creative mind, or the simple miracle of conscious awareness. Then, consider one person whose presence in your life deserves recognition. Mentally send them appreciation, whether they're someone you'll see today or someone distant from you.

- **Connect with the supreme:** Open your awareness to something larger than yourself, whatever that means. Reflect on one quality of the divine you've experienced recently, such as the vastness of the universe, a moment of compassion, or a feeling of being guided or helped. Express gratitude for this connection.

- **Connect with your foundation**: Acknowledge the people, traditions, and resources that have supported your growth. Consider acknowledging a teacher's influence, a perspective-changing book, a welcoming community, or even the supporting earth beneath you. Take a moment to recognize how these supports have enabled your journey.

As you practice, don't rush. Give each connection time to deepen. And don't just think these thoughts—speak them aloud, write them down, or express them through a gesture. The act of expression transforms internal gratitude into a living practice.

Try this for just seven consecutive days. You might be surprised at how consistently practicing the three-connection exercise slowly realigns your awareness, illuminating the previously overlooked web of support that has always sustained your journey. Start now—these few minutes might become the most transformative part of your day.

REMEMBER, GRATITUDE ISN'T ABOUT FORCED POSITIVITY OR DENYING LIFE'S CHALLENGES. IT'S ABOUT HONEST RECOGNITION OF THE INTERDEPENDENCE THAT MAKES YOUR LIFE POSSIBLE, EVEN IN DIFFICULT TIMES.

The Sacred Exchange

TAKE A DEEP BREATH. Now exhale. Taking a breath and releasing it unveils one of life's most fundamental principles. Our bodies function through this continuous rhythm of taking and giving, breathing in oxygen and releasing carbon dioxide. What would happen if we could only inhale but never exhale? It's not just impossible; it's contrary to the fundamental pattern of existence.

The pattern of giving and receiving doesn't stop at biology. It's embedded in the universe's very structure. The oxygen you breathe sustains your life, while the carbon dioxide you release nourishes plants. What you give differs from what you take, but giving back maintains the harmony of life.

The cyclical pattern of give and take reaches far beyond our physical bodies into our connections with others and our environment. We'll discover that charity—this sacred exchange of giving and receiving—isn't just something we do occasionally but is as essential to our spiritual wellbeing as breathing is to our physical existence.

Let's Dive Deeper

Many think about charity occasionally, perhaps when asked to donate or during the holiday season. But what if giving was as natural and automatic as breathing? For some fortunate individuals, it is. They give without calculation simply because it's integral to who they are.

For most of us, though, developing a charitable mindset requires conscious effort. I know this because I've struggled with it myself. For years, I never felt satisfied with my philanthropic actions. Something was missing until I discovered the right way and type of charity to practice.

The Gita and Upanishads offer profound insights about charity that have guided countless generations. Let's begin by understanding how different types of people approach the act of giving.

The Three Types of People

The *Brihadaranyaka Upanishad*, one of the most revered spiritual texts, offers guidance for three types of individuals:

- Those with abundance—people who have everything at their command

  For those with abundance, the emphasis is on self-control (*dama*). When you have too much of everything, you tend to splurge and lose control. Just as giving a race car to a child requires restraint, so too does having too much of a good thing.

- Those with ruthless power—people who wield significant influence

  For those with power, the focus is on compassion (*daya*). Power can corrupt, so compassion must accompany every decision and action.

- Those with a mix of abundance, passion, and lethargy—the majority of us

  For most of us, with our diverse mix of qualities, we tend to emphasize giving (*daana*)—charity.

These three principles (self-control, compassion, and charity) aren't just intellectual concepts but matters of the heart. Speaking of the heart, there is a beautiful insight in Sanskrit where "heart" (*hrudayam*) is composed of three syllables: *hr* (to take), *da* (to give), and *yam* (giving through knowledge, thought, and feeling). A spiritual being meditates on the heart, focusing on self-control, compassion, and charity.

When you step back and examine your life, you'll realize that whatever abundance or power you possess is essentially borrowed from the universe. You're not the owner but a custodian. You work hard to increase what you have, but there must be a way of giving back some of it. That's the essence of charity.

The Three Types of Charity

True charity manifests in three distinct forms, each with its significance and practice:

1. Charity through Distribution

Donating a portion of our possessions through charitable giving, organized fundraisers, or direct monetary contributions represents the most widely recognized form of charity. It's the simplest form of charity, requiring only seconds. Even governments recognize its importance by offering tax benefits!

Remember, it's not about how much you have or give, but whether you're giving a component of what you take rather than hoarding it all. Just like breathing, you can't just inhale; you must exhale too.

Distribution charity extends beyond financial giving to include sharing apparel, household items, practical tools, and various material belongings.

2. Charity through Sacrifice

The Bhagavad Gita guides us to perform every action as a sacrifice. Perform the action as an offering kindled and consumed by the correct type of fire. Take eating as an example: food is offered to the body and ignited by the fire of digestion.

Charity through sacrifice occurs when you give something without expecting a transactional outcome in return. Examples of sacrificial charity include providing meals or dedicating hours at spiritual centers, shelters for people experiencing homelessness, or community food resources. These actions are taken from principle rather than personal gain.

While charity of distribution may be transactional, charity of sacrifice has little or no expectation of return.

3. Charity through Austerity

Austerity-based charity manifests through conscious behaviors expressed via physical actions, mental attitudes, and verbal communications:

- Body: Serving through cleanliness, simplicity, and non-violence

- Speech: Speaking with empathy, listening without judgment, and understanding others' perspectives

- Mind: Acting with purity of intention, a steady hand, and bringing order to situations

Charity through austerity becomes an integral part of your daily routine, transforming into a fundamental aspect of your behavior in both personal and professional life.

The Right Way of Giving

Understanding the types of charity is essential, but equally crucial is knowing the right way to give:

1. Give to Worthy Recipients

Direct charity towards worthy individuals or organizations. Look for transparency and alignment with your values, provided those values benefit the broader society.

2. Give at the Proper Time and Place

Help people when they need it most. Don't over-analyze their needs based on your judgment. If there's a genuine need and the recipient isn't taking advantage, consider giving, whether that's your time or financial support.

3. Avoid Giving to Unworthy Causes

Regardless of popularity, charity to the wrong person or organization can be harmful. The only reason someone would give to such entities is a lack of evaluation or an expectation of something in return.

These principles apply to all forms of charity, distribution, sacrifice, and austerity. The only exception is food. When sharing food, give to those in need and those at your table. Lastly, once you've provided, consider it done. Please don't dwell on it. If you feel you've made a mistake by contributing to an unworthy cause, adjust your approach next time.

How Much Should You Give?

Being mindful of giving applies to both your financial contributions and time allocation, as these are tangible resources that can be effectively utilized. While ancient texts like the Gita and Upanishads don't specify exact amounts (they provide frameworks, not rulebooks), later scriptures suggest dividing what you have into five parts.

- One part for fulfilling desires and family responsibilities

- One part of saving, investing, and growing wealth

- One part for activities that could bring you recognition

- One part for activities that better society

- One part for charity through distribution and sacrifice

Remember, it's not about the quantity but the intent, type, and proper way of giving that matters.

Summary: The Breath of Charity

- Just as we naturally inhale and exhale, giving and taking should become a natural rhythm. Charity isn't just about money, but expands into how we distribute our resources, what we sacrifice, and the austerity we practice.

- True charity comes from understanding that we're custodians, not owners, of what we possess. We borrow everything from the universe, including our wealth, time, energy, and talents. It is our responsibility to give back.

- The right charity involves giving to worthy recipients at the proper time and place without expectation of return. We should embody this in our conduct through our actions, words, and thoughts.

- Whether you have abundance, power, or a mix of qualities, the principles of self-control, compassion, and giving apply to you. These aren't just philosophical concepts but practical guides for living a meaningful life.

Like breathing, charity follows a natural rhythm of taking and giving. When we align with this rhythm, we contribute to the well-being of others and enhance our sense of purpose.

Start Today: Your First Step

If there's one action I encourage you to take right now, it's this: **Perform a simple act of charity.** Don't wait for the "perfect" time or opportunity to practice charity. Start with simple acts.

Here's how to begin:

- Buy a coffee for someone who serves the community—a soldier, firefighter, or teacher.

- Share food openly with those around you, whether they're in need or not.

- Dedicate a few hours to serving in a temple, shelter, or food bank, not because you need to serve a deity, but because it's your moral obligation to serve divinity in all forms.

REMEMBER, TRUE WEALTH ISN'T MEASURED BY WHAT YOU HAVE BUT BY WHAT YOU GIVE. THE JOURNEY OF CHARITY BEGINS WITH A SINGLE ACT. LIKE BREATHING, ONCE YOU START THE RHYTHM OF GIVING, IT BECOMES EASIER AND MORE NATURAL.

Dreams

MORE REAL THAN YOUR WAKING LIFE?

I HAD THE MOST EXTRAORDINARY DREAM. I was flying over a city engulfed in flames, and somehow, I knew I had the power to save everyone below. With each dive through the smoke, I lifted people to safety, carrying them above chaos to a haven on the mountain. What struck me wasn't just the vivid detail, the weight of each person in my arms, the heat of the flames against my skin, the profound relief in their eyes, but how real it all felt. When I finally woke up, my heart was still racing with purpose, and I found myself doing what we all do: wondering what it meant, if anything.

Dreams have fascinated humanity since the beginning of recorded history. Ancient civilizations considered dreams to be messages from the gods or glimpses into other realms. Some viewed dreams as windows into the unconscious mind. But what if both perspectives contain elements of truth? What if dreams are neither random neural firings nor simple messages but a different state of consciousness as real as our waking life?

Most of us have experienced waking from a vivid dream and feeling its emotional impact lingering throughout the day. Perhaps you've had dreams so realistic that you needed a moment to determine which reality was "real upon waking." Or maybe you've experienced those rare lucid dreams where you suddenly realized you were dreaming and could control what happened next.

These experiences hint at something profound about dreams that goes beyond conventional understanding. And that's what we will explore in this chapter—dreams from a spiritual perspective, particularly through the lens of ancient wisdom found in the Upanishads.

Let's Dive Deeper

We'll tackle three essential questions about dreams:

> Are dreams real?
>
> Do dreams have meaning?
>
> Can dream events come true, and should we be concerned about them?

The answers might surprise you, challenge your assumptions, and transform your thoughts about that third of your life spent sleeping. Let's journey into the mysterious world of dreams, where the boundaries between reality and imagination, past and future, conscious and unconscious, become wonderfully blurred.

Are Dreams Real? The Upanishadic Perspective

Let's start with the most fundamental question: Are dreams real? Most of us think of dreams as "not real," mere fantasies or hallucinations that occur when our conscious mind shuts down. We dismiss them with phrases like "it was just a dream" or "back to reality now." But the ancient wisdom of the Upanishads offers a fascinatingly different perspective.

The Upanishads—philosophical texts that form the foundation of Hindu spiritual thought —approach this question by focusing not on the content of our various states of consciousness, but on who is witnessing them. They recognize three primary states of consciousness: the waking state, the dream state, and the deep sleep state.

Consider this: when you wake up from a dream, you might say, "I had a dream." When you wake up from deep sleep, you might say, "I slept well." And in your waking life, you say, "I am experiencing this." There's a consistent "I" witness who experiences each state in all three states. The Upanishads identify this unchanging witness as your true self, your soul, or what they refer to as the "atman."

The Mandukya Upanishad goes into beautiful detail about these three states:

> jagarithastanah (the waking state)

> svapnastanah (the dream state)

> suṣuptasthānah (the deep sleep state)

It speaks of a fourth state—the pure consciousness that witnesses all three, the true "you" that remains constant while states of consciousness come and go.

From this perspective, if the same consciousness witnesses both your waking state and your dream state, how can we say one is "real" and the other "unreal"? If the dream state is unreal, logically, the waking state must be equally unreal because the same unchanging consciousness witnesses both.

We are not discussing abstract philosophy. Modern neuroscience has demonstrated that brain activity during REM sleep closely resembles that of the waking state, during which most dreaming occurs. Your brain doesn't distinguish between waking and dreaming; it processes experiences in remarkably similar ways.

Are dreams real? According to the Upanishads, dreams are as real as your waking life, and your waking life is as unreal as your dreams. Both are simply different states of consciousness experienced by the unchanging witness, your true self. The Upanishadic lens prompts us to reconsider what we fundamentally assume about reality.

The Meaning of Dreams: Understanding Our Inner City

Let's explore our second question: Do dreams have meaning, and how do we make sense of them? To answer this, we must understand how our mind and body function during different states of consciousness. The Upanishads offer a fascinating metaphor: the body is a city with multiple entrances, gates, and energy stations.

This "city" operates with all systems engaged in the waking state. The Upanishads describe nineteen aspects of our being that keep this city alive and functioning:

- The five senses of knowledge (ears, eyes, skin, tongue, nose)

- The five organs of action (speech, hands, feet, organs of procreation, and digestion)

- The five energy stations or "fires" that sustain life (breath, digestion, excretion, bodily mass, and internal circulation)

- The four psychological centers (the mind that thinks, the intellect that decides, the ego that creates identity, and the capacity to retain past impressions)

While in the waking state, our knowledge is directed primarily toward external objects and experiences. The nineteen gates and energy stations work in an organized manner, processing information from outside and responding appropriately. But what happens during the dream state? Interestingly, most of these same systems remain active.

The five energy "fires" continue to burn, keeping the body alive and functioning. Most of the nineteen aspects of our being are still present, but with two critical differences:

- Information flows freely without the filters that operate in the waking state

- The rational faculty (intellect) is subdued

The Brihadaranyaka Upanishad compares the dream state to an emperor taking citizens and moving whimsically around the city. Past impressions, memories, desires, and fears intermingle freely without the organizing principle of reason.

The suspension of rational filtering explains those moments in dreams when one suddenly shifts from being human to an elephant, a mouse, or encounters impossible situations that feel entirely normal until one awakens. These observations provide us with clarity about what our dreams may signify.

When the organizing principle of reason is suspended, dreams aren't usually direct messages or prophecies but reflect our inner world. They reveal the contents of our mind—our memories, fears, desires, and unprocessed experiences—in a state of free flow.

When you wake up and try to make sense of a dream, you often apply waking-state logic to dream-state experiences. No wonder they usually seem absurd! It's like trying to read a book with its pages randomly rearranged.

But this doesn't mean dreams are meaningless. Far from it. Dreams give us glimpses into the contents of our minds when the usual filters are removed. They can reveal emotional states we're not fully acknowledging, concerns we're suppressing, or creative connections our rational mind wouldn't usually make.

Understanding dreams requires approaching them not as straightforward messages but as symbolic expressions of our inner landscape. This landscape encompasses not just recent experiences, but also the accumulated impressions of our entire lives.

Can Dreams Come True? The Influence of *samskaras*

Now, we arrive at our third question: Do dream events materialize, and should we be concerned about them? As we've discussed, most dream content is non-linear and lacks logical coherence. But there are exceptions, and understanding these exceptions requires us to explore the concept of *samskaras* or *vasanas*—our mental tendencies and impressions.

Both in waking life and dreams, we act based on memories, past impressions, and current experiences. In dreams, without current external experiences, we primarily work with stored impressions and memories. The quality of these impressions has a significant influence on the nature of our dreams. The Sanskrit tradition categorizes tendencies into three main types:

sattvic (pure, harmonious, balanced)

rajasic (active, passionate, restless)

tamasic (dull, lethargic, negative)

When our mind is cluttered with rajasic or tamasic tendencies, those charged with aggression, hatred, fear, or lethargy, our dreams become chaotic and disturbing. As an example, watching a violent movie before bed often leads to troubled sleep. Emotionally charged impressions even wake you from sleep.

However, our dreams take on a different quality when our tendencies are *sattvic*—peaceful, compassionate, and filled with goodness. They become more coherent, positive, and sometimes even insightful. Hindu mythology contains many stories of saints and sages receiving guidance or blessings through dreams, manifesting in their waking lives.

A crucial insight emerges here: meaningful connections between dreams and waking reality are more common when they arise from a sattvic mind characterized by clarity, peace, and stability. Not because dreams inherently foretell the future, but because a balanced, clear mind sometimes recognizes patterns or possibilities that our rational faculties miss.

Should you be concerned if you have a disturbing dream that predicts something negative? Generally, no. Most dreams, especially those that're chaotic or unsettling, are simply a reflection of the jumbled contents of a mind dealing with rajasic or tamasic impressions. They're more a reflection of your mental state than a window into the future.

However, if you occasionally have clear, positive dreams that later seem to connect with waking events, there's no need for surprise. A mind that approaches both dreaming and waking with clarity and balance can sometimes perceive connections and patterns across both states. A fundamental truth emerges here:

The nature of our dreams mirrors the nature of our consciousness

The Deep Sleep State: Beyond Dreams

Before we conclude, let's briefly touch on the third state of consciousness mentioned in the Upanishads: deep sleep (*suṣuptasthānah*).

In deep sleep, unlike in the dream state, most of the "gates" of our body-city go dormant. The senses, organs of action, and psychological centers temporarily shut down. However, the five "fires" or energy stations continue to function, keeping the body alive and warm. If these fires were to be extinguished, we would not be in deep sleep but dead.

Deep sleep represents yet another state of consciousness, one where individual awareness recedes completely. There are no dreams, no sense of self, and no experiences to process. Yet upon waking up, we say, "I slept well." That unchanging "I", the witness remains, even when nothing specific is being witnessed.

The state of deep sleep illuminates what may be the most profound Upanishadic wisdom regarding consciousness: your essential self transcends all forms of experience. Understanding the relationship between these three states (waking, dreaming, and deep sleep) provides a comprehensive picture of consciousness and helps us recognize that dreams are not separate from our "real" life, but are integral to our entire experience as conscious beings.

Summary: Dreams as a Gateway to Understanding Consciousness

Let's bring together the key insights we've explored about dreams from a spiritual perspective:

- Dreams are as real as waking life—and waking life is as "unreal" as dreams. Both are states of consciousness witnessed by the same unchanging awareness, which the Upanishads identify as your true self.

- Most of the same systems that operate in the waking state remain active during the dream state. The rational faculty is subdued, and information flows freely without the usual filters, causing dreams' non-linear, sometimes bizarre nature.

- Dreams aren't usually direct messages or prophecies but reflections of our inner mental landscape when the organizing principle of reason is temporarily suspended. They reveal the contents of our minds, the memories, fears, desires, and unprocessed experiences in a state of free flow.

- The quality of our dreams is directly connected to our consciousness. Minds cluttered with agitated or hostile tendencies (*rajasic* or *tamasic*) produce chaotic, disturbing dreams. Minds characterized by peace and clarity (*sattvic*) experience more coherent, positive, and occasionally insightful dreams.

- For individuals with predominantly *sattvic* tendencies, dreams can occasionally contain insights that prove meaningful in waking life, not because dreams are inherently prophetic but because a clear mind can perceive patterns and possibilities across different states of consciousness.

- All three states (waking, dreaming, and deep sleep) are witnessed by the same unchanging awareness, which points to a deeper understanding of our true nature as the consciousness that makes all experiences possible.

Dreams offer us a unique opportunity to gain insight into the nature of consciousness itself. By paying attention to our dreams and noticing the continuity of awareness across different states, we can recognize that our essential nature transcends any state or experience. Far from diminishing our waking experiences, such awareness enriches them.

It enriches our experience by helping us recognize that consciousness is deeper and more expansive than we typically realize. Dreams aren't a meaningless side effect of sleep but a different expression of the same consciousness we experience in waking life. By approaching dreams with this spiritual understanding, we can appreciate them as an integral part of our existence—a different room in the house of consciousness we all inhabit.

Start Today: Your First Step

If there's one action I encourage you to take right now, it's this: **Begin cultivating *sattvic* awareness in your daily life.** Since the quality of our dreams is directly connected to the quality of our waking consciousness, the most effective way to transform your dream experiences is to cultivate peace, clarity, and balance in your everyday awareness.

Here's how to begin:

Before going to sleep each night, take five minutes to consciously transition from the day's busy activities to a state of calm awareness. Sit comfortably, close your eyes, and gently focus on your breath. Imagine releasing the day's tensions, worries, and agitated thoughts with each exhale.

Then, recall three things from your day that brought you peace, joy, or a sense of connection. These don't need to be significant events, perhaps a moment of kindness from a stranger, the beauty of sunlight through leaves, or the satisfaction of completing a task. Briefly relive each positive experience, allowing the good feelings to permeate your awareness.

Finally, set an intention for your ideal state of mind. You might silently say, "As I sleep, may my mind rest in clarity and peace. May my dreams reflect the harmony I cultivate in my waking life." The evening ritual gradually transforms your tendencies from *rajasic* (agitated) or *tamasic* (dull) toward *sattvic* (clear, balanced, harmonious). Over time, you may notice your dreams becoming less chaotic and more coherent. You might experience fewer disturbing dreams and more peaceful, even insightful ones.

When aligned in this way, your various states of consciousness work in concert, revealing the unbroken 'I' that observes all states while remaining unbounded by them. Get started. The journey toward sattvic awareness is both simple and profound, and it starts with just five minutes of conscious transition before sleep. As your waking awareness becomes more *sattvic*, this quality also naturally extends to your dream state.

REMEMBER, THE GOAL ISN'T TO CONTROL OR MAKE YOUR DREAMS PROPHETIC. INSTEAD, IT'S TO BRING THE SAME QUALITY OF AWARENESS TO ALL STATES OF CONSCIOUSNESS—WAKING, DREAMING, AND EVEN DEEP SLEEP.

Horoscopes & Astrology

SHOULD YOU BELIEVE?

DO YOU FIND YOURSELF CHECKING YOUR HOROSCOPE before making an important decision? Or perhaps you've noticed friends postponing plans due to an unfavorable planetary position? You're not alone. Millions of people worldwide turn to the stars for guidance, despite scientific evidence indicating that there is no confirmed empirical basis to support astrological claims.

> *The stars may impel, but they do not compel — Ancient astrological proverb.*

Our ancestors consistently looked to the heavens for guidance, finding patterns and meaning in the movements of celestial bodies. Over the millennia, such observations evolved into astrology, the study of how celestial movements are believed to shape our lives and personalities.

The birth chart, or horoscope, represents a snapshot of the cosmos at the precise moment and location of your birth. Each planet, each celestial house, tells part of a story (your story, according to astrological tradition). But what drives us to seek meaning in these cosmic patterns?

Let's Dive Deeper

If you've ever paused to question astrological wisdom, you might have encountered some of the same philosophical tensions I've wrestled with over the years. Particularly for those who also hold theistic beliefs, a central question arises: If one believes in an all-powerful divine being, how can human-created calendars and almanacs override or predict the divine will?

The Bhagavad Gita offers insight into this paradox when Lord Krishna declares:

> *The Supreme Lord is situated in everyone's heart, O Arjuna, according to their actions, the supreme being is directing the wanderings of all living entities (Bhagavad Gita 18.61)*

Krishna's teachings imply that divine guidance works through an intimate, internal connection rather than via external celestial indicators. So why would we need planetary positions to guide us? Let's consider some questions worth pondering:

- At what point did humans acquire the authority to designate certain days as auspicious or inauspicious? By what mechanism did we determine that divine favor or grace follows astronomical patterns?

- What justifies the belief that divine presence or influence is stronger in specific directions or locations based on planetary positions? Can the divine truly be constrained by cosmic geography?

- How can a celestial configuration chart determine the compatibility of two individuals for marriage or other relationships? Does this not challenge notions of personal responsibility and free will?

- What logic supports the notion that certain days are more appropriate for prayer or spiritual connection than others? Is divine receptivity truly calendar-dependent?

The Spectrum of Belief

In my conversations with people from diverse backgrounds and cultures, I've noticed that astrological beliefs exist along a spectrum. Let me share with you the different types of believers I've encountered:

**Note: The names and personal stories shared in this chapter are used solely as examples to illustrate various perspectives on astrology. They are not meant to criticize or question anyone's beliefs.

1. The Devout Believers: Faith Above All

Meet Sid, a 46-year-old business owner who consults his astrologer before making any significant decision. For Sid and others like him, astrology represents an immutable cosmic law that governs human experience.

"I would never dream of starting a new venture without consulting my birth chart," Sid told me. "Twenty years ago, I ignored my astrologer's warning about an inauspicious time to expand my business, and the venture failed within months. I won't make that mistake again."

An absolute commitment to astrological guidance characterizes the relationship devout believers have with astrological principles. They integrate astrological principles into daily decision-making, attributing successes to astrological alignment and failures to misinterpretation.

2. The Fear-Motivated Disciple: Cosmic Insurance

"Better safe than sorry" might as well be the motto for this group. Take Mala, a 36-year-old engineer who describes herself as "scientifically minded" yet still checks her horoscope and astrological charts and reschedules essential events.

"I know it sounds contradictory," she explained, "but what if it's true? The cost of following astrological advice is small compared to the potential cost of ignoring it."

Fear-motivated disciples view astrology primarily as a risk-management tool, characterized by stress reduction through the practice of prescribed rituals and a focus on preventing unfavorable outcomes over pursuing favorable ones.

3. The Cultural Practitioners: Tradition Keepers

For many, astrology connects to cultural heritage rather than a literal belief system. Consider Shiv, whose family has followed the same astrological lineage for generations:

"When my daughter was born, we created her birth chart not because I believe planets control her destiny, but because it connects her to our traditions. It's about continuity, not prediction."

These cultural practitioners emphasize tradition and continuity with ancestral practices, engaging with astrological customs during significant life events.

4. The Convenience Users: Taking What Works

"I am checking if it's an auspicious day for my wedding," admits Neela, a doctor. "But if the only date available at my dream venue falls on an inauspicious day, I'll find a ritual to offset the negative influence and book it anyway."

The fourth category interacts with astrology adaptively. Adopting its guidance when advantageous, but working around it when it creates barriers. They perform a cost-benefit analysis of astrological compliance and utilize "ritual measures" to circumvent inconvenient predictions.

Which of these categories resonates with you? You may identify with more than one, or your relationship with astrology has evolved between these categories at different life stages.

Selective Application

Have you ever noticed that even the most devoted astrology believers don't consult star charts before brushing their teeth or choosing breakfast? Such inconsistent usage exposes a fundamental truth about how people think and behave.

Believers typically consult astrological guidance for significant life events, such as marriages, property acquisitions, business ventures, or religious ceremonies, while mundane daily activities proceed without astrological consultation. This suggests that even devoted believers recognize practical limits to astrological application.

In the words of Anita, a long-time astrology enthusiast: "Of course, I don't check my horoscope before deciding what to eat for lunch. Astrology is for life's big moments, not everyday choices."

But this raises an intriguing question: If celestial forces are powerful enough to determine the success of a marriage or business venture, wouldn't they also influence seemingly more minor decisions that might have significant cascading effects?

Finding the Middle Path

We need to adopt a mode of critical engagement that balances diverse perspectives. Several principles for this approach include:

Cultural Respect with Critical Thinking:

Honor astrological practices as cultural heritage while maintaining intellectual autonomy in decision-making. Traditions can have value beyond literal truth claims. They help keep the community together, and the softer benefits of a tight-knit community sometimes outweigh rational truth.

Awareness of Confirmation Bias:

Our minds naturally remember "hits" while forgetting "misses" in predictive systems, such as astrology. If you believe in astrology, consider keeping a journal of astrological predictions to track accuracy objectively over time.

Risk Assessment:

Evaluate the potential consequences of deferring important decisions (medical treatments, career opportunities) based on astrological guidance. What is the worst-case scenario if you follow or ignore astrological advice?

Integration with Core Spiritual Principles:

Examine whether astrological practices align with fundamental spiritual teachings. Do they enhance or potentially distract you from spiritual inquiry and core spiritual values?

What Do Spiritual Texts Say?

Notably, foundational spiritual texts like the Bhagavad Gita and Upanishads place minimal emphasis on astrological determinism. Instead, these texts emphasize ethical conduct, fulfilling one's duty, and spiritual self-realization as primary pathways to human flourishing.

The Bhagavad Gita offers several verses that seem to challenge the fundamental premises of predictive astrology:

> *You have a right to perform your prescribed duties, but you are not entitled to the fruits of your actions (Bhagavad Gita 2.47)*

> This teaching emphasizes performing one's duty without attachment to outcomes, which contrasts with astrological practices that often focus on securing favorable outcomes by choosing auspicious timing.

The wise see action amid inaction and inaction amid action with unified consciousness, and although they perform actions, there is complete awareness, and they are the masters of their actions (Bhagavad Gita 4.18)

This verse suggests that enlightened action transcends favorable and unfavorable timing, focusing instead on awareness and consciousness at any moment.

Indeed, miserable are those who are motivated only by desire for the fruits of action, for they are constantly anxious about the results of what they do (Bhagavad Gita 2.49)

The Gita's warning directly confronts the anxiety commonly found in astrological practices, where followers prioritize favorable timing over proper conduct regardless of the situation. The gap between widespread astrological customs and the core teachings of the Gita should prompt serious reflection among fervent adherents of astrology.

My Journey with Astrology

I grew up in a tradition where astrological consultations were a routine part of life. Before major family decisions, consulting the almanac or a priest and returning with favorable dates was a common practice. As a child, I accepted this as usual; as a teenager, I began to question; and as an adult, I've come to appreciate the psychological comfort these practices provided, while recognizing their limitations.

My relationship with astrology has evolved from an unquestioning acceptance to a skeptical rejection, and finally to a middle path where I appreciate astrology as a symbolic language and cultural practice while not deferring my decision-making authority to it.

My evolution of thought mirrors the nuanced relationship many people develop with ancestral knowledge frameworks in contemporary settings. We need not choose between wholesale acceptance or dismissal.

Summary: Beyond Simple Acceptance or Rejection

Whether to "believe in astrology" perhaps misframes the issue. Rather than approaching astrology as a binary proposition demanding complete acceptance or rejection, I propose viewing astrological systems as complex cultural phenomena worthy of engagement.

- These benefits need not be dismissed for those finding meaning, comfort, or connection through astrological practices. However, critical thinking remains essential, particularly when astrological guidance affects consequential life decisions.

- As we navigate our relationship with ancient predictive systems in the modern world, perhaps the wisest course lies not in blind faith and cynical dismissal, but rather in thoughtful engagement that honors both tradition and reason.

The Bhagavad Gita offers a final thought for consideration:

Whatever state of being one remembers when giving up the body at the time of death, that state is attained (Gita 8.6)

The scripture suggests that our state of mind at the time of death, rather than our natal chart, determines what follows. Perhaps our energy is better spent cultivating that consciousness through righteous living than anxiously consulting celestial calendars.

Start Today: Your First Step

If there's one action I encourage you to take right now, it's this: **Make a consequential decision based on your discernment rather than astrological timing.**

Here's how to begin:

Choose something meaningful but manageable, perhaps a decision you've been postponing while waiting for the "right time" astrologically. These could be applying for a job, having a difficult conversation, starting a creative project, or making a commitment you've been considering.

Make this decision consciously and with a full awareness of your values and priorities, rather than being influenced by external cosmic factors. Before making a decision, express gratitude to the divine for the opportunity it has provided you.

As you implement your decision, observe your thought patterns:

- Do you feel anxiety about not having astrological validation?

- Do you notice yourself looking for signs of "cosmic approval" or disapproval?

- How does it feel to claim full agency or responsibility in this decision?

- If challenges arise, do you attribute them to astrological factors or see them as normal aspects of any endeavor?

Document your experience in a journal, noting both the practical outcomes and your internal responses. Completing just one such experiment may uncover more profound insights about your connection to astrological beliefs than countless hours of abstract contemplation. As the Bhagavad Gita teaches:

For the doubting soul, there is no happiness either in this world or the next. The person of faith whose consciousness is unified burns all doubts through knowledge and proceeds steadily by performing the next righteous action (Bhagavad Gita 4.40)

REMEMBER, BY MAKING EVEN ONE DECISION FROM A PLACE OF SELF-TRUST RATHER THAN RELYING ON COSMIC CONSULTATION, YOU MAY DISCOVER A STEADINESS THAT TRANSCENDS THE FLUCTUATING FORTUNES PREDICTED BY THE STARS.

Fate

THE HUMAN SEARCH

"I GUESS IT WAS MEANT TO BE." "It must have been fate." We've all said these words after something significant happened. When life takes an unexpected turn, whether extraordinary or tragic, we often seek explanations that help us make sense of the seemingly random nature of existence. Fate becomes that convenient explanation, the invisible hand we imagine guiding our lives.

I want to share a story with you. I was walking on the streets of London with a friend when we witnessed the aftermath of a serious accident. A bus hit a pedestrian. We arrived just minutes after the collision. From what we gathered, the person had been walking on the sidewalk, decided to cross the road, and looked in the wrong direction, probably a visitor not accustomed to London traffic flowing in the opposite direction from what they were used to. Their life changed dramatically in that split second when the individual looked left instead of right.

As my friend and I walked back to our hotels, we discussed how a few nanoseconds can completely alter the course of someone's life. The natural human tendency is to find comfort in attributing such incidents to "fate" or a "predetermined plan." It feels reassuring to think that, as part of destiny, the person looked in the wrong direction at precisely that moment, that the bus was fated to arrive at that exact time, and that destiny had the medics respond quickly.

Viewing fate as a predetermined script provides comfort by suggesting that there is order within chaos and meaning within randomness. But is this truly what the ancient wisdom traditions teach us about fate? More importantly, does this concept withstand philosophical inquiry and our lived experiences? These are the questions we'll explore together in this chapter.

Let's Dive Deeper

Before delving deeper, let's clarify what we're discussing. The terms "fate" and "destiny" are often used interchangeably, but they carry subtly different connotations.

People often speak of "fate" as events that are predetermined and beyond an individual's control. They view it as a fixed sequence that will inevitably unfold, regardless of one's actions. It's the idea that somewhere, somehow, the significant events of one's life have already been written, and one is simply walking a path laid out before they were born.

"Destiny," on the other hand, is often understood as a predetermined endpoint that allows for some flexibility in how you get there. Many believe individuals have some influence over their future through choices and actions, but the guardrails of an ultimate destiny constrain them. You may choose different routes, but the final destination remains the same.

For much of my life, I have accepted phrases like "no one can change fate" and "what's meant to be will be" without question. These ideas became embedded in my thinking, particularly because they provided a convenient explanation when things didn't go my way. There's a certain comfort in attributing disappointments or tragedies to some greater plan rather than random chance or, more uncomfortably, to our choices.

A science student might refer to this as the "god of gaps" phenomenon, where we attribute unexplained phenomena to supernatural forces. Similarly, when we can't comprehend why certain events occur, we often find comfort in attributing them to fate.

But what do the Bhagavad Gita and Upanishads—those profound sources of ancient wisdom say about fate? The answer might surprise you.

Gita's Perspective on Fate

Krishna's message in the Bhagavad Gita is unambiguous, though it's often misunderstood or misinterpreted. Rather than endorsing the concept of fate, Krishna demystifies and negates it by asserting that no one can predict outcomes with certainty. According to Krishna, what matters is the action itself, not some predetermined result.

Interestingly, many people twist this message and claim that Krishna has already defined all outcomes as part of a divine plan. Such an interpretation fails to grasp the profound message that the Gita and Upanishads convey: our actions and moral choices constitute the foundation of existence, not some predetermined script authored by divine forces.

The Gita emphasizes *karma* (action) and *dharma* (moral duty) as the drivers of our experience. When Krishna tells Arjuna to focus on his actions without attachment to results, he's not suggesting that the results are already determined. Instead, he's acknowledging that results emerge from an incredibly complex web of intersecting causes and conditions, so complex that attachment to specific outcomes leads only to suffering.

The Gita's wisdom aligns impressively with contemporary scientific understanding. Quantum mechanics reveals elements of randomness and unpredictability at the subatomic level, challenging the notion that everything is predetermined. Neuroscience reveals that our decisions arise from complex brain processes rather than being predetermined. Studies have found that brain activity related to decision-making occurs before we're consciously aware of a choice. This suggests that our decisions are guided by our established neural patterns and behavioral tendencies, not by some external controlling force.

The principle of the Gita is elegantly simple: every action creates a modifying effect in the universe. Nothing we do is without consequence, but those consequences aren't predetermined. They emerge from countless factors.

The Chain Reaction of Action

Consider the conversation we're having right now through these pages. My writing creates ripples of effect. Some of you reading this may find it insightful and valuable, while others might dismiss it, preferring the comfort of believing in a predetermined fate. Some might read with open hearts, sending harmonious energy into the universe, while others might read with skepticism or distraction.

Throughout this exchange, I must decide: Will I worry about how everyone will receive these words, or will I focus on my duty to convey what I understand to be true based on the teachings of the Gita and Upanishads?

The identical principle extends to all aspects of your life, including job interviews, raising children, driving a car, or any other activity. Every action and thought creates a chain reaction. Each link in that chain has its modifying effect, which creates another chain reaction based on how others respond.

The result is an unimaginably complex web of infinite possible outcomes based on countless permutations. The more thoughts and actions involved, the more people participating, the greater the randomness, and the less certainty we have about outcomes. The desire to reduce experiential randomness explains why monks and *sanyasis* (renunciates) often limit their actions and engagements. It's also part of why meditation helps calm the mind; it temporarily reduces the chain of thought and action reactions.

If someone wants to call this unexplainable, complex map of chain reactions and outcomes "fate," they apply a label to complexity, rather than identifying a predetermined plan. To say the result is predetermined contradicts what Krishna emphasizes in the Gita: you can only perform your action; the outcome emerges from the totality of interacting forces.

"Divine Will" vs. Predetermined Fate

Those who have matured spiritually often refrain from using the term "fate" in the sense of a predetermined plan. Instead, they focus on performing their duty with excellence and then describe the outcome as *ishvara iccha,* the Divine's wish or will.

Such terminology doesn't imply that they believe someone is actively deciding outcomes. Instead, by saying *ishvara iccha*, they acknowledge that their role is to act to the best of their ability and then leave the outcome to the broader universe at play. Since that universe, with its fundamental elements, is divinity, the outcome becomes "Divine Will."

Interestingly, many traditional terms for fate align more closely with this perspective than with the idea of predetermination. In Hindi or Urdu, the term "Kismet" (derived from the Arabic "Qisma") means "the portion of modifying effects in one's life." Similarly, "Naseeb" means "one's share in life." In Sanskrit, *bhagya* represents the divisible share of modifying effects from a chain reaction. None of these traditional concepts claims that life follows a predetermined plan. Instead, they acknowledge that outcomes emerge from complex interactions beyond any individual's control.

Revisiting the London Accident

Let's return to the unfortunate accident I mentioned at the beginning. Consider the complex set of events that led to that moment: if the pedestrian was a visitor, there were the actions of traveling to London, the choice to walk rather than take a cab, the habit of looking in a particular direction before crossing, the bus driver's schedule and reaction time, the availability of medical help, and countless other factors.

Each person's action creates a chain reaction, leading to a set of outcomes that aren't final but rather more points in the ongoing web of cause and effect. The accident itself wasn't an endpoint but another beginning, setting in motion new chains of events affecting the injured person, their family, the bus driver, witnesses, medical personnel, and many others.

To attribute this complex web to "fate" or a predetermined plan dramatically oversimplifies what's happening. It also removes the profound truth that we are responsible for co-creating the unfolding reality through our choices and actions.

Finding Comfort Without Fate

Many people find comfort in believing in fate, as it provides an anchor in a seemingly chaotic world and offers a way to make sense of events that might otherwise seem random or meaningless. This can be exceptionally comforting when facing tragedy or injustice, as it suggests some greater purpose or design behind suffering.

However, there is another kind of comfort available, and that one stems from understanding life as an intricate, dynamic interplay between our choices and the larger forces of existence. A perspective that harmonizes with the ancient wisdom of the Gita and Upanishads, as well as modern scientific understanding, eliminates any need for unquestioning belief in predetermination.

Such a viewpoint encourages us to embrace full responsibility for our actions while simultaneously releasing attachment to specific outcomes. It enables us to act with wisdom, compassion, and moral integrity, not because these actions will lead to predetermined "good" results, but because they contribute positively to the unimaginably complex web of cause and effect.

Living this way doesn't mean we understand or control everything. It means we recognize our part in the cosmic dance, taking our steps with as much awareness and grace as possible while remaining humble about our limited perspective.

Summary: Beyond Fate to Freedom

As we've explored together, the concept of fate as a predetermined script doesn't align with the more profound teachings of the Gita and Upanishads, nor with our lived experience of choice and consequence. What these ancient texts teach is far more nuanced and empowering.

- Rather than being puppets in a predetermined play, we are active participants in an unfolding cosmic dance. Every thought, word, and action creates a ripple effect, interacting with countless other causes and conditions to produce outcomes that no single entity could predetermine.

- Our new perspective on fate doesn't diminish the importance of divine consciousness in the universe, but reshapes how we conceptualize that role. The sacred doesn't micromanage events by predetermining every detail of our lives. Instead, the divine establishes the fundamental principles by which existence operates and then allows for genuine freedom within that framework.

- A spiritual viewpoint encourages us to embrace full responsibility for our actions while simultaneously releasing attachment to specific outcomes. This responsibility stems from the fact that our choices genuinely matter and help shape what unfolds. It fosters humility by recognizing that outcomes stem from forces beyond our control or comprehension.

- When we release the concept of fate as predetermination, we don't lose meaning. We gain freedom. It is the freedom from the fatalistic mindset that our efforts are insignificant. Freedom from the burden of trying to align with some imagined predetermined plan. Freedom to act with integrity in each moment, without attachment to results that we cannot control.

- Most importantly, we are free to respond wisely to whatever life brings, not as passive recipients of a predetermined fate but as conscious co-creators of our experience. True wisdom from the Gita involves not escaping responsibility through fatalism but engaging fully with life through mindful, dharmic action.

Start Today: Your Next Step

If there's one action I encourage you to take right now, it's this: For the next week, approach each day with what I call "responsibility consciousness" rather than "fate consciousness."

Here's how to begin:

When you wake up each morning, take a moment before starting your day to acknowledge your agency. Say to yourself: "Today, I choose my responses. Each action I take creates ripples of effect. I cannot control all outcomes, but I act with awareness, integrity, and compassion."

Throughout the day, when you face small and large decisions, consciously recognize that you are making a choice, not following a script. Ask yourself: "What action would create the most positive effect? What would align most closely with my highest values?" Then, act from that awareness.

When unexpected events occur, whether positive or negative, resist the urge to immediately attribute them to fate. Instead, observe the complex web of conditions that may have contributed to this moment. Consider your role, the role of others, and the countless factors beyond anyone's control. Practice saying, "This has happened; now how will I respond?" rather than "This was meant to be."

At the end of each day, reflect on your actions without judgment. Notice the effects they created, recognizing that they will continue to ripple outward in ways you cannot fully predict or control. Release attachment to specific outcomes while remaining committed to acting with wisdom and integrity.

Implementing these daily reflections can fundamentally alter your relationship with life's events. Rather than seeing yourself as subject to a predetermined fate, you'll begin to experience yourself as an active participant in the unfolding of existence, responsible for your choices but humble about your limited perspective.

REMEMBER, MOVING BEYOND FATE CONSCIOUSNESS IS AN ONGOING AWAKENING TO YOUR PROPER ROLE IN COSMIC DANCE, OR ISHVARA ICCHA, AND IT BEGINS WITH CHOOSING RESPONSIBILITY OVER FATALISM, MOMENT BY MOMENT, DAY BY DAY.

Theism

FINDING DIVINE THROUGH NAME AND FORM

WHEN WE LOOK UP AT THE NIGHT SKY, filled with countless stars stretching into infinity, we often feel something profound — a sense of wonder, perhaps a recognition of something greater than ourselves. The cosmic vastness, this immensity that exceeds our comprehension, gives us a glimpse into what we might call the divine.

But how do we relate to something so vast? How do we connect with the infinite when our minds are developed for the finite? How do we speak to, pray, or worship something that transcends all categories and definitions?

At this point, theism enters the picture, not as a limitation on divinity but as a bridge between our human understanding and that which exceeds it. Theism offers us a way to relate to the incomprehensible through names, forms, and attributes we can grasp.

In this chapter, we'll explore the nature of theism and its relationship to divinity. We'll examine why humans across cultures have given names and forms to divine energy, how this shapes our spiritual experience, and what wisdom we can draw from this understanding. Whether you connect with a specific concept of God or prefer a more abstract approach to spirituality, understanding theism can deepen your appreciation for the diverse ways humans have sought connection with the divine.

Let's Dive Deeper

Before fully understanding theism, we must recall what we've discussed about divinity. As we explored earlier, divinity can be understood as an infinite energy field. The concept of divinity as an endless energy field is magnificent in its scope but challenging in its abstraction. It's like trying to comprehend the entire ocean at once, with all its depths, currents, ecosystems, and the intricate dance of its inhabitants. The mind struggles to hold something so vast and multifaceted.

Theism represents a natural human response to this challenge. It's not a rejection of divinity's infinite nature but rather a practical approach to relating to it. It's akin to focusing on a single wave or a particular shoreline, rather than trying to comprehend the entire ocean simultaneously.

As we delve deeper into theism, we'll explore how giving names and forms to aspects of divinity creates a focal point for spiritual connection by providing a way of channeling our attention and devotion that honors our human needs while still acknowledging the ultimately boundless nature of the divine.

What Is Theism? Divinity Given Name and Form

At its core, theism is an approach to divinity that gives name and form to aspects of that infinite divine energy. In Sanskrit, this is referred to as *nama and rupa*. It's understanding that the infinite can be approached through the finite, that the formless can be honored through form, and that the nameless can be addressed through names.

When we look at the vast array of divine energies and attributes, it becomes overwhelming for the human mind to comprehend, as there are infinite permutations of those eight fundamental elements and the full spectrum of emotions. How do we relate to something so abstract, so all-encompassing? Over time, humans have addressed this challenge across cultures by assigning names and forms to various aspects or combinations of divine attributes. These names and forms make the abstract tangible, the infinite approachable, and the cosmic personal.

Divinity is like a white light, containing all the colors of the spectrum. Theism is like a prism that separates this light into distinct colors we can recognize and relate to. Each color is still light (and divine) but presented in a way that our human senses can perceive and our minds can comprehend.

The Purpose of Name and Form

Why do we give names and forms to divinity? The answer lies in our human nature and the way we interact with the world. Here are four common purposes for humanizing divinity:

1. Creating an Anchor Point

First and foremost, names and forms provide a focal point for our attention, devotion, and spiritual practice. Rather than dispersing our energy across an infinite field, we can direct it toward a specific manifestation that resonates with us.

Having a focal point serves as a crucial anchoring function for spiritual practice. When we meditate, pray, or engage in rituals, having a clear focus helps us maintain attention and deepen our connection.

Whether that anchor is the form of Krishna or any other divine representation, it gives our mind something concrete to orient toward.

2. Making the Abstract Relatable

Names and forms also help us relate to divine qualities in ways that make sense to our human experience. When we envision a deity with specific attributes, such as wisdom, compassion, courage, and protection, we can more easily contemplate and cultivate these qualities within ourselves.

For instance, when divinity is represented as a mother figure, we can connect with the divine qualities of nurturing, protection, and unconditional love. When described as teachers, we access divine wisdom and guidance. These representations address various aspects of our human needs and aspirations.

3. Creating Emotional Connection

Most importantly, names and forms allow us to connect emotionally with the divine. As beings with hearts and minds, we naturally form deeper relationships with what we can visualize, name, and relate to personally.

The Bhagavad Gita recognizes this aspect of human nature. In Chapter 12, Krishna acknowledges that while the ultimate reality is formless and infinite, it is much easier for humans to connect with a personal form than an abstract concept. Our hearts respond to stories, images, and personalities in ways they cannot respond to philosophical abstractions.

4. Theism and Personal Resonance

One of the beautiful aspects of theism is that different names and forms resonate with various individuals in different ways. Just as the divine encompasses all attributes and energies, humanity includes a wide range of temperaments, needs, and spiritual inclinations.

Some people naturally connect with divine attributes of wisdom and discernment, others with divine love and compassion, and still others with divine strength and protection. Theistic approaches honor this diversity by offering various manifestations that speak to different aspects of our nature.

Being drawn to a particular representation of the divine often reflects something in your nature or something you aspire to develop. The characteristics of divinity in that name and form that resonate with you the most become a bridge for your connection with the infinite.

Personal resonance doesn't mean that one representation is better than another or that the divine exists in separate, distinct forms. Instead, these various names and forms are like different pathways up the same mountain. Each is valid, authentic, and ultimately leads to the same summit.

The Balance of Form and Formless

While theism emphasizes the value of names and forms, it's important to remember that these are gateways to, not replacements for, the ultimate reality. The map is not the territory; the finger-pointing at the moon is not the moon itself.

The most profound theistic traditions maintain this balance, honoring specific divine forms while simultaneously acknowledging that they are expressions of something that ultimately transcends all names and forms. They use the personal as a doorway to the transpersonal.

In the Bhagavad Gita, Krishna presents himself as a personal deity with whom Arjuna can relate, but he also reveals his universal form (*vishvarupa*), which encompasses all of existence. The *vishvarupa* scene illustrates the complementary relationship between a divinity's personal and universal aspects. It shows us the named and the nameless, the formed and the formless.

Advanced spiritual practitioners often move fluidly between these approaches, sometimes relating to the divine through specific names and forms and other times resting in awareness of the formless ground of being. Each approach supports and enriches the other.

Such an equilibrium reflects the wisdom at the heart of theism, using the personal as a doorway to that which transcends the individual.

Diverse expressions of theism reflect the universality of the human need to relate to divinity in accessible ways and the beautiful variety of cultural and historical contexts in which this need has been addressed.

Summary: Theism as a Bridge to Divinity

Let's recap what we've explored in this chapter:

- Theism is the approach to divinity that gives name and form (*nama* and *rupa*) to aspects of infinite divine energy, making the abstract tangible and the infinite approachable.

- Names and forms serve as anchor points for spiritual focus, make abstract divine qualities relatable, and enable emotional connection with the divine.

- Different names and forms of divinity resonate with individuals based on their temperaments, needs, and spiritual inclinations.

- While theistic approaches emphasize divine forms, they ultimately point toward divinity's infinite nature that transcends all categories.

- The Bhagavad Gita acknowledges that connecting with a personal form of divinity is easier for most humans than connecting with an abstract concept, even though both approaches lead to the same ultimate reality.

- Theistic approaches exist across diverse spiritual traditions worldwide, reflecting a universal human need to relate to divinity in accessible ways.

At its best, theism bridges our finite human understanding and the infinite divine reality. It uses the language of human experience to point toward that which transcends experience itself.

Whether you resonate with a particular theistic approach or prefer a more abstract understanding of divinity, appreciating the wisdom of theism can deepen your spiritual journey and broaden your knowledge of humanity's diverse approaches to the divine.

Start Today: Your First Step

If there's one action I encourage you to take right now, it's this: **Create a Personal Divine Imagery Practice.**

Creating personal divine imagery invites you to explore how divine forms resonate with you, helping you discover which aspects of divinity most powerfully support your spiritual connection.

Here's how to begin:

- Set aside time in a quiet space where you won't be disturbed. Begin with a few minutes of centered breathing to quiet your mind and open your awareness.

- Ask yourself: "If I visualize the divine in a way that speaks deeply to my heart, what form might it take?" Allow images to arise naturally without forcing or judging them.

- As images emerge, notice which ones evoke the strongest feelings of connection, reverence, or love. These might be traditional religious imagery, aspects of nature, abstract light or energy, or something unique to your experience.

- Select one image that feels particularly meaningful and spend time developing it in your imagination:

  What are its qualities and attributes?

  How does it move, speak, or express itself?

  What feelings does it evoke in you?

  What quality does it embody that you're drawn to?

After exploring this imagery, gradually allow it to dissolve into formless awareness. Recognize that while the form helped you connect, the divine ultimately transcends all forms. Practice this exploration once a week for a month, allowing your divine imagery to evolve naturally. You may find yourself drawn to different expressions at different times or discover one form that consistently resonates with your heart.

The power of this practice lies in honoring both the personal and transpersonal aspects of divinity. You're using theistic approaches of names and forms as bridges to connection, while recognizing that these bridges lead to something beyond all images and concepts.

REMEMBER, THERE'S NO "RIGHT" OR "WRONG" WAY FOR DIVINE IMAGERY TO APPEAR TO YOU. WHAT MATTERS IS THE AUTHENTICITY AND OPENNESS OF YOUR CONNECTION TO THE FORM AND THE FORMLESS.

Reality of Religion

NATURE AND PURPOSE

THE WORD "RELIGION" evokes different images in our minds. Perhaps you picture temples, sacred texts, spiritual leaders, rituals performed at dawn, or festivals celebrated by thousands. These visible elements are certainly part of religion, but they represent only the surface of something more profound and fundamental to the human experience.

Religion is one of humanity's oldest and most persistent creations. It's a phenomenon that has shaped civilizations, inspired art, sparked conflicts, and provided meaning for countless individuals across time and space. Yet, despite its ubiquity and importance, religion remains surprisingly difficult to define precisely.

Is religion primarily about belief in supernatural beings, a set of moral codes, a collection of rituals, or an explanation for life's mysteries? Or is it something else entirely, perhaps a way of creating community and shared identity?

In this chapter, we'll explore the core of religion, its function in human life, and why it continues to matter even in our increasingly secular and technological age. Whether you consider yourself religious or spiritual but not religious, agnostic, or atheist, understanding religion more deeply can help you navigate our complex world with greater awareness and empathy.

Let's Dive Deeper

Religion touches nearly every aspect of human culture, from our grandest architectural achievements to our intimate personal experiences. It's woven into how we mark time (think of our calendars and holidays), understand morality, and make sense of joy and suffering.

Yet for something so pervasive, religion can be surprisingly invisible to us, like water to a fish. We may practice religious rituals without fully understanding their origins or reject religion without fully comprehending what we reject. Religion shapes our thinking in ways we don't always recognize, influencing even those who consider themselves non-religious.

As we dive deeper into understanding religion, we'll move beyond simplistic views that reduce it to mere superstition or blind faith. We'll discover that religion is a complex, multifaceted human phenomenon that serves vital social and psychological functions, regardless of whether its theological claims are valid.

Understanding religion provides insight into specific belief systems and human nature. We see how humans across time and cultures have wrestled with fundamental questions about meaning, morality, and mortality. Additionally, we gain perspectives that may help us build bridges in a world often divided along religious lines.

Let's begin our exploration with a fundamental question: What exactly is religion?

Beliefs and Practices Grooved Together

At its most basic level, religion can be defined as a system of beliefs and practices that are deeply interconnected or, as we might say, "grooved together." These beliefs and practices are named and become an identity marker for the community that follows them.

A religion isn't just a set of ideas about the universe or merely a collection of rituals. It's the integration of theories about reality and methods for engaging with that reality. Beliefs inform practices, and practices reinforce beliefs, creating a cohesive system that shapes how adherents experience the world.

When a substantial population adopts a system of interconnected beliefs and practices, it becomes what we recognize as a religion. Hinduism, Christianity, Islam, Buddhism, Judaism, and Sikhism each represent distinct configurations of beliefs about the nature of reality and practices designed to align believers with that understanding of reality.

The Purpose of Religion: Creating a Common Fabric

If we examine religion from a functional perspective, its primary purpose is to create a shared fabric—something that binds a community together. Religion provides a shared language, values, experiences, and identity that help people feel connected across time and space.

The shared religious foundation serves several essential functions:

1. Providing Identity and Belonging

Religion offers a ready-made answer to one of life's most fundamental questions: Who am I? By identifying as a member of a religion and a faith tradition, a person gains a sense of place in the cosmic order and human society.

Religious identity connects the individual to something larger than themselves: a community with a shared history, values, and vision for the future. It provides the comfort of belonging and the security of knowing one's place in the grand scheme.

Of course, whether you feel the need for such an identity is your individual choice. Some find significant meaning and comfort in religious identity, while others prefer to construct their sense of self from different sources. However, the identity-providing function of religion helps explain its enduring appeal across cultures and periods.

2. Facilitating Human Connection

Religion offers opportunities for meaningful human interaction. Religious gatherings, whether weekly at temples, during holiday celebrations, or at rites of passage, bring people together through shared experiences and traditions. These gatherings foster bonds among community members, creating networks of support and care that strengthen the community.

Consider this: In a religious community, people who might otherwise have little in common come together regularly. They share important life events, such as births, coming-of-age ceremonies, weddings, and funerals. They engage in everyday activities, such as prayer, singing, meditation, study, and service projects. Through these shared experiences, they develop relationships that extend beyond the religious context into everyday life.

Religion's social dimension is so powerful that even as belief in traditional religious doctrines has declined in many societies, people continue to seek out the community aspects of religious life.

3. Establishing Moral Guidelines

Religion typically defines a set of dos and don'ts—operational practices often linked to concepts of morality. These guidelines structure individual and community life, helping adherents navigate complex ethical territories.

There's an ongoing debate about whether morality requires religion. Some argue that science alone cannot define morality, while others contend that moral principles can be derived from rational reflection on human well-being without reference to religious authority. What's clear is that throughout history, religious frameworks have been significant sources of moral guidance.

As we evolve and observe changes in our world, we develop moral sensibilities that may build upon or depart from religious foundations. The evolution of moral thinking influences laws, regulations, and social norms, regardless of whether they're explicitly connected to religious traditions.

Religion and Theism: Natural Partners

Religion and theism (the belief in one or more gods) often go hand in hand, although they're not identical or inseparable. Some theistic individuals don't identify with organized religion, and there are non-theistic religions, such as some forms of Buddhism.

Nevertheless, there's a natural affinity between religion and theism. When theism infuses characteristics and attributes into a name and form, creating concepts of specific deities with particular personalities and powers, it provides a powerful focal point for the religious community.

The gods or goddesses of a religion become central to its identity, narratives, and practices. They serve as a focal point around which the community can gather, further cementing the shared fabric among its members.

Consequently, a religion like Hinduism is defined in part by sacred texts such as the Upanishads and the Bhagavad Gita, which explore the nature of divinity and humanity's relationship to it. These texts establish a theological foundation that helps maintain cohesion among the religion's practitioners.

The Evolution of Religious Practices

Because religion defines specific practices, such as rituals, observances, and prohibitions, these practices can and do change over time. The rate of change depends mainly on the nature of the community following the religion.

An active, inquisitive, and thinking community will tend to rationalize religious practices, making them better suited to their particular geography and historical moment. They'll adapt ancient wisdom to contemporary circumstances, keeping the essence while updating the expression.

However, if a religious community remains passive and uncritical, its practices may become outdated and irrelevant to contemporary life. When this happens, people may move on, abandoning religion altogether rather than working to reform it from within.

The evolution of practices highlights an important truth: religion is not static. It's a living tradition that evolves through the active engagement of its practitioners. The most vibrant religious communities honor their traditions while thoughtfully adapting to changing circumstances.

Religion and Human Excellence

When religion is combined with philosophical and logical knowledge, as when Hinduism incorporates the profound insights of the Gita and Upanishads, it has the potential to drive human excellence.

> *"Religion excels when it doesn't simply tell people what to think but teaches them how to think."*

A religion that encourages critical thinking, personal experience, and individual discernment fosters a community of thoughtful practitioners. Rather than demanding irrational obedience, such a religion provides tools for deeper understanding, allowing individuals to form their conclusions within a supportive framework.

The thoughtful integration approach honors both tradition and personal agency, recognizing that spiritual growth requires a balance of guidance from the past and openness to new insights. The harmony between tradition and critical thinking helps religion fulfill its highest purpose: binding communities together and elevating human consciousness and potential.

Summary: Religion as a Living System

Let's recap what we've explored in this chapter:

- Religion is fundamentally a system of interconnected beliefs and practices, ideas about reality, grounded together with ways of engaging that reality.

- The primary purpose of religion is to create a standard fabric that binds communities together, providing identity, facilitating connection, and establishing moral guidelines.

- Religion and theism naturally complement each other, with concepts of divinity serving as focal points around which religious communities organize.

- Religious practices evolve, with the rate and nature of change depending on how actively and critically the community engages with its traditions.

- When combined with philosophical depth and critical thinking, religion can drive human excellence by teaching people how to think rather than merely what to think.

- At its best, religion is not a rigid set of dogmas but a living system that evolves through the thoughtful participation of its adherents. It provides structure and continuity while remaining responsive to the changing needs and circumstances of humans.

Regardless of whether you're a devoted practitioner, a casual participant, or someone who has chosen a different path, understanding the nature and functions of religion can help you engage more thoughtfully with the diverse religious expressions you encounter in our world.

Start Today: Your First Step

If there's one action I encourage you to take right now, it's this: **Cultivate Sacred Curiosity.** Commit to observing religious expressions with fresh eyes and an open mind for the next month. This practice will help you move beyond automatic judgments to see religious phenomena more clearly and understand them more deeply.

Here's how to begin:

Choose two religious expressions to observe. These might include:

A ritual or ceremony (whether one you participate in or one you observe)

A religious text or a conversation about religion with someone whose perspective differs from yours

For each observation, ask yourself these questions:

- What beliefs and practices are "grooved together" here? How do they reinforce each other?

- What type of community is being created or maintained through this expression?

- What values and moral guidelines are being communicated?

- How has this expression likely evolved, and how might it continue to grow?

- After your observation period, review your notes and consider: How has your understanding of religion deepened or changed? What new perspectives have you gained?

The power of this practice lies not in reaching a particular conclusion, but in developing a more nuanced understanding of religion as a complex human phenomenon. By observing with curiosity rather than judgment, you cultivate greater awareness of the visible forms of religion and the deeper human needs they address.

A nuanced understanding can serve you well, regardless of your religious stance. It can help you engage more meaningfully with your tradition if you follow one, find common ground with people of different faiths, or understand the religious dimensions of culture even if you don't personally embrace religious belief.

REMEMBER, UNDERSTANDING RELIGION ISN'T JUST AN ACADEMIC EXERCISE—IT'S A PRACTICAL SKILL FOR NAVIGATING OUR DIVERSE WORLD WITH GREATER INSIGHT, EMPATHY, AND WISDOM.

Tradition

TRADITIONS SHAPE OUR LIVES in ways both seen and unseen. They're the rituals that mark our holidays, the recipes passed down through generations, the stories we share, and the values we hold dear. Like threads in a tapestry, traditions weave together to form the cultural fabric surrounding us.

Many people view traditions as static customs from the past, actions we take simply because "that's how it's always been done." But traditions are far more dynamic and complex than this view suggests. They're living expressions of our collective wisdom, adaptable systems that have evolved over centuries to meet human needs.

In the pages ahead, we'll explore what tradition means, its origins, and its significance in our modern lives. We'll discover that tradition isn't simply about preserving the past—it's about carrying forward the best human experience while remaining open to growth and change.

Let's Dive Deeper

The word "tradition" comes from the Latin "tradere," meaning "to hand over" or "to deliver." Such etymology reveals something fundamental about tradition: it is a form of inheritance that transcends material possessions and is passed from generation to generation. But what exactly are we inheriting? Is it just a set of customs and practices? Or is there something deeper being transmitted?

As we explore tradition more closely, we'll see that it's not a monolithic concept but a complex interplay of various influences. Traditions don't emerge randomly; rather, they develop in response to specific conditions, needs, and beliefs. They encode wisdom gained through centuries of trial and error, preserving solutions that have proven valuable over time.

Yet traditions can also become rigid or outdated when they're followed mindlessly. The challenge for us today is to engage with tradition thoughtfully, honoring its wisdom while allowing it to evolve in response to changing circumstances.

Let's peel back the layers of tradition to understand its origins, purposes, and the potential it holds to enrich our lives today.

What Is Tradition? A Set of Practices

Tradition is a set of practices and ways of doing things that have been established over time and passed down through generations. These practices touch every aspect of our lives, from marking significant life transitions, such as births, weddings, and funerals, to the foods we prepare for holiday celebrations and festivals.

Our traditions encompass artistic expressions, such as music, dance, and storytelling, that carry cultural meaning across generations. They influence how we dress and adorn ourselves, the social etiquette we observe in our interactions with others, and even the methods we use to educate and raise our children. These practices, woven together, create the textured fabric of tradition that shapes our individual and collective identities.

But where do these practices come from? What shapes them and gives them their particular character? The traditions we inherit aren't random or arbitrary. They emerge from several key influences that interact and overlap in complex ways. Let's explore these influences one by one.

Religious Influences

Religion plays a profound role in shaping traditions. Every religion defines a set of dos and don'ts, practices that become integral to the daily lives of its followers. These practices might involve regular prayer or meditation that structures the day, observance of holy days and festivals that punctuate the year, or dietary regulations that influence daily meals.

Religious traditions often establish ethical guidelines that shape behavior, marriage customs that define family formation, and funeral rites that guide communities through loss and grief. For members of a religious community, these practices often become integrated into the traditions of their families and broader social groups. Even people who don't consider themselves religious usually inherit traditions with religious origins, such as the rituals of festivals or the symbolism used in wedding ceremonies.

The influence of religion on tradition runs deep, frequently persisting even as explicit religious beliefs evolve or fade.

Cultural DNA: The Macro Genetic Code

Beyond religion, traditions are shaped by what we might call the "macro genetic code" of a nation or culture—its distinctive character that has evolved over thousands of years.

Consider India, for example, which has developed a macro genetic code centered around family values. India's cultural orientation has given rise to practices that emphasize intergenerational connections, collective decision-making, and familial responsibility. These practices have become traditions that reinforce the underlying values of the culture.

Every culture has a macro genetic code, particular emphasis, and orientation that shape its traditional practices. Some cultures emphasize individual autonomy, while others emphasize communal harmony; some prize innovation, while others value continuity with the past. These broader cultural values become embedded in the traditions that emerge within a society, creating distinctive patterns that persist across generations, even as specific practices evolve and change over time.

Theistic Beliefs

Separating from organized religion, theistic beliefs about divine or supernatural powers influence traditional practices. For instance, a village might revere natural entities, such as trees, as sacred or holy. The sacred status gives rise to specific practices, including offerings left at the tree's base, prohibitions against cutting it down, and ceremonies conducted in its shade. For the villagers, these practices become traditions embedded in their way of life.

Theistic beliefs about reality, the origin of life, and the presence of divine forces shape how people interact with their world and what practices they develop and maintain across generations. These belief-based traditions often connect people to their environment and forces they perceive as greater than themselves, providing meaning and practical guidance for navigating life's challenges.

Geographic and Environmental Factors

The physical environment in which people live exerts a powerful influence on their traditions. People living in a cold climate develop different practices than those in a tropical region, from what they eat to when they wake up to how they construct their homes. Traditional clothing, for instance, often reflects climate conditions: loose, breathable fabrics in hot regions and layered, insulating garments in colder ones. Traditional cuisine also reflects the locally available ingredients and preservation methods that are suited to local conditions.

Even as technology has reduced some of these geographic constraints (with electricity, climate control, and global food distribution), these traditions, shaped by centuries of environmental adaptation, continue to influence our practices today. The landscape often becomes woven into cultural identity, with mountains, rivers, forests, or oceans playing a prominent role in traditional stories, celebrations, and worldviews.

Lineage and Family Heritage

The specific family line you come from—your lineage or *parampara*—also shapes your traditions.

Perhaps you come from a family of teachers who have valued education across generations. Or maybe your ancestors served in the military, instilling traditions of discipline, sacrifice, and service to the nation. These family legacies give rise to distinctive traditions within each family. One family might have traditions centered on academic achievement, with special celebrations for graduations, rituals marking the beginning of school years, and stories of intellectual accomplishment passed down through generations. Another family might emphasize athletic prowess, artistic expression, entrepreneurship, or other values reflected in their traditions.

These family-specific practices create a sense of continuity across generations, connecting family members to their shared history and values while distinguishing each family's culture from others in subtle but meaningful ways.

Balancing Family and Society:

sampradaya and samajam

Within a family unit, the set of traditional practices is referred to as *sampradaya*. In conjunction with other family members, each head establishes traditions that reflect their values, history, and aspirations.

These might include special ways of celebrating birthdays or anniversaries, Family recipes and meal rituals, Holiday customs specific to your family, Bedtime routines, Ways of welcoming new members into the family, Methods for resolving conflicts, approaches to education and discipline.

These family-specific traditions foster a sense of belonging and continuity within the family unit, establishing a distinctive family culture that helps members understand their identity and heritage.

But what happens when we step outside our homes into the broader society? Here is where *samajam* comes into play.

samajam refers to the broader social sphere that extends beyond the family. While rigorous adherence to family traditions (*sampradaya*) might be appropriate within the home, once we enter the larger community, we encounter people with different traditions shaped by other influences.

For the welfare of the broader society, we must strive to find balance, one that honors our traditions while respecting those of others. We seek commonalities that connect us across our differences, contributing to our nation's or community's shared cultural heritage.

Finding equilibrium between *sampradaya* and *samajam* allows traditions to serve their purpose without becoming divisive. It enables us to maintain distinctive family practices while still participating in a cohesive society with shared values and mutual respect.

How Tradition Contributes to Excellence

Traditions, when understood and practiced thoughtfully, contribute to both human excellence and cosmic excellence. They do this in several ways:

First, traditions encode wisdom accumulated over generations, representing solutions to human problems that have stood the test of time and preserving knowledge that might otherwise be lost.

Second, traditions provide structure and rhythm to life, marking transitions, celebrating milestones, and creating a framework for understanding our place in the world and our responsibilities to others.

Third, traditions connect us to something larger than ourselves, including our ancestors, the broader community, and the natural world. The connection combats isolation and reminds us of our interdependence.

Fourth, traditions offer a foundation for innovation. Knowing where we come from and what has worked in the past gives us a stable platform for creative thinking and thoughtful change.

When we engage with tradition in this way—neither rejecting it wholesale nor accepting it unthinkingly—we contribute to human excellence by carrying forward the best of our collective inheritance while remaining open to growth and adaptation.

The Interplay of Tradition, Religion, and Divinity

Tradition, religion, and divinity are distinct yet interconnected dimensions of human experience. Religion provides structures and practices that often become traditions. In turn, traditions can nurture an awareness of divinity by creating spaces for reverence, reflection, and connection to something greater than oneself.

Together, these dimensions create a rich ecosystem of meaning and practice. A religious ritual becomes a family tradition that fosters awareness of divine presence. A cultural tradition incorporates religious elements that evoke a sense of transcendence. A theistic belief gives rise to traditional practices that are integrated into religious observance.

Rather than seeing these as separate categories, we might view them as different facets of human efforts to make meaning, create community, and connect with deeper dimensions of reality.

Summary: The Living Stream of Tradition

Let's recap what we've explored in this chapter:

- Tradition is a set of practices passed down through generations. These practices emerge from multiple sources, including religious influences, cultural heritage, theistic beliefs, geographic factors, and family lineage.

- Within families, traditions (*sampradaya*) create a distinctive identity and sense of belonging. In broader society, we balance family traditions with respect for diverse practices (*samajam*).

- Traditions contribute to human excellence by preserving wisdom, providing structure, fostering connection, and establishing foundations for growth. Tradition, religion, and divinity interrelate in complex ways, forming an ecosystem of meaning and practice.

- Traditions are not static relics of the past but a living stream of wisdom and practice that flows through time. Each generation stands in this stream, receiving traditions, adapting them to present circumstances, and passing them forward into the future.

The challenge for us is to engage with tradition consciously—to understand its sources and purposes, discern which elements remain valuable and which might need to evolve, and participate in its ongoing development with reverence for what has come before and openness to what might be in the future.

Start Today: Your First Step

If there's one action I encourage you to take right now, it's this: **Decode a Family Tradition.**

Take time to investigate and reflect on one significant tradition in your family. The decoding practice will help you understand its origins, meaning, and evolution, making you more conscious of the role of traditions in your life.

Here's how to begin:

Select a critical tradition in your family, perhaps a holiday celebration, a special meal, or a ritual marking a life transition. Research its history by:

- Interviewing older family members about how the tradition was practiced in their youth.

- Looking for historical documentation (old photos, recipes, letters) related to the tradition.

- Research the broader cultural or religious context from which the tradition emerged. Reflect on what has remained constant about the tradition and what has changed.

- What does this tell you about its essential purpose? Consider how this tradition might continue to evolve while maintaining its core meaning.

Your investigation serves as a gateway to understanding not just a single tradition, but the broader role of tradition in your life. As you trace the story of one practice through time, you'll gain insights into how traditions preserve wisdom while adapting to changing circumstances.

The power of this practice lies in the awareness it creates. By deeply understanding just one tradition, you develop a template for engaging with all your traditions more intentionally, honoring their wisdom while ensuring they remain relevant and life-giving for today's world. Your thoughtful engagement with tradition contributes to its ongoing evolution, while remaining responsive to present needs.

REMEMBER, TRADITIONS ARE MEANT TO SERVE LIFE, NOT THE OTHER WAY AROUND.

Can We Prove the Existence of God?

BEYOND THE "GIVER ON DEMAND"

DEBATES ABOUT GOD'S EXISTENCE often reach frustrating impasses. Atheists present logical arguments against the possibility of proof, while believers offer what they consider compelling evidence. These discussions frequently stall because they center around a particular concept of Divinity: what I sometimes humorously call the *"Giver on Demand"*—a divine figure positioned somewhere above us, responding to prayers like a cosmic vending machine.

But what if we're asking the wrong question entirely? What if the very framework of this debate misses something essential about the nature of divinity? In this chapter, I invite you to approach this age-old question in a new way.

Instead of trying to prove the existence of a personified deity who grants wishes, let's explore a more profound inquiry: Can we validate and confirm the existence of divinity as the supreme consciousness that permeates all of existence?

Such a shift isn't about evading the question but about deepening it. It moves us from abstract arguments to the realm of direct experience, from theoretical debate to lived reality. In this shift, we may discover that the evidence we seek has been present all along, hiding in plain sight in our everyday experiences.

Let's Dive Deeper

Before we can discuss proving the existence of divinity, we need to clarify what we mean by "divinity" in the first place. As we explored in our earlier discussion about divine energy, the supreme reality isn't a separate being detached from creation but the substance and consciousness that constitute all that exists.

How do we understand electricity? We don't see electricity directly, but we experience its effects—lights illuminating a room, appliances powering on, devices charging. We don't doubt the existence of electricity just because we can't see the actual flow of electrons. Instead, we recognize it through its manifestations and effects.

Similarly, divinity isn't something we can point to as a discrete object among other objects. Instead, the underlying reality makes all experiences possible, the "substratum layer" or foundation upon which all phenomena appear.

With this understanding in mind, the question of proving God's existence transforms from locating a specific being to recognizing the divine nature of reality itself. This recognition doesn't happen primarily through logical arguments or physical evidence (though these have their place) but through direct experience.

Let's explore what this means and how we might approach it.

Divinity as an Experiential Reality

When discussing divinity or the supreme, we refer to something fundamentally experiential. Unlike a physical object that can be measured, weighed, and observed by anyone in the same way, divinity reveals itself through our inner experience of life.

Due to its experiential nature, divinity is both immediately accessible and challenging to convey. It's like the fragrance of roses in a garden, where you can experience it directly, but describing that experience to someone else in words will always fall short of capturing its essence.

When you walk into a rose garden, you don't need someone to prove that the fragrance exists. You experience it directly. Similarly, the existence of divinity isn't proven through abstract reasoning alone but through direct recognition of your lived experience.

Experiential nature doesn't mean it is purely subjective or arbitrary. Just as people generally agree on the presence of a rose's fragrance (even if they might describe it differently), there are common patterns in how people across cultures and throughout history have experienced divinity. The experiential nature of divinity doesn't make it less real—it simply means we access it differently than physical objects.

How Divinity Manifests in Experience

In the Bhagavad Gita, Krishna provides numerous examples of how divinity manifests in our everyday experience. Rather than pointing to some distant realm, Krishna directs Arjuna's attention to the world immediately before him. Krishna suggests divinity is present in the taste of water, in the syllables of a song, and in the tune of music.

Krishna's guidance invites us to look beyond the surface of things to the deeper reality they express. When you drink water mindfully, experiencing its taste and texture, you're connecting with something more fundamental than just a chemical compound. You're experiencing the divine quality that manifests as the essence of water.

Significantly, Krishna doesn't limit divine manifestation to what we typically consider good or virtuous. He clarifies that divinity encompasses the entire spectrum of existence, virtues, and vices. The all-encompassing nature doesn't mean that harmful actions are divinely endorsed, but rather that even challenging aspects of life manifest on the same divine foundation.

Even the villain in a movie appears alongside the hero on the same screen. The screen doesn't judge or take sides. It allows all characters to appear. Similarly, divinity is the consciousness that enables all experiences to manifest, whether we label them as positive or negative.

Mindfulness as a Path to Recognition

The practice of mindfulness is a powerful approach to recognizing divine presence in everyday experience. When you engage with life mindfully through activities like drinking water, listening to music, watching a sunset, or engaging in conversation, you move beyond surface perceptions to a deeper level of awareness.

In mindful awareness, you recognize there's more to your experience than sensory data. There's a quality of presence, a depth of being that transcends the physical properties of what you're experiencing. The deeper dimension is where divine reality becomes palpable.

When you mindfully drink a glass of water, for instance, you might notice its clarity, feel its coolness, taste its subtle flavors, and sense how it quenches your thirst. But beyond these physical sensations, you might also recognize something more: a quality of harmony, refreshment, and life-sustaining goodness that points to a deeper reality. The deeper recognition is not adding something to your experience but simply perceiving what's already there at a deeper level.

Mindfulness enables us to peek behind the curtain of ordinary perception, allowing us to glimpse the divine nature of reality. It's not about having spectacular spiritual experiences, but rather about recognizing the extraordinary nature of what we typically consider ordinary.

Beyond Physical Evidence

It's essential to recognize that the existence of divinity cannot be proven through physical evidence, as we demonstrate the existence of a new planet or chemical element. The unprovability of divinity isn't because it's somehow less real, but because it belongs to a different order of reality.

Physical evidence can only demonstrate physical realities. Consciousness, meaning, values, beauty, and love, though undeniably real, aren't physical phenomena that can be weighed or measured. Yet few would deny their existence because we experience them directly.

As the supreme consciousness, divinity falls into this category of non-physical but experientially real phenomena. We recognize it not through instruments that measure physical properties but through our awareness, insight, and our ability to derive meaning.

The non-physical nature of divinity doesn't mean we abandon reason or critical thinking. Instead, we apply these faculties appropriately, recognizing that different aspects of reality require different approaches to knowledge. Just as you wouldn't use a thermometer to measure distance or a ruler to measure temperature, you wouldn't use physical measurement to discern divine presence.

Summary: Experiencing the Divine

Let's recap what we've explored in this chapter:

- Divinity is fundamentally experiential—like the fragrance of roses, it's directly perceived rather than logically deduced.

- Rather than trying to prove the existence of a "Giver on Demand" God, we've shifted our inquiry to recognize divinity as the supreme consciousness pervading all existence.

- The divine manifests through countless expressions in our everyday experience—from the taste of water to the harmony of music to the full spectrum of life's experiences.

- Just as we recognize electricity through its effects rather than seeing it directly, we recognize divine presence through its manifestations in consciousness and physical reality.

- Mindfulness is a powerful approach to recognizing divine presence. It allows us to move beyond surface perceptions to deeper levels of awareness.

- The existence of divinity isn't proven through physical evidence but through direct experience of non-physical but real dimensions of existence.

Our perspective doesn't dismiss the importance of reason or evidence but reframes our understanding of what constitutes valid knowledge in different domains of experience. It invites us to trust our direct recognition of divine reality while remaining open to the continuous deepening of that recognition.

The question "Can you prove the existence of God?" transforms from a demand for physical evidence or logical proof to an invitation for direct recognition: Can you experience the divine nature of reality already present in every moment? The transformed question isn't about believing in a concept but perceiving what already is.

Start Today: Your First Step

If there's one action I encourage you to take right now, it's this: **Anchor Yourself Through the Senses.** Sensory awareness is a simple yet profound exercise that invites you to experience the divine quality that manifests through ordinary sensory experiences. By bringing heightened awareness to your senses, you can begin to recognize the deeper reality that's always available but often overlooked.

Here's how to begin:

Choose a time when you can be fully present—perhaps early in the morning, during a lunch break, or in the evening. Select one sensory experience to focus on. This could be:

- Drinking a glass of water or a cup of tea

- Eating a piece of fruit

- Listening to a piece of music or watching a sunset, or observing nature

- Feeling the sensation of your breath in your skin

As you engage with this experience, bring your full attention to it, noticing every aspect with fresh awareness. If you're drinking water, for example:

- Notice its clarity and how light passes through it

- Feel its temperature against your lips and in your mouth

- Taste its subtle flavors as it moves across your tongue

- Sense how it flows down your throat and the feeling of refreshment it brings

- Observe any changes in your body's sensations after drinking

Once you've thoroughly explored the physical sensations, gently shift your awareness to a deeper level:

- Beyond the physical properties, what qualities or essence do you sense?

- Is there a feeling of harmony, aliveness, or rightness in the experience?

- Can you sense how this simple experience connects to something larger?

- Can you directly recognize a divine quality in this ordinary moment without analyzing or labeling it?

After your exploration, take a few moments to reflect on the experience. What did you notice that you might typically overlook? Was there a moment when you sensed something beyond physical properties?

Try this practice for a week, dedicating 2-3 minutes daily to a focused sensory exploration, using different sensory experiences. You may be surprised at how this simple practice alters your perception, enabling you to recognize the divine presence that pervades your everyday experiences.

The divine doesn't need to announce itself with thunder and lightning—it's already speaking through the quiet miracle of each moment, waiting for us to listen.

REMEMBER, THE EXERCISE ISN'T ABOUT HAVING DRAMATIC SPIRITUAL EXPERIENCES BUT RECOGNIZING WHAT'S ALREADY PRESENT WHEN WE BRING OUR FULL AWARENESS TO ORDINARY MOMENTS.

A Day with God

WHAT DOES GOD DO ALL DAY? It seems like such a simple question. Yet, it opens the door to some of the most profound insights about the nature of divinity and our place in the universe. Let's take a moment to consider this question together. Look around at the vastness of the cosmos—billions of galaxies, trillions of stars, and countless planets—and here on Earth, an intricate web of life in constant motion. Surely, the force behind these must be incredibly busy, right?

And that's before we even consider the human element. Think about the billions of prayers ascending every moment—requests for healing, guidance, and intervention in matters both monumental and mundane. Add to that the tracking of good and bad actions, the distribution of karma, and the maintenance of cosmic order, and the divine to-do list seems endless! But what if we've been thinking about this all wrong? What if the question itself reveals more about our limited human perspective than it does about the true nature of divinity?

Let's Dive Deeper

Our human minds naturally conceive of God as a sort of cosmic manager, a mighty being who oversees the universe the way a CEO might run a vast corporation. We imagine that divine attention is divided among countless tasks, and divine energy is expended on maintaining creation.

It's mind-boggling to consider how such an administration would work. How could any entity, no matter how powerful, keep track of every particle in the universe, every thought in every mind, every cause and its effects stretching across time and space?

Of course, the most straightforward explanation is to invoke omnipotence. God can do all these things effortlessly because God's power is unlimited. But the omnipotence explanation only brings us back to our original question with even more urgency: if God handles all universal management effortlessly, what does God *do* with divine time?

Wisdom from Ancient Traditions

Fortunately, we don't have to speculate unquestioningly about this. The Bhagavad Gita and Upanishads offer profound insights that reframe the question entirely.

According to these texts, we commit a fundamental category error when we imagine God having "days" or engaging in "activities" in the same manner as humans do. The divine doesn't manage the universe like we manage our affairs by dividing attention, expending energy, and parceling out time among different tasks. Instead, divinity is best understood as the fundamental energy that enables the universe to exist and function. It's not a manager, but a foundation; not a doer, but a being.

The Two Energies of Creation

As we discussed earlier in this book, the Gita describes two types of divine energy that comprise all existence. The first is material energy, composed of eight components: earth, water, fire, air, space, mind, intellect, and individual identity. Material energy is the tangible, visible aspect of creation—the hardware of the universe, if you will.

However, hardware needs software to function, and this is where the second type of energy comes in—spiritual energy, the life force that animates material existence. Without this animating principle, the universe would be like an empty highway, all infrastructure but no movement, all potential but no actuality.

These two energies, material and spiritual, continuously interact, creating patterns we experience as the events and outcomes of life. The flow of these energies and the way they intersect determine what we perceive as cause and effect.

The Divine Non-Intervention

Here's where we encounter a perspective shift that might challenge many traditional religious viewpoints: According to this understanding, divinity doesn't actively intervene in daily affairs. The divine role is to provide the highway and the energy that allows movement, and after that, there is no divine micromanagement happening on a moment-to-moment basis.

When you pray or make a request to the divine, you might imagine your petition entering a celestial queue, waiting for divine attention and action. But that's not how it works. Whether your prayer seems "answered" depends on how effectively your efforts and those of others channel or disrupt the flow of divine energy.

When energy flows are appropriately channeled, leading to your desired outcome, you might say, "God has responded to my prayer." When flows are disrupted, leading to disappointment, you might attribute it to karma or bad luck. But in both cases, divinity hasn't changed its behavior—only the energy patterns have shifted, influenced by countless factors, including your actions, attitudes, and state of being.

Your Role in the Cosmic Dance

If divinity isn't actively managing affairs, then what determines the course of your life? According to the Gita, several key factors come into play:

Samskaras: The characteristics you develop and embody

Vasanas: The tendencies and inclinations you manifest

Jnana: The knowledge you acquire and apply

Bhakti: The devotion with which you live out that knowledge

Prapatti: Your surrender to the process—doing your best while releasing attachment to specific outcomes

These elements shape how you interact with material and spiritual energies, which create patterns that manifest as your lived experience. Your choices, behaviors, beliefs, and level of commitment all contribute to how these energies flow through and around you.

The True Nature of Divinity

So, what does God do all day? Nothing. Because doing isn't part of divine nature. Divinity isn't a doer but a sustainer. Not an actor but a foundation. The entity we call God is the substratum of all existence: the unchanging background against which all change occurs, the eternal present in which the past and future unfold.

The divine foundation sustains everything. It was, is, and will be. Compared to this foundation, everything else seems small because nothing else has an independent existence. Through the material energy of this foundation, we have our bodies; through the life energy of this foundation, we have our consciousness, spirit, and sense of being alive.

Which brings us to the more critical question: Given this understanding of divinity, what do *you* do all day? How do you use the material and spiritual energies flowing through you? What patterns are you creating through your choices, attitudes, and actions?

Summary: Being, Not Doing

As we conclude this exploration of divine nature, let's reflect on the key insights that can guide your spiritual journey.

- First and foremost, divinity is not a cosmic manager but the very foundation of existence. Understanding this fundamentally shifts your relationship with the divine from petitioning an external authority to aligning with the foundation of your being. This foundational understanding invites you to look for the divine, not in an imaginary, exalted location in the clouds, but in the ground beneath your feet, the breath within your lungs, and everything around you.

- Your life is shaped by the interaction of material and spiritual energies. By becoming more conscious of these energies and how they flow through you, you can participate more intentionally in creating your experience. Think of yourself as less of a petitioner and more like a conductor of divine energy, influencing its expression through your awareness and intention.

- The elements of your being matter deeply. Your characteristics, tendencies, knowledge, devotion, and surrender determine how you channel divine energy, creating patterns that manifest as the circumstances and events of your life. Your spiritual development isn't separate from your life development; they are the same process.

- When you understand this interplay of energies, you recognize that prayers and intentions work not because they change God, but because they change the flow of energy. Your spiritual practices are effective to the extent that they align you with divine energy, allowing it to flow more freely through your being. The power of prayer lies in its ability to align you with divine energy.

- Perhaps most importantly, the question isn't what God does, but what you do with the divine energy flowing through you. Your choices, moment by moment, determine how this energy manifests in your life and the world. The recognition isn't about taking control away from God, but about acknowledging your role in expressing the divine nature.

By understanding divinity as the substratum of existence rather than a cosmic CEO, you free yourself from waiting for divine intervention and step into your power as a conscious channel of sacred energy. The practice isn't about controlling outcomes, but about showing up fully, acting with wisdom and compassion, and trusting the process even when you can't predict the results. It's about dancing with divine energy rather than waiting for it to move you.

Start Today: Your First Step

If there's one action I encourage you to take right now, it's this: **Become the conduit.**

Here's how to begin:

Sit quietly, close your eyes, and feel the life energy flowing through you, the same energy that animates all existence. As you breathe, imagine yourself as a conduit for this divine energy, neither creating nor controlling it but allowing it to flow freely through you and express itself in your thoughts, words, and actions throughout the day.

Don't worry about doing this perfectly. The practice itself will guide you over time, revealing insights and opening up possibilities you might not have currently imagined.

REMEMBER, WHAT MATTERS IS YOUR WILLINGNESS TO BEGIN SEEING YOURSELF NOT AS SEPARATE FROM DIVINITY, BUT AS AN EXPRESSION OF IT—NOT ASKING WHAT GOD WILL DO FOR YOU TODAY, BUT HOW THE DIVINE WILL EXPRESS ITSELF THROUGH YOU.

True Spirituality

THERE'S A PROFOUND DIFFERENCE between living a routine, mechanical life and one filled with meaning and purpose. You've likely experienced moments when you felt a deeper connection to everything around you, moments that transcended your everyday experiences. Those glimpses, my friend, are what we're exploring in this chapter.

When I began thinking about spirituality, I imagined it involved mystical experiences or religious rituals. But as I delved deeper, I discovered something far more practical and accessible. Spirituality isn't about floating above the realities of life but about navigating them with a heightened awareness and intention.

Let's embark on this journey together to understand what spirituality truly means, how it differs from religion, and, most importantly, how you can cultivate a spiritual mindset in your everyday life. The truth is, spirituality isn't something reserved for monks or mystics; it's available to all of us, right here, right now, amid our ordinary lives.

Let's Dive Deeper

Now that we've set the stage for our exploration, it's time to go beneath the surface. The concept of spirituality can seem abstract or elusive at first glance. Some associate it with religious practices, others with meditation or yoga, and others with a vague sense of connection to something greater than themselves.

But what if spirituality were something more fundamental that touches every aspect of how we move through the world? What if it were less about what we believe and more about how we live? These are the questions that guide our journey in this chapter.

As we delve deeper, we'll discover that we don't need to incorporate spirituality into our busy lives. Instead, it's a dimension of awareness always available to us, a way of being that transforms ordinary experiences into opportunities for growth, connection, and meaning.

Let's take a deep breath together and plunge beneath the surface appearances of life to explore the rich depths of a spiritual mindset.

What Is Spirituality? A Behavioral Mindset

At its core, spirituality is a mindset that influences behavior. But what does that mean?

Throughout your life, you've acquired tendencies that manifest as behaviors from childhood onward. You've watched your parents, observed your environment, made intellectual decisions, and noticed what brings you joy versus what doesn't. All these experiences have shaped your tendencies, which in turn have influenced your behaviors and actions.

Over time, these tendencies accumulate and form your overall mindset and your approach to life. According to the Bhagavad Gita and the Upanishads, these tendencies don't develop over a single lifetime, but rather across multiple lifetimes. Life is seen as a continuum, with our current physical form being just one phase of that ongoing journey.

However, let's focus on the present moment, on the tendencies you've developed throughout this lifetime, and on how they manifest in your actions. Spirituality comes into play precisely at this point. When it comes to expressing our tendencies through actions, we can operate on two distinct levels:

The First Level: The Material Plane

On the first level, what we might call the material or earthly plane, your actions are solely based on what's right in front of you. You make quick judgments based on surface impressions, and when you reencounter the same situation, you replay your previous response. Operating this way is not inherently wrong. It's efficient for handling routine matters, but lacks depth and reflection.

Let me give you an example: Imagine driving to work, and someone cuts you off in traffic. You might immediately react with frustration or anger on this first level because that's your established pattern. The next time someone cuts you off, you react the same way without considering alternatives.

The Second Level: The Higher Plane

The second level represents a higher plane of consciousness. Here, you still have your tendencies and impressions, but you take a moment to pause before acting. In that pause, you reflect, think, and then act. You're not just making snap judgments; you're engaging your prefrontal cortex, your intellectual discriminating faculty, to validate your impressions before responding.

The realm of spirituality exists precisely here as a behavioral mindset that operates on a higher plane.

Of course, not every situation requires this level of reflection. Brushing your teeth or making your morning coffee can become a routine that runs on autopilot. But there are countless moments throughout your day when the reflective approach would serve you well.

Spirituality in Action: A Practical Example

Let's make this concrete with a practical example: preparing for a meeting or an interview.

The Non-Spiritual Approach

With a non-spiritual mindset (the first level), you might approach the meeting with tension and anxiety, focusing solely on answering questions correctly and appearing perfect. Your internal dialogue might sound like: "I need to nail every question, every query. I can't make any mistakes. Gaining acceptance is everything." You're operating from a place of fear and attachment to outcomes.

The Spiritual Approach

With a spiritual mindset (the second level), you would:

- Research the company beyond surface information to understand its values, culture, leadership, and financial health. You're using your intellectual discriminating faculty.

- Approach the meeting with confidence in your values, seeking to understand how the company aligns with your values system and what they can offer you. You're going in for a meaningful exchange, not just to please or impress.

- After the meeting, you wouldn't anxiously await the outcome or obsess over your performance. Instead, you'd recognize that you gave your best effort and that the result depends on many factors beyond your control, such as the other person's perception, the company's budget, and external economic factors.

Acknowledging that the outcome isn't entirely in your hands frees you from unnecessary anxiety. You've done your part; now, you can let go of attachment to the result. Such non-attachment represents the essence of a spiritual mindset in action.

Ten Aspects of Spiritual Mindset

Now, let's explore ten different aspects that can help you gauge your current position on your spiritual journey. Self-reflection here isn't about judging yourself as "right" or "wrong," or "high" or "low" on some spiritual hierarchy. It's simply a framework for self-reflection and measurement.

1. Seeing Unity in Diversity

A spiritual mindset recognizes the unity behind diversity. Recall what we discussed about divinity being composed of eight fundamental elements and twenty different emotions, resulting in an infinite number of permutations and combinations? A spiritually minded person looks beyond the surface of diversity to perceive the underlying fabric that connects us all.

Instead of seeing only differences between yourself and others, you begin to recognize the shared essence. The recognition of shared essence naturally leads to greater compassion and understanding.

2. Cultivating Mindfulness in Personal Experiences

Spirituality encourages you to be fully present in your experiences. When you drink a glass of water, you appreciate its taste, temperature, and clarity. When you walk outdoors, you notice the sensation of air on your skin and the sounds around.

The practice of mindfulness isn't about adding something new to your life, but it's about removing the veil of inattention that keeps you from experiencing the richness already present in every moment. Through mindfulness, even ordinary experiences become extraordinary.

3. Aligning Thoughts with Actions

A spiritual person demonstrates consistency between inner thoughts and outer actions, particularly in significant matters. You're not one person in private and another in public; instead, integrity runs through all aspects of your life.

Alignment doesn't mean you never make mistakes or experience negative emotions. Instead, you're aware of the gap between your ideals and reality, and you work to narrow that space.

4. Distinguishing Between Love and Attachment

Distinguishing between love and attachment represents a vital aspect of a spiritual mindset. Love and attachment seem similar, but they're fundamentally different energies. Love is an open, expansive feeling that wants the best for the beloved without condition. Attachment, on the other hand, is based on how the other person or object fulfills your needs or desires.

As a parent, for example, you can deeply love your child while setting boundaries and allowing them to face the natural consequences of their actions. Your love is not contingent upon their meeting your expectations or making you proud. You love them unconditionally, even as you guide them toward making good choices.

A spiritual mindset cultivates this kind of love, one that is unconditional, unattached, and unencumbered by expectations of control or possession.

5. Practicing Non-Judgment

Spiritual people strive to observe without immediately labeling experiences as "good" or "bad." They recognize that what appears negative at the moment may later reveal unexpected gifts, and what seems positive might carry hidden challenges.

Non-judgment doesn't mean you become passive or indifferent. Instead, you develop the ability to respond thoughtfully rather than react automatically based on your likes and dislikes.

6. Embracing Impermanence

Everything changes, and that includes your body, thoughts, relationships, and circumstances. A spiritual mindset acknowledges this fundamental truth, rather than resisting it.

By embracing impermanence, you can hold your experiences more lightly. You can enjoy pleasant moments without clinging and move through difficult times, knowing that all situations, good or bad, eventually pass.

7. Cultivating Gratitude

Gratitude is a cornerstone of spiritual practice; instead of focusing on what's missing or what could be better, a spiritual mindset is oriented toward an appreciation for what it is.

The practice isn't about forcing positivity or denying difficulties. It's simply the recognition that there are countless things to be grateful for at any moment — from the functioning of your body to the beauty of the natural world to the kindness of others.

8. Seeking Growth Through Challenges

A spiritual person views challenges not as punishments or obstacles but as opportunities for growth and learning.

When facing difficulties, rather than asking, "Why is this happening to me?" they might ask, "What can I learn from this experience?" or "How can I grow through this challenge?"

Viewing challenges this way doesn't eliminate pain but transforms your relationship with it, allowing difficulties to become doorways to greater wisdom and compassion.

9. Practicing Selfless Service

Spirituality naturally expresses itself through service to others without expectation of reward or recognition. Selfless service isn't about grand gestures, but about bringing a service-oriented attitude into everyday interactions, like listening deeply to a friend in need, offering a kind word to a stranger, or contributing your talents to causes you believe in.

Through selfless service, you transcend the limitations of self-centeredness and emerge into an interconnected way of being.

10. Developing Inner Stillness

Amidst the noise and busyness of modern life, a spiritual mindset cultivates moments of inner quiet. Inner quiet might be cultivated through formal meditation or taking regular breaks from external stimulation.

In these moments of stillness, you connect with something more profound than your thoughts and emotions, namely a stable presence that remains constant amid life's changes.

How Spirituality Differs from Religion

It's essential to recognize that spirituality is parallel to, yet distinct from, religion. A spiritual person doesn't discount or shun religion; instead, they see it as a potential vehicle for developing discipline and community.

For the spiritualist, religion offers a set of practices, dos and don'ts, and community connections that can support their inner journey. Instead of debating religious doctrines or finding fault with traditions, they focus on how religious frameworks might help instill self-discipline in their behavioral mindset.

Think of religion as offering a structure, like the banks of a river, that can help channel the flow of spiritual experience. The structure isn't the experience itself, but it can help guide and support it.

The Divine Experience of Spirituality

Remember, spirituality is an experience. A mindset that manifests through one's actions and thoughts. You cannot simply read about or intellectualize; it must be lived.

Similarly, divinity is also an experience. When you engage with life from a spiritual mindset, you're having a divine experience right here and now. You don't need to wait for some future state or afterlife because the Divine is accessible now through your way of being in each moment.

As Krishna says in chapter 7, verse 19 of the Bhagavad Gita, the ability to see beyond the surface appearance to the unity underlying all diversity is rare. But the capacity to perceive unity lives within each of us, waiting to be developed through conscious intention and practice.

Summary: Beyond the Surface Appearance

Let's recap what we've explored in this chapter:

- Spirituality is a behavioral mindset that involves approaching life from a higher plane of consciousness, with reflection before action.

- The spiritual mindset develops through the tendencies we acquire over our lifetime(s) and how we choose to express them.

- We can operate on two levels: the material plane (automatic reactions based on surface impressions) or the higher plane (thoughtful responses based on deeper understanding).

- A spiritual approach involves doing your best while releasing attachment to outcomes, recognizing that many factors beyond your control influence results.

- Ten aspects of a spiritual mindset include seeing unity in diversity, practicing mindfulness, aligning thoughts with actions, distinguishing love from attachment, and cultivating inner stillness.

- Spirituality differs from religion but can complement it, using religious frameworks as vehicles for developing discipline rather than objects of debate.

- Living with a spiritual mindset provides a divine experience in the present moment, rather than waiting for a future state.

The journey toward a spiritual mindset isn't linear or finite. It's an ongoing process of awakening to greater awareness and intention in how you live. Each moment offers a fresh opportunity to choose the higher plane, pause before reacting, and see beyond surface appearances to the deeper reality.

Start Today: Your First Step

If there's one action I encourage you to take right now, it's this: **Start a Two-Plane Journal.** Begin documenting your journey between the material and higher planes by keeping a simple journal dedicated to this awareness practice. Keeping a journal will help you track your growth and identify patterns in your responses to life's situations.

Here's how to begin:

Each evening, take 5-10 minutes to reflect on 2-3 significant interactions or decisions from your day. For each situation, answer these questions:

- Did I operate from the material plane (automatic reaction) or the higher plane (thoughtful response)?

- What triggered my reaction/response?

- What emotions were present?

- What might a higher plane response have looked like if I operated from the material plane?

- What enabled me to do so if I operated from a higher plane?

- Notice patterns over time: Are there specific people, situations, or emotions that tend to pull you into material plane reactions? What conditions support your higher-plane responses?

The power of this practice lies in its simplicity and consistency. You're not trying to force yourself to operate from the higher plane continuously, as that would create unnecessary pressure and judgment. Instead, you're developing awareness of when and how you move between these planes.

The awareness itself will gradually shift your responses. As the Bhagavad Gita suggests, simply witnessing your patterns with compassion begins to transform them. After a week of journaling, review your entries and celebrate your growth. Even small shifts toward a higher plane can lead to meaningful changes in your relationships and life experiences.

REMEMBER, SPIRITUALITY ISN'T ABOUT PERFECTION BUT PRESENCE AND AWARENESS. EACH MOMENT OF RECOGNITION IS A STEP ON YOUR JOURNEY TOWARD A MORE SPIRITUAL MINDSET.

PART FOUR

Practical Wisdom For Daily Life

Choices

THE ART OF DECISION MAKING

A CONVERSATION WITH A FRIEND the other day prompted me to think about how we make decisions. She told me about a significant career move she was considering and how she'd been going back and forth for weeks, unable to commit one way or the other. "I just don't feel confident making the right choice," she confessed.

I bet you've been there too. We all struggle with decisions at times, whether it's something as simple as what to have for dinner or something as life-changing as deciding whether to move across the country for a new opportunity. And let's be honest: in today's world, we're making more decisions than ever before. Our grandparents didn't have to choose between 50 streaming services or hundreds of breakfast cereals!

What I've discovered over the years is that decision-making isn't just about weighing the pros and cons, but it is about developing a spiritual muscle to examine the consequences. When we approach our choices from a deeper place of wisdom, something remarkable happens within us. We transform not just our decisions but our entire experience of life.

Becoming a spiritually centered person involves several interconnected elements: intellect, gratitude, and grace. In previous chapters, we explored how gratitude opens the door to divine grace. Now, let's focus on how to harness your intellect to develop something I call "the power of proper decision-making."

What if I told you that making better decisions doesn't require more information, more analysis, or more options? What if the secret lies in understanding yourself at a deeper level and following three simple and yet profound steps that spiritual masters have practiced for centuries?

Let's Dive Deeper

In this chapter, I will share with you a framework for decision-making that goes beyond pros and cons lists or gut feelings. Grounded in ancient wisdom yet perfectly applicable to modern life, our framework will help you develop what the Bhagavad Gita calls "firm wisdom" or *sthitha prajna*—a state of being where your decisions flow naturally from a place of inner clarity and spiritual alignment.

In the Bhagavad Gita, the warrior Arjuna poses a profound question to Krishna: What are the characteristics of a person with firm wisdom? How do they speak, conduct their lives, and behave?

Krishna's response outlines four distinct stages an individual passes through on the path to becoming a *sthitha prajna*—a person of unwavering wisdom. Let's explore each stage and see how they progressively enhance our decision-making power.

Stage 1: yatamaana samjna — Awareness Before Action

The first stage is about developing the ability to pause before reacting. Like a tortoise that withdraws its limbs when sensing danger, a person in this stage learns to catch and direct sense responses appropriately.

Think about those times you've said something in anger that you immediately regretted, or made an impulsive purchase that didn't align with your budget or values. These are examples of decisions made without that crucial moment of awareness.

In the first stage, you develop what I call a "response gap," a small space between the stimulus and the response where a proper choice becomes possible. Anger or hate is no longer an automatic reaction; there is a momentary recognition of one's behavior before action is triggered.

In this stage, you won't always succeed in pausing. You'll still make impulsive decisions and react in ways you later wish you hadn't. But the critical difference is that awareness exists. You notice when you've reacted automatically, and this noticing is the beginning of change. Known as *yatamaana samjna* in Sanskrit, this stage provides the foundation for all that follows. Without this initial development of awareness, no further growth in decision-making is possible.

Stage 2: vyatireka samjna — Emotional Balance

In the second stage, you develop restraint from excessive likes and dislikes. Developing emotional balance doesn't mean becoming emotionless or indifferent; it means cultivating a balanced approach to emotions. Instead, it means developing what we might call emotional equanimity, the ability to experience preferences without being controlled by them.

A person in this stage understands their constitutional rights and responsibilities. They recognize the interplay between body, soul, and the divine (what some traditions call the Supersoul). When you realize this interplay, you naturally develop more balanced emotional responses.

When making decisions, someone in this stage isn't swayed dramatically or ignores emotions or temporary circumstances. They can acknowledge their feelings while still maintaining perspective on the bigger picture.

Consider how different your decisions might be if you were not caught between strong attractions and aversions. How might you approach a difficult conversation if you weren't afraid of the discomfort it might cause? What goals might you pursue if you weren't so attached to comfort and security? At *vyatireka samjna*, you experience new freedom in decision-making because you're no longer a prisoner to your strongest emotions.

Stage 3: ekendriya samjna — Proactive Mindset

The third stage represents a significant shift in consciousness. Here, you develop a proactive rather than reactive approach to life. Your mind is no longer dramatically affected by sorrow or happiness, even when you can see them coming.

Joy and sadness remain integral to your experience, but the difference lies in how they influence your decisions. Instead, it means these emotions no longer dictate your choices. You can receive good news without becoming giddy with excitement (and making poor choices as a result). You can face challenges without becoming despondent (and making fear-based decisions).

A person in this stage makes decisions based on principles and purpose rather than emotional weather. They ask, "What's the right thing to do?" rather than "What will make me feel better right now?"

When you reach *ekendriya samjna*, your decision-making becomes notably consistent. Your choices begin to form a coherent pattern aligned with your deepest values rather than zigzagging according to circumstances.

However, it's essential to note that in this third stage, remnants of material desires persist. If these are unmanaged, they can expand and cause regression to earlier stages. Like a pot that once held oil, even when emptied, a residue remains that can attract more of the same.

Stage 4: vaseekara samjna — Unwavering Concentration

The fourth and final stage, preceding full maturation into a *sthitha prajna*, is characterized by unwavering concentration and focus. Your mind is fully engaged in action and inquiry into the real purpose of life.

At this stage, decision-making becomes remarkably clear and almost effortless. Why? Because your concentration is no longer divided among competing values and desires. Your actions, thoughts, and contemplations all pivot around a unified understanding of your purpose.

At the *vaseekara samjna* stage, meditation and concentration manifest as union with the soul or divinity. You become what the scriptures call an *aparoksha jnani*—a person with the ability to perceive direct knowledge without being judgmental.

Unlike the third stage, where traces of material desire remain, purity overflows the fourth stage. Using our pot analogy, it's as if the pot has been thoroughly washed with detergent and all traces of oil are gone. The transformation is permanent; there is no going back.

In this stage, you see unity in diversity. The distinctions between man, woman, and other entities fade, and what remains is recognition of the universal energy that pervades all living beings. When you view things from this unified perspective, decision-making becomes profoundly clear because you naturally consider the highest good of all parties involved.

Approaching Decision-Making Differently

Step 1: Actions with Purpose

The first and perhaps most crucial step is to recognize that you are not your body. The self, your soul or inner energy, is distinct from the physical form it inhabits. The self-body distinction isn't just a philosophical concept; it's a practical realization that changes how you approach every decision.

When you identify solely with your body, your decisions tend to revolve around physical comfort, immediate gratification, and survival instincts. But when you recognize yourself as a spiritual being having a human experience, your decision-making expands to include higher considerations.

If you're just a body, then decisions are simple. Choose whatever feels good at the moment. But if you're a soul with a purpose, then decisions become about aligning with that purpose, even when they don't offer immediate physical comfort.

Although initially abstract, the distinction between self and body proves practical when making decisions, such as whether to stand up for your values even when it's uncomfortable or whether to sacrifice short-term pleasure for long-term growth. Understanding the distinction between the self and the body gives you a broader perspective from which to evaluate your choices.

Step 2: Intention of Actions

Once you understand the distinction between self and body, the next step is to focus intently on your actions. Not just on what you do, but on how and why you do it.

In our distracted world, we often act on autopilot, letting habits and conditioning guide our behavior. Real decision-making power comes from bringing conscious awareness to our actions. Like physical fitness, this awareness grows stronger the more you exercise it.

When you focus on your actions, you begin to notice patterns. You see how certain decisions lead to specific outcomes. You recognize the difference between actions that drain your energy and those that replenish it. You understand which choices align with your deeper values and which ones create internal conflict.

Like physical fitness, this awareness grows stronger the more you exercise it. The more you practice being present with your actions, the more naturally you'll make decisions that serve your highest good.

Step 3: Validate

The third step is the most overlooked in our busy lives: creating space for reflection. Proper decision-making requires regular time for contemplating your actions and their effects. Don't confuse contemplation with ruminating or overanalyzing. It's about creating a sacred pause where you can honestly assess:

How did my actions align with my values?

What were the effects of my decisions on myself and others?

What wisdom can I gain from both my successes and my mistakes?

Without this contemplative space, we miss the lessons our own lives are trying to teach us. We repeat patterns without understanding them, and we forfeit the opportunity to refine our decision-making capacity.

Even a simple reflection can be transformative. Even 10-15 minutes of quiet journaling or meditation at the end of each day can transform how you approach decisions over time.

When you consistently practice these three steps (taking actions with purpose, being intentional about your actions, and setting aside time for contemplation), you develop what spiritual traditions refer to as "firm wisdom." Firm wisdom transcends intellectual knowledge by becoming an embodied understanding manifesting in all areas of life through transparent and confident decision-making.

The Challenge of Maintaining Firm Wisdom

Is it easy to attain and maintain this state of firm wisdom? Probably not. At least not without a life of discipline.

A person in the first stage can easily sway back to unconscious living, much like a recovering addict might return to old patterns without disciplined recovery practices. Even those in the second and third stages aren't immune to regression.

That's why the three foundational steps we discussed earlier— realizing the self-body distinction, focusing on your actions, and setting aside time for contemplation must become daily practices, not occasional efforts.

Think of developing firm wisdom like building any other kind of strength. You don't become physically strong by lifting weights once a month. Similarly, you don't establish firm wisdom by practicing awareness or contemplation only when you face major decisions.

It's the daily, consistent practice that transforms your decision-making capacity over time. Each small choice becomes an opportunity to exercise your wisdom muscles. Each moment of awareness, each intentional action, and each period of reflection contribute to your growth.

The beauty of this approach is that it integrates seamlessly into ordinary life. You don't need to retreat to a mountain cave or spend hours in meditation (though these certainly help!). You need to bring a new quality of awareness to the life you're already living.

Summary: The Path to Proper Decision-Making

Let's review the key insights we've explored about developing the power of proper decision-making: You develop "firm wisdom" or *sthitha prajna* through four progressive stages:

- *yatamaana samjna* — Developing awareness before action, creating a response gap between stimulus and reaction.

- *vyatireka samjna* — Cultivating emotional balance and restraint from excessive likes and dislikes.

- *ekendriya samjna* — Establishing a proactive mindset that remains unaffected by anticipated pleasure or pain.

- *vaseekara samjna* — Achieving unwavering concentration with a mind fully engaged in purpose-driven action and inquiry.

You approach decision-making differently by:

- Acting with Purpose - Recognize that the self (soul) is distinct from the body. While the self-body distinction may seem abstract, it becomes concrete when faced with day-to-day decisions.

- Intention of Actions — Bringing conscious awareness to what you do creates space for intentional choice.

- Validate — You set aside time for contemplation. Regular reflection allows you to learn from experience and refine your capacity for wisdom.

Throughout this journey, your decision-making capacity transforms from reactive and inconsistent to clear, purposeful, and aligned with your highest values. While you'll undoubtedly make better practical decisions, the deeper benefit involves aligning your entire life with your spiritual nature.

When you make decisions from firm wisdom, you experience less inner conflict, greater peace, and a profound sense of living in alignment with your purpose. Your actions and choices naturally contribute to both your well-being and the well-being of those around you.

Remember that growth in decision-making happens progressively. No one moves immediately from unconscious reaction to unwavering wisdom. Be patient with yourself as you develop these capacities and celebrate each small victory along the way.

Start Today: Your First Step

If there's one action I encourage you to take right now, it's this: **Establish a Response Gap.**

Here's how to begin:

Choose one common trigger in your life, something that typically causes an automatic reaction (e.g., someone cutting you off in traffic, a specific tone of voice from a family member, or a work email that arrives late Friday afternoon).

- For one week, make a special effort to notice when this trigger occurs.

- When you encounter your chosen trigger, try to create a tiny pause—even just a breath—before responding.

- During that pause, notice your physical sensations, the urge to react, and any thoughts or emotions present.

- Then, choose your response consciously rather than reacting automatically.

Each evening, journal about your experiences:

- When did the trigger occur?

- Did you create a pause?

- What did you notice during the pause?

- How did your conscious response differ from your typical automatic reaction?

After a week with one trigger, choose another and repeat the process. As this practice becomes habitual, you'll notice a subtle but significant shift in how you approach decisions throughout the day. Knowing that you'll be reflecting later creates a natural incentive to stay more aware of the moment. It's like telling yourself, "I'm going to be thinking about this choice later, so let me be more conscious about it now."

Over time, this simple practice will strengthen all aspects of your decision-making capacity. You'll become more aware before acting, more balanced in your emotional responses, more proactive in your mindset, and eventually, more focused on what truly matters.

Start today. Don't wait for the "perfect" time or method. An honest reflection can be the first step toward developing the kind of firm wisdom that transforms not just your decisions but your entire life.

REMEMBER TO DEVELOP THE HABIT OF PAUSING BEFORE REACTING IN VARIOUS SITUATIONS. DON'T APPROACH THIS AS A SELF-JUDGMENT SESSION. THE GOAL ISN'T TO CRITICIZE YOURSELF FOR MISTAKES BUT TO LEARN FROM ALL YOUR EXPERIENCES WITH COMPASSIONATE AWARENESS.

Passion vs. Interest

WHICH PATH TO FOLLOW?

I RECEIVED A THOUGHT-PROVOKING QUESTION from an individual that speaks to something many of us struggle with. The question was multilayered but centered around a fundamental dilemma: Should we build our lives around our interests or follow our passions? How do we even identify what these are, and which approach is more sustainable for the long journey of life?

These aren't just abstract philosophical questions. The answers shape our career choices, how we spend our time, what we commit to learning, and ultimately, how we define a meaningful life. The confusion between interests and passions isn't surprising. These terms, often used in motivational speeches and career counseling sessions, are frequently defined without clarity. What exactly is the difference between an interest and a passion? How does one transform into the other? And which should we prioritize when making life's big decisions?

In this chapter, I want to explore these questions through the lens of ancient wisdom from the Gita and Upanishads, which offer surprisingly practical insights into this modern dilemma. The perspective I'll share isn't about choosing between passion and interest, but it's about understanding their relationship and aligning both with deeper principles that lead to a truly fulfilled life.

Let's Dive Deeper

Before we can decide whether to follow our interests or passions, we need clarity about what these terms mean and how they relate to each other. Let's start by examining each concept.

Interest is an attraction to something that feels enriching or gratifying. When you encounter an activity or subject that promises a rewarding outcome, whether that's enjoyment, learning, accomplishment, or some other benefit, you feel interested. There's a spark of excitement about the potential results.

For example, you might become interested in photography after seeing stunning images on social media and thinking, "I'd like to create beautiful pictures like that." The anticipation of creating something beautiful draws you in.

Passion goes deeper. It emerges when you've moved beyond initial interest into sustained engagement with something. When you continue to put effort into an activity despite challenges, experience satisfaction from the progress you're making, and your conviction about its value deepens over time, that's when interest transforms into passion.

Continuing with our photography example, interest becomes passion when you find yourself willingly spending hours learning about camera settings, experimenting with different lighting conditions, and feeling deeply fulfilled by the process of improving your skills, not just the results.

What's crucial to understand is that passion typically doesn't appear instantaneously. Rather than being something you discover fully formed, passion typically develops through a process that begins with an initial interest. The journey often follows this path:

- A thought arises, sparked by your intellect, encountering a possibility

- That thought leads to an action—trying something out

- The action, if gratifying, develops into an interest

- With continued engagement and satisfaction, that interest evolves into passion

The initial thought that starts this chain reaction can come from many sources. Perhaps you've noticed someone else doing something that seems fulfilling. You could read about it in a book or an article. Or you may have been exposed to it through education or family traditions. Whatever the source, when that initial spark gives you a sense of potential gratification, and you decide to act on it, the cycle begins.

However, this progression isn't always so linear or conscious. Sometimes, you might feel an instinctive pull toward certain activities without clearly understanding why. Such a "gut feeling" about what interests you often emerges from your accumulated experiences and memories. The people you've surrounded yourself with, the experiences you've had, and the impressions stored in your mind all contribute to these instinctive attractions.

Even when interest seems to arise spontaneously as an instinct, the same fundamental process is at work. Instinctive interest leads you to take action. When that action is executed with conviction and yields satisfaction, it gradually develops into passion through repeated cycles of engagement and improvement.

The Three Fundamental Components

Whether we're talking about interests or passions, three fundamental components are always involved: intellect, action, and outcome. Understanding these components through the wisdom of the Gita and Upanishads can help us approach both our interests and passions more consciously and meaningfully.

The Role of Intellect

You are endowed with the intellect to make choices, which is one of the most profound gifts of human consciousness. But the key question is: Are you using this intellect consciously?

Many of our interests and even supposed "passions" can emerge from the more primitive parts of our brain, the parts drawn to immediate pleasure, status, or security. The Gita encourages us to engage our higher intellectual faculties, what modern neuroscience might locate in the prefrontal cortex, to make more conscious choices about what we pursue.

Such thinking means asking more profound questions about our interests and passions: Does this align with my values? Is this something I genuinely want to develop, or am I pursuing it due to social pressure or a fleeting desire? What are my true motivations?

When we engage our intellect in this reflective way, we're more likely to develop interests and passions that truly resonate with our authentic selves rather than following unconscious conditioning or impulsive attractions.

The Nature of Action

Once intellect has helped us identify an interest, action brings it to life. However, the Gita provides profound guidance on the quality of this action, encouraging us to ask: Is the action I'm taking righteous? Does it cause harm to others? Does it contain elements of kindness and compassion?

Such a perspective transforms how we approach our interests and passions. Instead of evaluating them solely based on personal gratification, we consider their broader impact. Does my business solve meaningful problems for others? Does my musical talent bring joy and healing to listeners?

Gita also invites us to ask whether our actions contain an element of service. Of course, not every interest must be explicitly charitable, but it suggests that the most fulfilling pursuits generally involve contributing something valuable to others or the world beyond ourselves.

Interests that meet the criteria of righteousness, harmlessness, compassion, and service tend to develop into more sustainable and meaningful passions than those focused solely on personal benefit or achievement.

The Relationship to Outcomes

The third component of how we relate to outcomes is perhaps where the Gita's wisdom is most distinctive and potent. While having a vision of desired outcomes is natural and necessary, the Gita advises undertaking action without attachment to specific results.

Gita's guidance acknowledges a fundamental truth: while you can control your effort and approach, the outcome is never entirely within your control. Numerous factors beyond your control influence the results, including the decisions of others, timing, available resources, and unexpected events, among others.

The scriptural texts offer a beautiful metaphor for this relationship to outcomes: Be like a water droplet on a lotus leaf, which sits like a pearl on the surface but is detached from it. You can fully engage with your interests and passions while maintaining this inner freedom from attachment to particular results.

Maintaining inner freedom from attachment helps you cope with life's inevitable disappointments and surprises. When outcomes don't match your expectations, as it often happens, you can adjust and continue rather than becoming dejected or abandoning your path entirely.

The Transformation from Interest to Passion

Understanding the above three components helps clarify how interest transforms into passion and why some interests never make this transition.

Interests often begin with attraction to potential outcomes—the beautiful photographs you might create, the music you might play, and the business you might build. But if your engagement remains primarily outcome-focused and you find the process itself tedious or unpleasant, this interest is unlikely to develop into passion.

Passion emerges when you find fulfillment in the process itself, when the actions involved in pursuing your interest become intrinsically rewarding, not just a means to an end. You're no longer just seeking the photograph; you're enjoying the craft of photography. You're not just working for a paycheck; you engage in the challenges and learning of your field.

Moving from the outcome to process appreciation doesn't happen instantly. It develops through repeated cycles of effort, progress, and satisfaction. Each slight improvement or insight creates positive reinforcement that deepens your commitment and enjoyment.

Gita's wisdom about non-attachment to outcomes is particularly relevant in this context. When you're less fixated on specific results and more engaged in the present reality of your actions, you're more likely to discover the intrinsic rewards that fuel passion. You notice subtle pleasures and meanings in the activity itself rather than constantly measuring against external benchmarks of success.

Such freedom from specific outcomes also makes you more resilient in the face of setbacks, which are inevitable in any meaningful pursuit. Instead of becoming discouraged when outcomes disappoint, you can learn, adjust, and continue, maintaining the continuity of engagement that allows interest to mature into passion.

Which Should Guide Your Life?

Now we return to our original question: Should you follow your interests or your passions? The answer emerges from understanding their relationship.

Interests provide breadth—they allow you to explore various possibilities and discover what rcsonatcs with you. Passions provide depth. They enable profound engagement, mastery, and fulfillment in particular areas. Both have essential roles in a well-lived life.

In practical terms, understanding their connection points leads to a dual approach:

- Explore your interests broadly, especially in the early phases of life. Try different activities, subjects, and environments to discover what naturally engages you. Pay attention not only to the outcomes but also to how you feel during the process itself.

- Develop selected interests into passions by committing to continued engagement over time. Not every interest needs to become a passion. That would be impossible. However, dedicating yourself to developing deeper engagement with a few areas that particularly resonate with you creates a solid foundation for a fulfilling life.

The key insight from the Gita is to pursue one's interests or passions with awareness of the three components we've discussed. Whether you're exploring new interests or deepening existing passions, bring awareness to:

The quality of your intellectual choices

The righteousness and compassion in your actions

Your relationship to outcomes

Conscious engagement transforms even ordinary interests into meaningful engagement and prevents passions from becoming obsessive or harmful attachments.

Summary: The Wisdom of Both/And

We began with what seemed like an either/or question: Should you follow your interests or your passions? The wisdom of the Gita suggests transcending this dichotomy with a both/and approach that recognizes the relationship between interests and passions while grounding both in deeper principles.

- Interests and passions aren't competing alternatives but different stages of engagement. Interests provide the seeds from which passions can grow. Not every interest will or should develop into a passion, but without initial interests, deep passions cannot emerge.

- Both interests and passions involve the same three fundamental components: intellectual choices, action in the world, and relationship to outcomes. Gita's guidance applies to both, encouraging us to:

  Make conscious intellectual choices rather than following conditioning or impulsive behaviors.

  Take righteous action that avoids harm and incorporates compassion and service.

  Maintain non-attachment to specific outcomes while fully engaging with the process.

- Following this guidance transforms how we relate to both our interests and our passions. Instead of pursuing interests solely for personal gratification or following passions with an obsessive attachment to results, we engage in a more balanced way that creates sustainable fulfillment.

- The question isn't whether to follow your interests or your passions, but how to approach both with the consciousness that transforms ordinary activities into meaningful engagement with life. When pursued with awareness of these principles, both interests and passions contribute to a life of purpose, growth, and fulfillment.

- Like the water droplet on the lotus leaf, you can fully engage with your interests and passions while maintaining the inner freedom that comes from righteous action and non-attachment to outcomes. Maintaining this equilibrium, neither apathetic nor obsessive, creates the conditions for a genuinely sustainable and meaningful life.

Start Today: Your First Step

If there's one action I encourage you to take right now, it's this: **Undertake a purposeful activity evaluation.**

Here's how to begin:

Select three activities that occupy significant time in your life right now. These might be related to your work, hobbies, relationships, or other areas of focus. For each activity, ask yourself these questions:

- Intellectual Choice: Am I engaging in this consciously, or am I doing it out of habit, obligation, or unconscious conditioning? Does this activity align with my authentic values?

- Quality of Action: Is my approach to this activity righteous? Does it involve harming others or contributing positively? Does it incorporate elements of compassion or service?

- Relationship to Outcomes: How attached am I to specific results in this area? Can I engage fully while maintaining inner freedom from particular outcomes?

- Process vs. Outcome: Do I find fulfillment in the process itself, or am I only focused on results? Does this activity feel more like an interest or a passion based on my engagement with the process?

After reflecting on these questions, choose one specific change you could make to bring more consciousness to each activity. You may need to clarify your intellectual motivation for one pursuit, incorporate more service into another, or practice non-attachment to outcomes in a third.

Implement these changes over the next week, paying careful attention to how they affect your experience. Notice whether activities that previously felt like obligations or mere interests begin to develop more qualities of passion as you engage with them more consciously.

Making these mindful changes puts the wisdom of the Gita into practical action in your daily life. Instead of making dramatic changes based on abstract ideals about interests versus passions, you're bringing greater consciousness to your existing engagements, which often naturally clarifies which activities merit more profound commitment, and which might be released or transformed.

REMEMBER, THE GOAL ISN'T TO TURN EVERY INTEREST INTO A PASSION OR TO IMMEDIATELY ABANDON ACTIVITIES THAT DON'T INSTANTLY FEEL PASSIONATE. IT'S ABOUT ENGAGING WITH BOTH YOUR INTERESTS AND DEVELOPING PASSIONS IN A MORE CONSCIOUS WAY, WHICH GRADUALLY REVEALS YOUR AUTHENTIC PATH.

Dance of Compassion

FINDING BALANCE WITH RIGHTEOUSNESS

The human experience is marked by countless moments where emotion and reason seem to war within us. I've certainly felt this tension, particularly when facing the choice between what feels right in my heart and what I know to be right in principle.

Imagine you're a teacher and your student has broken a rule, but you know they're going through a difficult time at home. Or perhaps you're a parent, and your child has done something wrong, yet punishing them feels almost as painful for you as it does for them. These moments compel us to confront a profound question: Do we follow the path of compassion, which our emotions urge us toward, or do we adhere to righteousness, which our reason dictates is necessary?

In this chapter, we'll explore this timeless tension through the lens of one of humanity's most enduring spiritual texts, the Bhagavad Gita, and discover that perhaps the choice isn't as binary as we might think. The ancient wisdom contained in this text provides a framework for navigating these challenging waters, one that may help us integrate both compassion and righteousness into our daily lives.

Let's Dive Deeper

What do Compassion and Righteousness mean?

Compassion is deeply emotional. It's that pull you feel in your chest when you see someone suffering, that instinctive desire to alleviate pain. It's subjective and personal, arising from our shared humanity and capacity for empathy. When we act with compassion, we respond to our feelings.

Righteousness, on the other hand, is a more objective concept. It's about aligning our actions with principles of justice, duty, and moral truth. Righteousness isn't just about what feels good; it's about what is right, regardless of how difficult it might be. When we act from righteousness, we respond to what we know.

But here's where things get interesting: righteousness isn't a fixed target. It shifts depending on the role you're playing at any given moment. Think about it—you take on multiple roles each day, don't you? You might be a parent, a professional, a friend, a citizen, a student, or a teacher - sometimes all within the same day.

The same person (you) plays each of these roles, but what constitutes righteous action varies with each one. As a parent, your natural inclination may be to love your child unconditionally. But as a teacher or coach to that same child, righteousness might require that you point out their mistakes, even when it hurts both of you.

Righteousness gives us a moral compass, but compassion, especially overwhelming emotion, can sometimes make it hard to read that compass.

The Battlefield Dilemma: Arjuna's Struggle

To better understand this tension, let's turn to one of history's most famous moral dilemmas, portrayed in the Bhagavad Gita.

Picture this: a battlefield where two armies stand ready for war. On one side is the warrior prince Arjuna, accompanied by his charioteer, who happens to be Krishna, an incarnation of the divine. As Arjuna surveys the battlefield, he sees not just enemies but family members, teachers, and respected elders whom he loves and honors.

Despite having access to divine wisdom through Krishna, despite commanding a righteous army, and despite knowing that his cause is just, Arjuna falters. Confusion overwhelms him. Should he show compassion toward his enemies, who are his relatives, or should he fulfill his duty as a warrior and fight?

In moments like these, Arjuna experiences what we all do when faced with difficult choices: fear, anger, and anxiety. His compassionate heart prompts him to think beyond the immediate battle to the consequences of war on future generations. He envisions a terrible future: elders killed, younger generations growing up without proper guidance, families destroyed, and society becoming unethical and immoral.

"How can we even think of committing such a sinful act?" Arjuna pleads with Krishna. "For the sake of humanity, I would rather be kind and compassionate than righteous; I would rather die than fight. Let me die."

Arjuna's momentary quandary, though painful for him, delivered a gift for all of humanity. His unique relationship with divinity became the trigger for Krishna to impart timeless knowledge, the wisdom of the Bhagavad Gita.

Krishna's Framework: Integrating Compassion and Righteousness

What's fascinating about Krishna's response is that he doesn't frame the choice as "either/or" but rather "both/and." Through his teachings, Krishna provides a framework for righteousness that naturally includes compassion.

Krishna explains that on an absolute path of righteousness, kindness is not separate but rather an ingrained and embedded component. Being kind alone doesn't necessarily mean you are righteous. However, when you are truly virtuous, you are also kind and compassionate.

It's a subtle but profound distinction. True righteousness isn't cold or detached. It encompasses compassion. And genuine compassion isn't merely emotional indulgence. Righteous principles must guide it.

But how do we know what's righteous in any given situation? According to the Gita, righteousness largely depends on our role and the responsibilities that accompany it. Your duty as a parent differs from your duty as a colleague, which differs from your duty as a citizen. Recognizing and fulfilling the responsibilities of your current role, while maintaining compassion, is the path to righteousness.

Krishna's guidance to Arjuna reveals another crucial insight: the importance of action without attachment to outcome. The Gita teaches that unconditional surrender, performing one's actions according to one's duty, and leaving the outcome to the divine, is the only way to lead a truly righteous life.

The focus, then, is on our responsibility and the actions we take. Not on what will happen as a result, not on how others will judge us, not even on whether we'll succeed. We're just doing what is right for the role we're in at this moment.

Finding Your Way: The Role of Guidance

Standing before the ocean of wisdom, that is the Gita, each of us takes what we need based on our current stage on the journey. Some may need only a handful of water to quench an immediate thirst. Others might fill vessels to carry away for sustained nourishment. A blessed few might absorb the knowledge of the entire ocean.

But to fully absorb and apply the message of the Gita, most of us need guidance from someone special. Someone who can illuminate the path for us based on these ancient tenets. Someone who can shine a light on the road so that we can walk it confidently. Someone who can help us understand the components and milestones of that path.

That "someone" might be an Acharya (a preceptor who leads by example), a Guru (who dispels the darkness of ignorance), or a Teacher (who imparts knowledge systematically). Finding such a guide can be transformative in our quest to strike a balance between compassion and righteousness.

Summary: The Integrated Path

Are compassion and righteousness mutually exclusive?

- The wisdom of the Gita suggests they are not. Instead, they are complementary virtues that, when properly understood and integrated, lead us to more fulfilled and moral lives.

- Compassion without righteousness can become mere sentimentality, potentially causing more harm than good despite the best intentions. Righteousness without compassion can become rigid dogma, losing touch with the humanity it aims to serve.

- The path forward lies in understanding our roles and the responsibilities that come with them, acting under those responsibilities while maintaining compassionate awareness, and surrendering attachment to outcomes.

- Righteousness varies by the role you take on. True righteousness includes compassion as an essential component

- Focus on your responsibility and action, not on outcomes

- Seek guidance from those who can illuminate this path for you

- By embracing both compassion and righteousness—allowing them to coexist rather than compete, we move closer to living with both moral clarity and an open heart.

Start Here: Your First Step

If there's one action I encourage you to take right now, it's this: **Strike a balance between duty and empathy**. Identify one role in your life where you feel the tension between compassion and righteousness most acutely. Perhaps it's as a parent, a leader, a friend, or a citizen.

Here's how to begin:

For the next week, consciously approach this role with the integrated perspective we've discussed. When faced with a decision, ask yourself: "What is my duty in this role right now? How can I fulfill that duty while maintaining compassion?" Then, act accordingly and surrender attachment to the outcome.

Notice how this approach feels different from either following pure emotion or adhering to rigid principles. Journal about your experience. Where did you find clarity? Where did you still struggle? Such mindful practice can rewire how you approach the dance of compassion and righteousness in your daily life.

REMEMBER, THE JOURNEY IS NOT ABOUT PERFECTION BUT ABOUT PRACTICE. EVEN ARJUNA, WITH DIVINE GUIDANCE LITERALLY AT HIS SIDE, STRUGGLED WITH THESE QUESTIONS. BE PATIENT WITH YOURSELF AS YOU EXPLORE THIS INTEGRATED PATH OF COMPASSION AND RIGHTEOUSNESS.

From Goals to Objectives

THE PATH TO HEALTH AND HAPPINESS

WE'VE ALL EXPERIENCED THAT FEELING when chasing after something big, like a promotion, a relationship, or a financial milestone, and you can almost taste it. There's that rush of anticipation, the mental calculations of how your life will change once you've achieved this goal. Then, when you finally reach it (if you do), there's that brief moment of satisfaction before the horizon shifts again, revealing a new peak to climb.

But what about when you don't reach it? When, despite your best efforts, the promotion goes to someone else, the relationship crumbles, or the financial goal remains frustratingly out of reach. That sinking feeling of disappointment can be crushing, yet oddly familiar, as it feels like another stop on the emotional rollercoaster of ambition.

I lived in this constant pursuit for years. Setting goals, reaching them, briefly celebrating, and then setting new ones immediately, and sometimes failing spectacularly, picking myself up, and throwing myself back into the chase with renewed determination. It was exhausting. More importantly, I noticed something strange—my happiness wasn't increasing in proportion to my achievements, nor was my disappointment diminishing with my failures. The emotional highs weren't getting higher, and the lows, while painful, weren't as devastating as I'd feared. I was in a cycle that moved me forward, but never seemed to change how I felt about my life.

That's when I stumbled upon a distinction in the Bhagavad Gita that completely transformed my approach to life. It was so simple that I almost missed its profundity: the difference between goals and objectives. It's not just semantic wordplay. It's a fundamental shift in how we approach life, and it's the key to that elusive combination of health and happiness that we're all seeking.

Let me share with you what I've discovered and how the ancient wisdom of the Gita offers us a prescription for living that feels remarkably relevant to our modern challenges. Along the way, I'll introduce you to what I call the "four medicines," practical applications of this wisdom that can transform your physical health and mental well-being.

Let's Dive Deeper

Here's the revelation that changed everything for me: Goals fixate on outcomes, while Objectives focus on actions.

Think about it for a moment. When we set goals, we become attached to specific outcomes such as losing 20 pounds, securing a particular job, or buying a certain house. But as the Gita so wisely teaches, outcomes aren't actually within our control. There are too many variables in the complex equation of life.

What we can control are our choices and actions, the steps we take each day. These are our objectives. When we shift our focus from the destination to the path itself, something remarkable happens. The pressure lessens. The joy increases. We find ourselves more present and engaged with the journey.

I remember my desperate pursuit of spiritual awakening. I'd set a goal of reaching a specific state, and each day, I'd evaluate with anxiety. My mood and outlook hinged on whether I'd made progress or experienced any profound insights. Not surprisingly, the pressure was blocking my spiritual growth.

When I shifted my focus to objectives, processing my thoughts before responding, practicing mindfulness during routine activities, and reading wisdom teachings without expectation, everything changed. The "depth" of my spiritual experiences became just one aspect of my practice, not the measure of my worth or progress. Ironically, once I released my attachment to achieving enlightenment, my spiritual life began to unfold more naturally and meaningfully.

Krishna teaches Arjuna exactly this principle in the Gita. Your journey is uniquely yours, and the only person you're competing with is yourself. Others' achievements can inspire you—I certainly am! Please take what you can learn from their experiences, but remember that your path is yours alone to walk.

That's why I've become such a devoted advocate for setting objectives rather than goals. It's not just semantics, it's liberation.

The Four Medicines for a Fulfilled Life

Whether or not you choose to think about life in terms of objectives, I encourage you to consider what we all universally desire: a healthy and happy life. Who doesn't want that? Why wouldn't we want to enjoy everything this beautiful universe has to offer?

What I love about the Gita is that it offers an incredible prescription for achieving exactly this. Krishna is the most outstanding psychiatrist who has ever existed, offering a path forward through what I like to call spiritual medicine.

Once you begin adopting these prescriptions, you'll notice they naturally become your default habits and way of life. The Gita provides us with four essential medicines. Two for the mind (spiritual) and two for the body (physical).

You might wonder, "Why focus on the body when the Gita is supposed to be about the mind?" The answer is beautifully simple: without an efficient, functioning body, it's tough to experience spiritual growth and inner peace. The mind and body aren't separate entities but interconnected aspects of our whole being.

Let's explore these four medicines together, and you'll see why they form such a comprehensive approach to well-being.

The First Medicine: Eliminating Hatred

In my experience, the first medicine I want to share with you is the most powerful. Even if you don't follow anything else from the Gita, this alone will lead you to remarkable health and happiness, and that's getting rid of hatred.

When I talk about eliminating hatred, I mean this: see other people, and even objects, for what and who they truly are. You may have different opinions about their behavior or attitudes, but refrain from harboring hatred, jealousy, or anger toward them.

You can call out undesirable behavior. I'm not suggesting you become a doormat! But in your heart and mind, don't hold onto those feelings of hatred. Because hatred is essentially a poison pill that you're taking, and it impacts you far more than the person you're directing it toward.

I learned this lesson the hard way. For years, I carried resentment towards a few individuals who I felt had betrayed me. They had moved on, seemingly unaffected, while I remained stuck in a loop of anger and bitterness. Every time I thought about the situation, my blood pressure would rise, my jaw would clench, and I'd feel that familiar knot in my stomach.

One day, while reading the Gita, I came across chapter 5, verse 6, where Krishna states that we need to elevate ourselves through the power of the mind, rather than degrade ourselves, because the mind can be either our greatest friend or our worst enemy. It hit me like a lightning bolt: I was the one suffering from my hatred. Probably, the others were just fine.

The Gita identifies three doors that lead us to hell: lust, anger, and greed. Every sensible person should release these, as they lead to the degradation of both body and soul. Particularly, rage and greed rapidly transform into hatred.

The first medicine given by Krishna is critical, getting you at least 50% of the way toward health and happiness. The remaining three medicines will take you the rest of the way.

The Second Medicine: Nourishing the Body

The second medicine Krishna prescribes is for the body. It focuses on food, exercise, and discipline.

Krishna tells us that there is no possibility of becoming spiritually inclined if we eat too much or too little, sleep too much, or not enough. We must be conscious of our habits in eating, sleeping, working, and recreation. Through this awareness, we can mitigate all material suffering.

In chapter 17, Krishna teaches that foods that increase life, purify our existence, and give strength are dear to those in the mode of goodness. Foods that are overly bitter, sour, salty, hot, pungent, dry, or stored for too long are preferred only by those in the mode of passion. Such foods cause distress, misery, and disease.

Our increased intake of salty, excessively sweet, and heavily processed foods is a major contributor to today's health challenges. The ancient wisdom of the Gita aligns perfectly with modern nutritional science on this point.

Exercise naturally complements proper nutrition. Our bodies need to be in a mode of physical movement and action. In Sanskrit, four terms describe a healthy physical rhythm: *upavishathi, uttishthati, tishtathi, and chalathi*—sitting, getting up, standing, and moving. Our bodies need to cycle through these states throughout our waking hours. As the saying goes, don't become a "couch potato," perpetually sitting like a stone!

Simply being mindful of these four states and intentionally moving through them throughout my day has made a tremendous difference in my energy levels and overall physical well-being. It doesn't require an elaborate exercise routine, just awareness and intention.

The Third Medicine: Practical Health Consciousness

The third medicine is again for the body and ensures you're living with common sense and rationality regarding your health in this modern world.

This means not getting carried away by any rhetorical or emotional statements about medicine and science, but instead having the simple objective of getting a thorough health checkup done each year. I'm referring to a comprehensive head-to-toe examination.

You need to understand and know the status of your "vehicle," your body. Without a well-maintained body, you will, unfortunately, lack the means to execute the actions and choices necessary to eliminate hatred, as we discussed in the first medicine.

How you correct any problems discovered during your checkup is up to you, since there are many science-based and natural options available. However, first, establish a baseline understanding of your health.

Krishna emphasizes the need for self-discipline as part of the mode of goodness, and for goodness to deliver its desired results, the body must be healthy.

I'll admit that I used to neglect this medicine. I'd only see a doctor when something was wrong, operating under the assumption that "no news is good news." But after a close friend had a serious health scare that was avoidable with regular screenings, I changed my approach. Now, my annual checkup is a non-negotiable part of my health routine, and it has also given me peace of mind, as it provides early warnings about potential issues I might otherwise have missed.

The Fourth Medicine: Spiritual Learning

The fourth medicine Krishna offers us is about embarking on the path of spiritual learning. This medicine is for the mind.

At a basic level, this means dedicating some time each day to reading about the Gita, listening to or watching teachings about the Gita and Upanishads, and most importantly, putting these teachings into practice.

I've observed many people who listen to or watch ritual practices or pujas and perform them as mere routines without considering their spiritual aspects. While these rituals can be helpful tools for developing discipline and can serve as a good first step, they don't substitute for genuine spiritual learning.

Without spiritual learning, one cannot develop a thinking mind. Instead, one will become a victim of emotions. Without a thinking and rational mind, there's no possibility of peace. And how can there be any happiness without peace?

The fourth medicine doesn't require you to become a scholar or spend hours in meditation. It simply asks that you dedicate some time each day to connect with spiritual wisdom.

In my case, I enjoy reading a verse from the Gita and contemplating how it might apply to my day ahead. Sometimes, I journal about it; other times, I mentally carry the teaching with me. This small practice has gradually transformed how I respond to challenges and how I perceive my place in the world.

Summary: Prescription for Living

Here are the four medicines for a healthy and happy life:

- Get rid of hatred — See people for who they are, respond to behaviors without harboring negative emotions that primarily harm you

- Focus on food, exercise, and discipline — Nourish your body with foods that promote well-being and maintain a healthy physical rhythm.

- Take a common-sense approach to health — Get regular checkups and address issues as they arise, using whatever methods align with your values.

- Dedicate time to spiritual learning — Spend at least 15-30 minutes daily to understand and implement spiritual teachings.

I've found that incorporating these four medicines into my daily life has transformed not just my health but my entire perspective on what it means to live well. The beauty of these teachings lies in their simultaneous antiquity and complete relevance to the modern challenges we face.

- When I reflect on why this approach works so well, it comes down to balance. The Gita doesn't ask us to renounce the world or devote ourselves entirely to spiritual pursuits. It recognizes that we are complex beings with physical, mental, emotional, and spiritual dimensions, all of which need tending.

- By shifting from goals (outcomes) to objectives (actions) and consistently applying these four principles, we create the conditions for both health and happiness to flourish. We stop postponing our well-being until some future achievement and instead cultivate it right here, right now, through our daily choices.

- The journey isn't about perfection. There will be days when you fall short in one area or another. The key is to approach this journey with compassion for yourself and a willingness to begin again each day. As Krishna teaches Arjuna, it's not about the perfection of your actions but the sincerity of your effort that matters most.

As you move forward on your journey, I encourage you to experiment with these medicines. Start small—perhaps with just a few minutes of spiritual reading or by being conscious of how you respond to someone who triggers negative emotions in you.

Notice the subtle shifts that begin to occur in your body, mind, and spirit.

The path to health and happiness isn't a destination we reach once and then reside in forever. It's a daily practice, a moment-by-moment choice to align with these timeless principles. And in that consistent choosing, we find our way to the peace and fulfillment we all seek.

Start Today: Your First Step

If there's one action I encourage you to take right now, it's this: **Three-Minute Release.** A simple exercise like this one addresses the first and most powerful medicine: eliminating hatred.

Here's how to begin:

- Set aside three uninterrupted minutes. Close your eyes and take three deep breaths.

- Think of someone who has recently triggered negative emotions in you—perhaps anger, frustration, or resentment. See their face clearly in your mind.

- Now, mentally separate the person from their behavior. Say to yourself: "This person, like me, is seeking happiness. Their actions may have upset me, but they are not their actions."

- Feel the weight of the negative emotion you've been carrying. Please recognize that this heaviness affects your well-being, not theirs.

- Complete by wishing this person well, not because they deserve it, but because your heart deserves peace.

As Krishna teaches, we elevate ourselves through the power of the mind. The Three-Minute Release is your first objective toward that elevation —a practical application that you can control completely, regardless of the outcomes. It's about taking action that aligns with the highest teachings of the Gita.

Try it right now. Then, try it again tomorrow. Before long, you'll wonder how you ever lived without it.

REMEMBER, BY SHIFTING TO EXECUTION ON OBJECTIVES INSTEAD OF BEING FIXATED ON GOALS, WE CONSISTENTLY BEGIN TO REWIRE OUR NEURAL PATHWAYS. THE FIRST FEW TIMES MAY FEEL MECHANICAL—THAT'S PERFECTLY NORMAL. WHAT MATTERS IS THE INTENTION AND THE PRACTICE ITSELF.

PART FIVE

Daily Spiritual-Traditional Living

Creating Sacred Space

DO I NEED A PUJA ROOM?

THE QUESTION OF SACRED SPACE in our homes speaks to the very essence of how we practice spirituality in daily life. Throughout my early years, I encountered many well-meaning but often unexplained directives about prayer spaces: "The *puja* room must face east," they'd say, or "Keep the deities in the northeast corner." These instructions came without context, leaving me with questions that lingered for years.

Why should a home prayer space face a particular direction? Does divinity truly care which way we face when we pray? If the divine is all-pervading, why designate a specific room for worship at all? These questions might sound familiar if you've ever found yourself arranging a prayer space while wondering about the deeper meaning behind these traditions.

In this chapter, we'll explore the concept of the *puja* room, not just as a physical space but as a focal point for spiritual practice in your home. We'll examine both the traditional guidance and the underlying principles that give these practices their true significance.

Let's Dive Deeper

The Sanskrit term *puja* derives from the root word *puj*, which means honor. At its core, *puja* is about creating a moment and space of honor, whether for the divine, for your spiritual journey, or for the act of contemplation itself.

Think about the various dedicated spaces in your home. You might have a home office for work, a kitchen for cooking, and a bedroom for rest. These designations aren't arbitrary. They help focus our energy and attention on specific activities. Similarly, a space dedicated to spiritual practice helps focus our spiritual energy and intention.

The question isn't really about whether divinity needs a special room but whether having such a space serves our human need for focus, structure, and ritual. Let's explore how this traditional practice can enrich your spiritual life, regardless of the complexity or simplicity of your sacred space.

The Purpose of Sacred Space

A dedicated worship space serves several vital functions in a household:

- **Focus:** Just as a dedicated office helps you concentrate on work, a *puja* room creates an environment specifically designed for prayer, meditation, and contemplation.

- **Community:** The *puja* room often becomes a gathering place for family members to come together in shared spiritual practice, especially during festivals and celebrations.

- **Energy:** Regular worship, meditation, and prayer in a specific location create positive vibrations that "kindle godliness" in those who enter or live in the home.

- **Consistency:** Having a designated space helps establish and maintain a regular spiritual practice. You see it daily, and that can serve as a reminder to take time for your inner life.

When we understand these purposes, we can see that the *puja* room isn't just about following tradition. Instead, it is a practical tool for enhancing our spiritual practice.

Directional Considerations: East, North, and Northeast

One of the most frequently asked questions about *puja* rooms concerns their orientation. Traditional beliefs suggest placing the *puja* room in the northeast or east of the home. But why?

The primary reason is simple and symbolic: the sun rises in the east. In many traditions, including those reflected in the Upanishads, the sun is the most visible form of divinity. It's the cosmic source of light, energy, and life that we can directly perceive. Facing east during prayer symbolically acknowledges this visible manifestation of divine energy.

The northern direction also holds special significance. In chapter 8 of the Bhagavad Gita, Krishna speaks of the "northern path" or the "path of light" that spiritually engaged souls take after death. This concept extends beyond our physical lifetime, connecting our daily practice to our spiritual journey beyond this life.

These directional preferences aren't arbitrary rules but symbolic gestures that connect our practice to larger cosmic rhythms and spiritual concepts.

What If East Isn't Possible?

Here's where we need practical wisdom: while traditional directions have symbolic value, they're not absolute requirements. The Upanishadic understanding of divinity describes an all-pervading presence that exists in all directions, not just in the east.

Who are we, as mere mortals, to say it's only in the East that you have God or divinity? If your home layout makes an eastern or northeastern *puja* room impossible, that's perfectly fine. What matters more than direction is the cleanliness of the space, a sense of focus and commitment, regular practice and contemplation, and creating a peaceful environment for worship. These elements, together, form the foundation of a meaningful sacred space, regardless of its orientation.

The essence of the *puja* room is the intention and energy you bring to it, not its compass orientation. If you have space in the east, by all means, follow that tradition. But if not, create your sacred space wherever it works best in your home.

Creating Your Own Sacred Space

A *puja* room doesn't need to be elaborate or take up an entire room. Even a small shelf, a corner of a room, or a dedicated cabinet can serve as your sacred space. What matters is that you designate this area specifically for spiritual practice and treat it accordingly. Start with these basic elements:

- A clean, uncluttered space

- Images or symbols that hold spiritual meaning for you

- A place for a lamp or candle

- Perhaps a small platform for offerings

- Making It a Focal Point

Whatever the size of your *puja* space, consider how to make it a focal point for spiritual practice in your home. Creating a focal point might mean:

Positioning it so family members can gather around

Making it visible enough to serve as a daily reminder

Keeping it accessible for regular practice

Designing it to be beautiful and inviting

During festivals and special occasions, this space naturally becomes the center of celebration, serving as a gathering point to bring the family together around shared spiritual values.

Regular Maintenance

A sacred space requires regular care. Regular maintenance isn't just about physical cleanliness (though that's important too), but about maintaining the energy and intention of the space:

Keep the area clean and free from dust

Refresh flowers or offerings regularly

Light lamps or candles during prayers

Periodically reassess and renew the space as needed

Such maintenance becomes an integral part of your spiritual practice and a way of showing respect for both the space and what it represents.

Summary: The True Meaning of a *puja* Room

When we look beyond rigid rules about directions and setups, we discover that a *puja* room or sacred space fulfills a profound human need for focus, consistency, and community in spiritual practice. The essence of this tradition isn't about appeasing gods who demand specific orientations but about creating conditions that help us connect more deeply with the divine presence that pervades everything. A *puja* room offers:

- A dedicated space that helps us focus our attention

- A symbolic connection to larger cosmic rhythms

- A gathering place for family and community

- A daily reminder of our spiritual commitments

Whether your sacred space faces east, west, north, or south, and whether it's an entire room or just a small shelf, what truly matters is the sincerity, commitment, and regular practice you bring to it. The divine, being all-pervading, is certainly not limited by direction. Our practice is enhanced by tradition but not confined by it.

Start Today: Your First Step

If there's one action I encourage you to take right now, it's this: **Create or renew a dedicated space for spiritual practice** in your home.

Here's how to begin:

If you don't already have a *puja* space, start small. Choose a shelf, a corner, or even a small table that can be dedicated solely to this purpose. Clean it thoroughly, and place one or two items that hold spiritual significance for you—perhaps an image, a sacred text, or a small lamp.

If you already have a *puja* room or space, take time this week to refresh and renew it. Clean everything thoroughly, replace any worn items, and consider adding one new element that enhances your practice—perhaps a new lamp, a meaningful image, or a fresh arrangement.

The key is to approach this process mindfully and with intention. As you create or renew your space, reflect on what this area will mean in your daily life. How will you use it? When will you incorporate it into your routine? How might it serve as a focal point for your family's spiritual practice?

REMEMBER, BY CONSCIOUSLY CREATING A SACRED SPACE IN YOUR HOME, YOU'RE COMMITTING TO REGULAR SPIRITUAL PRACTICE AND CREATING THE CONDITIONS THAT WILL SUPPORT YOUR INNER GROWTH, RATHER THAN MERELY FOLLOWING A TRADITION.

Illuminating Truth

THE REAL MEANING OF LIGHTING A LAMP

THE SIMPLE ACT OF LIGHTING A LAMP carries profound meanings that most of us never pause to consider. Growing up, I was told with unwavering certainty, "You have a *puja* room, so you should light a lamp. Period." No explanation was offered, and no questions were welcomed.

The rules seemed oddly specific yet inconsistent. Two lamps were mandatory, not one, because an accidentally extinguished single flame foretold disaster, possibly even death. Yet somehow, blowing out a lamp during a power outage was perfectly acceptable. And when someone passed away, the requirement suddenly shifted to one lamp instead of two.

These contradictions created a quiet confusion that followed me for years. I followed the traditions faithfully while harboring unanswered questions that slowly accumulated in the back of my mind. Perhaps you've experienced something similar, participating in rituals passed down through generations without fully understanding their significance.

Today, let's illuminate this practice! We'll explore what the Gita and the Upanishads teach us about this seemingly simple act of lighting a lamp and how it connects to profound spiritual concepts that can transform our understanding and deepen our practice.

Let's Dive Deeper

What appears on the surface as a simple ritual contains layers of meaning that connect us to ancient wisdom. When we light a lamp, we're not just creating physical light; we're participating in a tradition that goes back thousands of years, one that connects us to the fundamental elements of nature and our inner selves.

The beauty of examining these practices through the lens of the Gita and Upanishads is that we can move beyond blind faith and gain a deeper understanding of the rational, spiritual, and experiential dimensions of these customs. When we understand the 'why' behind our practices, they become more meaningful and powerful in our lives.

Let's approach this exploration with an open mind and a sense of curiosity. Whether you've been lighting lamps your entire life or you're just learning about this practice, there's something profound to discover about this seemingly simple act of illumination.

The Evolution of Lamp Lighting

The Three Sacred Fires

In Upanishadic or Vedantic times, daily life centered on understanding one's true nature and purpose. Rituals weren't empty gestures. They connected humans to the fundamental elements of nature: earth, fire, air, water, and space. The divine itself was often referred to through these elemental forms.

Fire, as the most visible manifestation of energy, became a natural focus for offerings and worship. The ancient texts refer to fire as *agni*, and it played a central role in household spirituality. Each household maintained a sacred fire altar and made offerings to three distinct fires:

- The Earthly Fire: Families kept this physical flame burning continuously in their homes.

- The Atmospheric Fire: Kindled from the earthly fire, this flame was used for cooking and worship aimed at material desires—wealth, health, offspring, and prosperity. Households maintained this fire facing east.

- The Celestial Fire: Families used this flame specifically to honor their ancestors. It represented our connection to the cosmos and was kept facing south.

These three sacred fires formed the backbone of household spiritual practice in ancient times. Today, when we light a lamp in our homes or at temples, we're symbolically continuing this ancient tradition of honoring these three fires.

From Fire Altars to Oil Lamps

Maintaining three distinct sacred fires isn't practical in modern apartments and houses. But the tradition continues in a simplified form through the lighting of oil lamps. The open lamp, with its cotton wick and oil, represents the fundamental elements of nature combined.

Lighting these lamps at dawn or dusk acknowledges the transitional moments of the day, times when the cosmos shifts from one state to another. While most homes have replaced fire altars with simple oil lamps or even electric lights, many temples still maintain the traditional Agni altars alongside the more accessible oil lamps.

The Deeper Meaning: Beyond Tradition

There's an even more profound reason for lighting lamps, one that requires deeper contemplation in two significant ways:

The Divine Light (divya jyoti)

First, the lamp represents the supreme light, showing the path of inquiry for those seeking truth. Since the supreme consciousness is referred to as *paramatma*, this guiding light is often called *divya jyoti* (divine light). You'll notice many temples maintain an eternal flame outside for precisely this reason, as it symbolizes the divine presence that is always accessible to devotees. The ever-burning lamp reminds us that spiritual guidance is always available to those who seek it.

The Inner Light (atma jyoti)

From another perspective, the lamp represents the divine spark that exists within each of us. It serves as a reminder that we all carry an internal light, our true self or *atman*.

Each time we see the lamp, we're reminded to shift our attention from the distractions around us to the stillness within. Because this light pertains to the inner spark within us, it's also called *atma jyoti* (the light of the self).

Common Questions About Lamp Lighting

How Many Lamps Should I Light?

> Here's something interesting: from a spiritual standpoint, the number of lamps doesn't matter. Lighting one lamp or a thousand carries the same symbolic significance. Anything beyond one lamp is simply a matter of personal preference, decoration, or creating a pleasing appearance.

How Many Wicks Should a Lamp Have?
The number of wicks comes down to what resonates with your practice. You might see lamps with one, two, or three wicks, and each number carries its symbolic meaning:

> Three Wicks: Represent the three modes of nature— goodness (*sattva*), passion (*rajas*), and ignorance (*tamas*).

Two Wicks: Symbolize the duality between the supreme consciousness and individual consciousness.

One Wick: Represents the singular source of all energy, which is divinity itself.

From a practical standpoint, multiple wicks work better. A single wick tends to slide around in the oil, while twisted strands of two or three wicks have better grip and stability. So there's both symbolism and practicality at work here.

Summary: The True Meaning of Lighting a Lamp

When we strip away superstitions and blind faith, we find that lighting a lamp connects us to profound spiritual truths:

- It represents the fundamental element of fire (*agni*), continuing an ancient tradition of honoring the forces of nature.

- It symbolizes the divine light (*divya jyoti*) that guides us on our spiritual journey.

- It reminds us of our inner light (*atma jyoti*), that divine spark within each of us.

- It serves as a physical anchor for contemplation and spiritual inquiry.

The next time you light a lamp, don't worry too much about the number of wicks or how many lamps you should light. One is enough, though more is certainly fine if that brings you joy.

Start Today: Your First Step

If there's one action I encourage you to take right now, it's this: **Establish a Daily Ritual of Mindfully Lighting a Lamp.**

Here's how to begin:

Choose a time, perhaps at dawn or dusk when day transitions to night, and create a small ritual around lighting your lamp. As you light it, take a moment to reflect on what this flame represents:

- First, acknowledge it as a connection to the ancient tradition of honoring the elemental forces.

- Then, see it as the divine light illuminating your path of spiritual inquiry.

- Finally, recognize it as a reminder of your inner light—the true self that remains constant beneath the fluctuations of daily life.

Start with just seven days of this practice. Don't worry about getting it "right." There's no correct number of lamps or wicks. What matters is the intentionality and awareness you bring to this simple act.

After a week, notice if this mindful approach to lamp lighting has shifted anything in your perspective or your relationship to this ancient practice. Has it become more than just a ritual? Has it begun to serve as that anchor for contemplation that the tradition intended?

REMEMBER, BY LIGHTING A LAMP, YOU UNDERSTAND THAT YOU'RE NOT JUST ILLUMINATING YOUR PHYSICAL SPACE, BUT ALSO ACKNOWLEDGING BOTH THE DIVINE LIGHT THAT GUIDES AND THE INNER LIGHT THAT DEFINES YOU.

The Five-Step Path to Spiritual Discipline

PANCHA KALA KRIYA

SPIRITUAL KNOWLEDGE AND DAILY PRACTICE often exist in separate worlds, creating one of life's most common inconsistencies. Many of us possess the map but never use it to find our way. I've experienced this myself. Our fast-paced world makes it all too easy to accumulate spiritual concepts without truly embedding them into our daily lives. We read books, watch videos, and attend lectures, yet somehow that wisdom remains separate from our everyday experience.

That's why I want to share something transformative with you: a simple five-step discipline that bridges this gap, offering a practical solution even the busiest among us can implement. It's called *pancha kala kriya*, a five-step process that uniquely combines spirituality and ritual, segmenting your entire day into meaningful touchpoints with the divine.

Now, you might be thinking: "ritual and spiritual in the same sentence? Isn't that a contradiction?" You're right. Spirituality, by definition, focuses on the characteristics or *tattvas*, as referred to in the scriptures. Ritualism has no place there. However, here's the thing: to embark on a spiritual journey, discipline serves as our compass. Particularly for those of us juggling careers, families, and numerous other responsibilities, we need something practical and simple that can anchor our spiritual development.

While this practice of *pancha kala kriya* has roots in orthodox Hindu traditions, I've designed this approach specifically for those who find it challenging to follow traditional practices due to time constraints. Regardless of your background, these five simple steps can help you incorporate spirituality into your daily routine.

Let's Dive Deeper

Before we explore each step of the *pancha kala kriya*, it's essential to understand why this approach matters so profoundly in our modern context. Throughout my years of sharing spiritual wisdom from the Gita and Upanishads, I've observed a recurring pattern: many people accumulate spiritual knowledge but struggle to translate it into lived experience.

Knowledge without application creates a peculiar form of spiritual poverty. You might have all the verses of the Gita, yet still face each day with anxiety, fear of the future, and even blind superstition. This disconnect occurs because we rarely take the time to integrate learning into our daily patterns. The five steps of *pancha kala kriya* are:

abhigamana: approaching divinity

upadana: preparation and collecting

ijya: worship

svadhyaya: spiritual learning

yogadhyana: body-mind connection

In traditional practice, these five steps would occupy an entire day: *abhigamana* in the early morning, *upadana* in early noon, *ijya* at noon, *svadhyaya* in the afternoon, and *yogadhyana* at night. Many orthodox Hindus, as well as *sanyasis* (renunciates), still follow this schedule. But for those of us balancing work, academics, and family life, dedicating an entire day to spiritual practice seems impossible.

That's precisely why we need to adapt these ancient practices to our contemporary reality. The essence remains unchanged, but the implementation becomes practical for modern living. Instead of spreading these five steps throughout the day, we'll condense them into two daily segments—morning and evening —without diluting their transformative power.

> In the morning, we'll practice *abhigamana* (approaching divinity), *upadana* (preparation), and *ijya* (worship).

> In the evening, we'll revisit those three steps in a simplified form, then add *svadhyaya* (spiritual learning) and *yogadhyana* (body-mind connection).

This practical adaptation allows us to maintain spiritual discipline without abandoning our worldly responsibilities.

Remember, spiritual growth doesn't require dramatic life changes or hours of complex rituals. It thrives in small, consistent practices woven thoughtfully into your existing routine. The beauty of *pancha kala kriya* lies in its simplicity and adaptability. A spiritual framework that is both robust enough to transform your consciousness and flexible enough to fit into your busy schedule.

Step 1: *abhigamana* – Approaching divinity

abhigamana means "approaching near," but approaching near to what? It's about approaching our true self, a deity, God, or simply the overall divinity that permeates everything. The practice begins immediately upon waking and focuses on purifying your internal temple (your body and mind) as a preparation for the day ahead.

Each morning presents us with an opportunity, a fresh wave of hope, a chance to reset, to build strength for a peaceful present. The Upanishads describe this wakeful state as *taijasa*, a conscious life filled with light. Our goal is to wake up each day with gratitude, confidence, and faith rather than fear or superstition.

Here are five simple ways to connect with divinity as soon as you wake up. Adopt any one or all of them:

- **Palm Gazing with Mantra:** Before your feet touch the ground, look at your palms and utter *om tat sat*, acknowledging that divinity exists everywhere, including within you.

- **Extended Mantra:** For a more profound connection, you might recite "*karagre vasathe lakshmi, karamadye vignana, kare mule sthitho govinda, prabhate karadarshanam,*" which recognizes that auspiciousness, knowledge, and divine sustenance exist within you.

- **Simple Devotion:** A brief offering to Krishna, the divinity, through the mantra "*om kleem krishnaya govindaya gopi jana vallabhaya.*" By reciting this mantra, you are sending vibrations that connect to the supreme energy.

- **Internal Visualization:** Envision your chosen deity internally rather than relying on external images. Internal visualization builds your spiritual capacity from within rather than creating dependence on external objects.

- **Parental Connection:** Visualize the faces of your parents, acknowledging them as the instruments that have shaped your physical existence, allowing you to experience divinity.

Once you've performed this mental cleansing and divine connection (which takes mere seconds!), stretch your body while still in bed. Express gratitude for this physical vessel that allows you to live purposefully. Take a moment to remember your loved ones, let that bring a smile to your face, and then rise to begin your physical cleansing.

The complete first step, approaching divinity, readies you both mentally and physically for the day ahead.

Step 2: *upadana* — Preparing for the day

upadana means preparing, collecting, and getting ready. In traditional practice, *upadana* would occur at early noon. But for us modern practitioners, we need to adapt, and for that we'll accomplish *upadana* in the morning.

What exactly are we preparing for in this second step? We're preparing for the day's variations and movements, as well as the challenges and opportunities that lie ahead. Still, we're approaching this preparation with a sense of worship, commitment, devotion, and connection to the divine. *upadana* consists of three key elements:

- **Physical Cleansing as Worship:** This fundamental step involves purifying your body through bathing and dental care. As an ancient scripture states, "One should first purify the body by cleansing one's teeth and bathing. Then one should perform a second cleansing through chanting and by relating to divinity." Physical cleanliness serves as a necessary foundation for spiritual development.

- **Mental Cleansing:** After physical preparation comes mental focus. You might meditate for a few minutes, perhaps chanting *om* while exhaling and focusing between your eyebrows. Another approach is to express gratitude to visible forms of divinity, such as the sun.

- **Preparation for Worship:** Finally, gather the basic ingredients for deity worship: water in a small container, flowers (if available), a lamp with a wick and oil, and perhaps food items that have been freshly cooked but not yet consumed. You can substitute food items with fruit or water. Such food offerings, called *naivedyam*, become *prasadam* (or grace of the divine) when consumed after worship.

These three elements—physical cleansing, mental focusing, and gathering worship materials—complete the *upadana* step, readying you for actual worship.

Step 3: *ijya* — The Act of Worship

ijya is the third step in our *pancha kala kriya* journey, and that is the actual act of worship to a deity. However, here's where many misunderstand that worship isn't merely an external action, but rather a state of being or a process of becoming. While performing the ritual aspects, the key is to become immersed in the experience.

Think of it like attending a symphony. You could analyze the technical aspects, noting the tempo, watching the conductor's movements, and observing the musicians' techniques. Alternatively, you could immerse yourself, feeling the music resonate through your body, letting the melodies stir your emotions, and experiencing the complete sensory journey. True worship is this immersion, where we connect deeply with the divine rather than going through the motions. The *ijya* practice consists of five stages:

- *mantra-asana*: Begin with an invocation to connect with the divine. You might recite a mantra like *om krishnaya namah* (I offer my salutations to Lord Krishna) or consult a scriptural book like *vishnu sahasranama* and recite a verse from it that acknowledges the all-pervading, divine source illuminating the universe in all directions with the calm, serene grace of moonlight. If that seems complex, simply reciting *om tat sat* while contemplating these meanings works beautifully.

- *snana-asana*: Using the water prepared during *upadana*, symbolically offer a drop to the deity. The water offering symbolizes both a ceremonial bath for a revered guest and your commitment to approach the day with cleanliness, truthfulness, and non-judgment.

- *alankara-asana*: Decorate the deity with the flowers you prepared and light the lamp. Offering flowers and lighting the lamp symbolize honoring a guest with beauty while representing your readiness to face the day illuminated by spiritual knowledge.

- *naivedyam*: Offer the prepared food items, symbolizing both hospitality to a divine guest and recognition that food itself connects us to universal divinity. After offering, consume it as *prasadam* to receive the divine grace.

- Closing Invocation: Conclude with a verse from the Gita (chapter 18.66) acknowledging that you surrender everything to the divine, recognizing yourself as a custodian rather than an owner, and that complete immersion in divine energy is your true purpose.

After completing these five stages, bow respectfully to the deity before beginning your day. Following this complete practice brings remarkable balance and equanimity to your life, not because you've asked for peace but because, through worship, you've aligned yourself with divinity.

Step 4: *svadhyaya* — Spiritual Learning

The fourth step of our *pancha kala kriya* journey is *svadhyaya*—spiritual learning through listening, reading, and contemplation. Spiritual learning forms an essential part of your daily routine and proves simpler than you might imagine.

But what exactly do we mean by "spirituality"? At its essence, spirituality means becoming one with the spirit. Imagine the universe as a fabric or cloth. We are individual threads within that fabric, all connected by an unseen energy. The universal energy pervades everything, animate and inanimate, revealing the commonality that links all existence.

We refer to the energy of the individual thread as the self-energy or *atman*, while the energy that pervades everything is referred to as the divine or *paramatma*. When we give this divine energy a name and form, we call it *ishvara*, which takes various names, such as Krishna, depending on the cultural context. The love for this divinity is spirituality itself, an unselfish dedication that emerges through truth-seeking.

For most of us with busy lives, finding time for spiritual learning in the morning proves challenging. That's why *svadhyaya* typically occurs in the evening when we can dedicate time to structured learning. Without this practice, we remain in a state of constant spiritual turmoil, experiencing fleeting moments of happiness followed by persistent worry and concern.

Spiritual learning provides an anchor for every action, strengthening your connection to the universal fabric of life. Without it, you become like a thread tearing away from the cloth by being indecisive, fearful, and prone to chronic worry.

The Bhagavad Gita explicitly prescribes *svadhyaya*, or spiritual learning, as an essential practice (chapter 8, verse 8 and chapter 6, verse 35). Spiritual learning doesn't require sitting for hours in ritualistic study. Instead, it's about inquiry and developing awareness and understanding of divinity. Do you recognize the divinity in those with whom you interact? Do you harbor hatred? Do you discriminate based on identity?

Authentic spiritual learning dissolves divisions while acknowledging differences. Differences highlight characteristics for understanding, with righteous characteristics gaining acceptance, while unrighteous behavior remains intolerable. Divisions, however, create harmful "us versus them" mentalities.

Think of differences as adding beautiful colors to the fabric, while divisions tear the cloth apart.

How does this learning occur? Through engaging your senses via reading and listening, followed by contemplation that transforms knowledge into wisdom. In spiritual terminology, this process involves:

sravana (listening)

manana (contemplation)

nidhidyasa (experiencing)

Set aside focused time daily for spiritual reading or listening. Don't worry if you don't grasp the concepts initially. Just listen again and read again. The understanding develops gradually. How can you determine whether a message, video, book, or ritual is truly spiritual? Ask yourself:

After engaging with it, does it instill fear and dependency?

Does it subtly ask you to set aside your intellect in favor of unquestioning belief?

If you answer "yes" to either question, recognize that the material isn't truly spiritual and is not helping you understand your true self, but rather imposing its perspective.

Genuine spiritual wisdom liberates. It's anchored in love based on detachment, and where there's detachment, there's nothing to lose. Attachment always leads to fear of loss. The concept isn't merely theoretical but represents a profound mindset shift: using your house, money, car, and even life itself without unhealthy attachment.

When should you practice spiritual learning? In our practical world, learning can occur at any time. Even routine activities can strengthen your spiritual muscles. The famous parable reminds us that "when washing dishes, one should wash the dishes," in other words, becoming fully immersed in whatever you're doing. As the Gita states (chapter 4, verse 34):

> *tad viddhi pranipatena pariprashnena sevaya upadekshyanti te jnanam jnaninas tattva-darshinah*

> *Approach a spiritual master to inquire and learn the truth. Adopt an attitude of reverence. An enlightened spiritual master imparts righteous knowledge, helping you see beyond names and forms into the cosmic universal person*

Make *svadhyaya* part of your daily practice. Even small steps taken consistently by listening to spiritual messages and integrating them into your life will yield remarkable results.

Step 5: *yogadhyana* — Body-Mind Connection

We've arrived at the final step of our *pancha kala kriya* journey: *yogadhyana*. In contemporary terms, this step establishes the body-mind connection as part of your evening routine and is a simple practice performed for a few minutes before bedtime. The final step proves particularly valuable for those who experience disturbed sleep patterns due to excessive dreaming. *yogadhyana* encompasses two key aspects:

- Gratitude and Grace: Lying in bed, acknowledge in your inner voice that the waking, dreaming, and deep sleep states all exist through divine grace. The brief contemplation connects your daily consciousness to its divine source.

- Explicit Gratitude to the Body: The practice, also known as *yoga nidra*, expresses appreciation for the physical vessel that enables spiritual experience. The process takes only a few minutes:

Lie on your back and begin with the right side of your body. Bring your inner focus to each body part in a clockwise direction, starting with your right foot, then moving to your right thigh, right abdomen, right hand, and so on. Continue to your chest, neck, face, and head, and then down through the left side of your body.

As you focus on each part, maintain a smooth rhythm of inhaling and exhaling without exertion or stress. Most likely, you'll fall asleep before completing the process. This is a natural outcome that demonstrates how a relaxed body-mind state leads to deep sleep, where only the real "you" remains.

Many have unnecessarily complicated *yoga nidra* with elaborate rituals and routines. Keep it simple. Bring awareness to the forefront and remain in a state of being rather than doing.

As Krishna says in the Bhagavad Gita (chapter 2, verse 69):

What others consider a typical day is a night of ignorance for the spiritual seeker, and what all other creatures see as night is a day for the spiritual seeker

Although deeply philosophical, the above statement reveals how the spiritual practitioner breaks through the darkness of ignorance to perceive the daylight of knowledge. Don't worry if you don't immediately grasp this meaning. As your spiritual journey continues, you'll not only understand it intellectually but experience it directly.

Summary: From Spiritual Concepts to Daily Habits

The *pancha kala kriya* offers a beautifully structured approach to spiritual practice that adapts ancient wisdom to modern life.

- Through five simple steps—*abhigamana*, *upadana*, *ijya*, *svadhyaya*, and *yogadhyana* - we create a framework that transforms ordinary days into spiritual journeys.

- We begin our day with *abhigamana*, approaching divinity through intentional morning practices that connect us to our higher selves.

- We continue with *upadana*, preparing ourselves physically, mentally, and spiritually for the day ahead.

- *ijya* follows as we engage in actual worship, not as a mere ritual but as an immersive connection with the divine.

- In the evening, we dedicate time to *svadhyaya*, spiritual learning that strengthens our understanding and dissolves harmful divisions.

- Finally, we close our day with *yogadhyana*, harmonizing body and mind as we prepare for restorative sleep.

- Unlike traditional practices, where these steps might occupy an entire day, the adapted approach fits seamlessly into busy modern schedules. The morning steps take only a few minutes to complete. In contrast, the evening practices require just half an hour. Yet despite their brevity, these practices gradually transform our relationship with ourselves, others, and the divine.

The beauty of *pancha kala kriya* lies in its simplicity and adaptability. It doesn't demand hours of ritualistic practice or extensive theological knowledge. Instead, it offers practical touchpoints throughout the day that anchor us to our spiritual core. With consistent practice, these five steps become second nature and get embedded in our DNA rather than remaining abstract concepts.

Through this discipline, we bridge the gap between spiritual knowledge and lived experience. We move beyond merely knowing spiritual truths to embody them. We manifest confidence instead of fear, connection instead of division, and peace instead of turmoil. We learn to see divinity not just in temples or texts but in every interaction, every challenge, and every moment of our daily lives.

Start Today: Your First Step

If there's one action I encourage you to take right now, it's this: **Start tomorrow morning with *abhigamana*.** Don't wait for the "perfect" time to begin your spiritual journey.

Here's how to begin:

As you wake up, before your feet touch the ground, look at your palms and recite *om tat sat,* acknowledging the divinity within and around you. A straightforward action takes less than ten seconds but sets a powerful tone for your entire day. The most profound transformations begin with the most straightforward steps. Don't procrastinate. The journey of a thousand miles begins with a single step. Everything else will follow naturally as you build this foundation of spiritual discipline.

REMEMBER, SPIRITUAL GROWTH DOESN'T COME FROM GRAND GESTURES BUT FROM SMALL, CONSISTENT PRACTICES. COMMIT TO TAKING THE FIRST STEP OF PANCHA KALA KRIYA TOMORROW MORNING AND EXPERIENCE THE DIFFERENCE IT MAKES IN YOUR LIFE.

God Realization

A SACRED JOURNEY

INNER PEACE RADIATES almost tangibly from specific individuals who maintain unwavering joy despite life's challenges. Have you noticed how some people seem to carry this remarkable serenity with them wherever they go? Inner peace is not just for saints or yogis who have spent decades in meditation, but it is available to each of us through the journey of God realization.

I know what you might be thinking: "God realization sounds like something for deeply religious people, not for someone like me." But here's the beautiful truth you will see emerge in this chapter: God realization is universal and deeply personal at the same time. It doesn't demand theological expertise or years of religious study. Instead, it asks for something much simpler yet profoundly powerful: a willingness to experience the divine nature that exists beyond our everyday perception.

In our modern world, we're constantly chasing modern definitions of success, such as better jobs, bigger homes, and more impressive achievements. We are conditioned to believe that intellectual excellence and material accomplishments are the ultimate goals. But what if our understanding of success has been incomplete all along? What if the most profound form of achievement isn't found in what we can acquire or accomplish but in how deeply we can experience life itself?

In this chapter, we'll explore the transformative journey of God realization, not as an abstract concept or religious doctrine, but as a practical path that can enrich every aspect of your life. We'll discover how God realization doesn't require you to abandon your worldly pursuits but rather infuses them with new meaning and brings unexpected blessings to your professional and personal life.

Let's Dive Deeper

Before we explore the specific stages of God realization, let's understand why this journey holds such profound significance. Many people pursue spiritual practices simply because they are told it's the right thing to do or because they seek relief from suffering. While these motivations can initiate the journey, sustainable spiritual growth requires something more.

What truly transforms us is direct experience, not intellectual understanding alone, not blind faith, but moments of genuine connection with something greater than ourselves. These experiences might come as fleeting glimpses at first. They could show up as a profound sense of peace during meditation, an overwhelming feeling of gratitude while watching a sunset, or a moment of perfect clarity amidst life's chaos. Each of these experiences plants a seed in our consciousness. As we nurture these seeds through continued practice and openness, they grow and eventually bloom into a sustained awareness of the divine presence that permeates all existence.

The beauty of this process is that it doesn't require you to reject your rational mind or scientific understanding. Instead, it enriches your perspective by adding depth and meaning to everything you already know and experience.

As we proceed, I invite you to approach these ideas not just as concepts to be understood but as invitations to experience. Let each word be a doorway rather than merely information. The actual value of what we're exploring together isn't in the knowledge itself but in how it transforms your lived experience day by day.

The True Nature of Success

Let's start by challenging our conventional understanding of success. In academic and professional realms, we're taught that intelligence, expertise, and dedication are the keys to achievement. And yes, a high degree of intellectual excellence certainly helps you climb the corporate ladder or excel in academic pursuits.

But when it comes to spiritual life, to finding lasting fulfillment and inner peace, the requirements are remarkably different. All you need is a genuine willingness to experience the transcendental nature of the divine. The desire to experience transcendence is not about intellectual understanding but about opening your heart to possibilities beyond the material world.

Here's the surprising part: when you dedicate yourself to spiritual growth, you'll often find that success in your professional and personal life naturally follows. Not because you're specifically pursuing it, but because your entire approach to life undergoes a transformation. There's a beautiful paradox at work here—by focusing less on material success and more on spiritual connection, you create a foundation for holistic success in all areas of life.

Spiritual dedication doesn't mean abandoning your ambitions or goals; it means embracing them with a deeper understanding and appreciation. Instead, it means pursuing them from a place of contentment coupled with a passion for evolution. You're no longer driven by fear, insecurity, or the need to prove yourself. Instead, you're motivated by a sense of purpose, gratitude, and a desire to make a meaningful contribution.

The Level Playing Field

One of the most beautiful aspects of spiritual life is its inherent fairness. God puts everyone on a level playing field. Your education, wealth, social status, or even your religious background doesn't give you any special advantage on this journey. The divine doesn't favor the intellectual over the simple-hearted or the wealthy over the poor.

The level playing field of spiritual life is what makes God realization so remarkable. It's not reserved for a select few but is available to anyone with an open heart. The janitor can achieve the same depth of spiritual realization as the CEO, and the high school dropout can experience the same divine connection as the university professor.

The key that unlocks this experience is grace, and grace comes most readily to those who cultivate gratitude. Do you see how beautifully interconnected this process is?

As I've articulated repeatedly, gratitude leads to grace; grace leads to self and God realization, and when that happens, a natural alignment occurs in both your professional and personal life.

The Unfolding Lotus: The Process of Experiencing Divinity

Think of yourself as an unblossomed lotus flower waiting to experience the fullness of divinity. Just as the lotus contains within itself all the potential for its eventual magnificent bloom, you already possess everything needed for your spiritual awakening. The journey is about allowing that inherent potential to unfold.

When you begin to experience divinity, you start to radiate a special kind of energy, like a lotus in full bloom. You glow with grandeur and ecstasy that others can sense, even if they can't quite name it.

It's important to understand that experiencing divinity isn't primarily an intellectual process. It's not something you can prove through scientific methods or adequately capture in words. It's an emotional and experiential journey that transcends our limited vocabulary. *Faith opens the door to comprehending what logic alone cannot grasp.*

Though God realization is ultimately beyond sequential steps, we can describe it as a process to help our understanding:

The First Step: Divine Contemplation

The journey begins when you genuinely contemplate the divine. Starting the journey isn't about forcing religious beliefs or adopting theological positions. It's simply about opening your mind to something greater than yourself.

In this stage, you begin to admire the opulence, grandeur, and supreme divinity of the universe. You find contentment in conversations and thoughts about spiritual matters. Your mind becomes captivated by the possibility of something greater, something divine.

In the words of a mystic poet, "The moment I found love, I gave up my soul, my heart, and my eyes." That's what happens in this first stage, falling in love with the divine. Your thoughts naturally drift toward spiritual matters, not out of obligation but out of genuine attraction. As this attraction deepens, you naturally engage in three practices:

Listening to wisdom about the divine

Chanting or verbally expressing your spiritual connection

Engaging in continued devotion

These practices aren't forced or mechanical; they flow naturally from your growing spiritual interest, just as someone in love naturally wants to talk about and connect with their beloved.

The Second Step: Awakening of the Inner Being

As your love and dedication deepen, something remarkable begins to happen. Your inner being, that part of you that has always been connected to the divine, but perhaps dormant or inaccessible, begins to awaken.

Think of it like a seed sprouting into a sapling. Something hidden and contained suddenly made its presence known. You begin to feel your inner self in a way that was previously impossible.

This stage often brings physical sensations that are difficult to explain. It is a feeling that "gushes through the entire body," a radiance that seems to emanate from within. It's as if divinity is bubbling up like a fountain, "merging through the crevices of a rock." Your being is preparing to receive even deeper grace.

Have you ever experienced moments when you felt inexplicably connected to something greater? Perhaps while watching a sunset, listening to music, or in a moment of profound silence? These might have been glimpses of this second stage.

The Third Step: Divine Intervention and Transformation

The third step represents a profound shift. Here, "the divine intervenes and wipes out the darkness of ignorance through the lamp of divinity and wisdom." Divine intervention isn't something you achieve through effort alone, as it's a gift of grace that transforms you from within. In this stage, you experience a series of paradoxical states:

Attachment with detachment

Desire replaced by a sincere effort

The divine becomes both the path and the destination of every activity

A peaceful calm settles within you. The divine isn't an occasional visitor to your consciousness. It's a constant presence that you see, hear, feel, and experience in all things and at all times. The separation between soul consciousness and body consciousness begins to dissolve. You're not divided between spiritual and physical existence. You experience them as integrated aspects of a unified life. This is the actual state of God realization.

In this realized state, you perceive God as the supreme being with six limitless qualities: Strength, Knowledge, Beauty, Fame, Opulence, and Renunciation. You understand God as a personal being, the creator and sustainer of all things, the master of the universe, and you experience the monotheistic nature of divinity, the oneness that underlies all existence.

The Foundation of Faith and Intellect

It's worth noting that God realization isn't about abandoning your intellect. Instead, it's "a product of faith on a foundation of intellect and vice versa." Your rational mind and your capacity for faith aren't enemies. They're partners in this journey.

Your intellect helps you discern, question, and understand. It keeps you from mindlessly following or succumbing to superstition. But faith allows you to transcend the limitations of pure rationality and experience dimensions of reality that lie beyond what can be measured or proven.

Together, faith and intellect create a balanced approach to spiritual life, one that is neither naively innocent nor coldly skeptical but open, discerning, and alive to the full range of human experience.

Summary: The Interlinked Path to Fulfillment

Let's bring together the key insights from our exploration of God realization. The journey to God realization is accessible to everyone, regardless of intellectual capacity or social standing. It requires not academic excellence but a willingness to experience the transcendental. This journey unfolds in three main stages:

- Divine contemplation, where we begin to think about and love the divine

- Awakening of the inner being, where we start to feel our spiritual nature

- Divine transformation, where grace changes us from within

Throughout this process, we discover that:

- Gratitude leads to grace

- Grace leads to self and God realization

- God realization brings alignment to our professional and personal lives

- The divine becomes both our path and our destination

- Faith and intellect work together rather than in opposition

Perhaps most importantly, we learn that success in spiritual life doesn't require abandoning worldly pursuits. Instead, it infuses those pursuits with new meaning and often brings unexpected blessings to all aspects of our lives.

God realization isn't about escaping the world. It's about experiencing it more deeply, more consciously, and with greater appreciation for its divine nature. It's about becoming fully alive to the miracle of existence and allowing that awareness to transform how you live, work, and relate to others.

Start Here: Your First Step

If there's one action I encourage you to take right now, it's this: **Notice Something Beautiful Every Day.** It doesn't require special knowledge, equipment, or circumstances—just opening your eyes to the wonder that's already around you.

Here's how to begin:

Each day, make it a point to notice one beautiful thing. It might be the way morning light streams through your window, how your child laughs, the kindness in a stranger's smile, or even how good your first sip of coffee tastes.

- When you notice it, pause for just a moment and let yourself feel genuinely appreciative. You might even say a quiet "wow" or "thank you."

- This simple practice does something remarkable: it trains your attention to see abundance instead of scarcity. It opens your awareness to the gifts that surround you, even during difficult times. And most importantly, it creates the perfect conditions for grace to enter your life.

Grace isn't something you can demand or force, but you can prepare your heart to receive it. Noticing beauty is that preparation. It softens your perspective, quiets your worries, and attunes you to the gentle presence of the divine in your everyday experience.

Begin today. Don't wait for perfect understanding or ideal circumstances. The journey of a thousand miles begins with a single step, and appreciating beauty is the most natural first step on your path to God realization.

REMEMBER WHAT WE DISCOVERED EARLIER? "GRACE COMES WHEN WE HAVE GRATITUDE."

Beyond Caste

THE SPIRITUAL ESSENCE OF VARNA

THE BHAGAVAD GITA DESCRIBES CATEGORIES (VARNA) of human nature, representing one of the most misunderstood teachings in ancient wisdom. For centuries, these have been interpreted as a rigid caste system, but that's not what Krishna taught Arjuna. There's something much deeper going on here that speaks directly to human psychology and spiritual development.

Whether you've heard about these categories before or you're encountering them for the first time, the real question is: what was Krishna talking about? Gita's perspective on human nature and purpose offers wisdom that transcends cultural boundaries and speaks directly to our lives today, revealing insights about how we can understand ourselves and our unique path in this world.

Let's Dive Deeper

Let me start by clearing up a fundamental misconception: The Bhagavad Gita doesn't create categories as a rigid social structure based on birth. Such an interpretation, which unfortunately became common practice in specific periods of Indian history, completely misses Krishna's teachings. Krishna advocated a classification based on the nature of one's actions, tendencies, and innate qualities. Think about how we categorize people today. We use demographics all the time, right? Age, gender, income, education, occupation, ethnicity, these are the boxes we typically check on forms and surveys. Marketers use these categories to target us with products. Governments use them to make policies. Political campaigns use them to craft messages.

However, Krishna's categorization in the Gita extends beyond these surface-level groupings. His classification speaks to the essence of human action and purpose, the natural tendencies and qualities that drive our contributions to the world.

What are these four categories about? Let me walk you through them, not as rigid social classes but as different expressions of human nature and purpose.

The *brahmanas*: Our Guiding Light

Picture someone whose primary purpose revolves around seeking truth, cultivating wisdom, and sharing knowledge. Someone who naturally gravitates toward learning, teaching, contemplation, and ethical discernment. That's the essence of the *brahmana* quality.

In ancient times, kings would seek counsel from those embodying the *brahmana* quality before making important decisions. Why? These individuals were unbiased, not swayed by material desires or political pressures. They lived and focused on wisdom.

What's interesting is that society had an understanding that the other three groups would take care of the *brahmana's* basic needs. The support system wasn't about privilege but about freeing these wisdom-keepers from material concerns so they could focus on their important work without conflicts of interest.

I see reflections of the *brahmana* energy in many people who live unassuming lives but transform countless lives through their service and teachings, or in ethical advisors who guide organizations toward more sustainable and humane practices.

The Brahmana quality isn't about intellectual superiority. It's about dedication to truth, wisdom, and ethical clarity that benefits everyone.

The *kshatriyas*: Passionate Protectors

Now imagine someone whose natural tendencies include courage, leadership, protection, and decisive action. Someone who isn't afraid to stand up for what's right, to defend others, to make tough decisions when necessary. That's the *kshatriya* energy.

Historically, these were the warriors and rulers in ancient societies. Please don't get caught up in the literal translation. It is the essence that matters. *kshatriyas* showed courage, confidence, and valor. A *kshatriya* without these qualities wouldn't be effective in their role. They protected people and places, fought when necessary, and maintained order.

Arjuna from the Gita was a *kshatriya* grappling with his duty on the battlefield. His crisis of conscience, stemming from his reluctance to fight against people he respected, is a perfect example of the *kshatriya* wrestling with the responsibilities that come with power.

However, there's something crucial to note—*kshatriyas* didn't act alone. They often took advice from those embodying *brahmana* qualities when developing strategies. It was a balance of power and wisdom.

I see the *kshatriya* spirit in individuals who left lucrative careers to become public defenders, fighting for those who can't fight for themselves. I see it in community leaders who stand up to powerful interests when neighborhoods are threatened. The *kshatriya* energy is about courage and protection, not domination.

The *vaisyas*: Engines of Growth

What about people whose work naturally involves creation, organization, entrepreneurship, and resource management? Those who have a talent for trade, commerce, agriculture, and generating prosperity? These characteristics embody the *vaisya* quality.

The *vaisyas* weren't just businesspeople; they were the economic engine of growth in society. While *kshatriyas* might win battles and expand territories, it was the *vaisyas* who built the financial foundation that made society prosperous. They understood then, as we do now, that an economy's strength and a nation's overall stability and well-being are tightly linked.

I see the *vaisya* energy in entrepreneurs who create jobs while addressing real human needs, in farmers who steward the land while feeding communities, and in business leaders who understand that long-term success comes from making genuine value, not exploiting people or resources.

The *vaisya* quality isn't about greed or materialism. It's about the creative energy that transforms resources into goods and services that enhance our collective well-being.

The *sudras*: The Power of Execution

Finally, consider those whose natural gifts involve consistent, precise execution, like work that's both mentally and physically demanding, requiring attention to detail and reliability. Such abilities represent the *sudra* energy.

The *sudras* were the dedicated workforce, the ones who turned plans into reality through their commitment and hard work. Without their focused execution, the strategies of *brahmana* s, the protection of *kshatriyas*, and the economic initiatives of *vaisyas* would remain just ideas. They made things happen, keeping society functioning through their reliable service.

I see the *sudra* quality in the master craftspeople whose precision and dedication create objects of lasting beauty and utility. I see it in healthcare workers who show up day after day, performing critical tasks with unfailing attention to detail. I see it in the countless essential workers who keep our world running smoothly, often without recognition.

The *sudra* quality isn't about inferiority; it is about the dignity and absolute necessity of skilled execution and service.

The Interdependent Whole

What I find most fascinating about this system is how it recognizes that all four qualities are necessary for a thriving society. Each depends on the others:

- What good is the *brahmana's wisdom without the kshatriya's* courage to implement it?

- What use is the *kshatriyas'* valor without the economic foundation built by the *vaisyas*?

- How would the *vaisyas* create prosperity without the guidance of *brahmana* s and the protection of *kshatriyas*?

- And what would any of it matter without the *sudras* turning plans into reality through dedicated execution?

Gita presents these categories as an interdependent ecosystem where each role carries its dignity and purpose. No single group can succeed without the support of the others. It's not a hierarchy, but rather a recognition of different yet equally necessary forms of contribution.

Our Modern Integration

Here's where many interpretations go wrong: There is no reference in the Gita suggesting that *varna* is determined by birth. None. Zero.

The Gita explicitly emphasizes that actions (*karma*) and natural qualities (*guna*) define us, not our birth. In chapter 4, verse 13, Krishna states that he created the four *varnas* based on *guna* and *karma* (qualities and actions), rather than by family lineage.

The son or daughter of someone who displays *brahmana* qualities might naturally gravitate toward *kshatriya* energy, *vaisya* ingenuity, or *sudra* reliability. Each person finds their path based on their natural tendencies and abilities.

If anyone tries to tell you that the Gita promotes a rigid birth-based caste system, they've missed the essence of Krishna's teaching. The criticism that the Gita is casteist or racist is, quite frankly, incredibly short-sighted and not supported by the actual text. In today's complex world, many of us embody aspects of all four *varnas*, don't we? Think about your own life:

- When you're seeking knowledge, reflecting on ethical questions, or sharing wisdom with others, you're expressing *brahmana* energy.

- When you stand up for yourself or others, make tough decisions, or protect what you value, you're channeling *kshatriya* qualities.

- When you create, organize resources, or build something of value, you're manifesting *vaisya* tendencies.

- And when you execute tasks with precision, provide reliable service, or bring projects to completion, you're embodying *sudra's* strengths.

We might lean more strongly toward one *varna*, but we contain elements of all of them. In doing so, we align with the teachings of the Gita. These aren't rigid boxes but fluid expressions of human nature that we all access in different proportions.

I've noticed this in my own life. As I write this chapter, I'm drawing upon the *brahmana* energy. I certainly tap into *kshatriya* qualities when advocating for others or standing up for myself, *vaisya* skills when managing projects and resources, and *sudra* dedication during execution.

The Spiritual Purpose

At its heart, the Gita's message about these categories is spiritual, not social. It's about understanding that everyone has a role to play based on their natural qualities (*gunas*) and the work they're suited for (*karma*). The goal isn't social stratification. It is each person's responsibility to fulfill their purpose with righteousness (*dharma*).

The aim? Self-realization, divine-realization, and spiritual growth. The Gita teaches that by performing our natural duties with dedication and without excessive attachment to outcomes, we advance on our spiritual journey.

In chapter 18, verse 45, Krishna makes this clear: *"By devotion to one's particular duty, a person can attain perfection. Hear now how one can attain perfection by devotion to their natural duty."*

The spiritual message here is profound: Your path to growth and realization lies not in trying to be someone else or performing duties that are misaligned with your nature but in embracing your authentic qualities and expressing them with skill and devotion.

Summary: Wisdom of *varna* for Today

As we've explored in this chapter, Gita's teachings on *varna* offer wisdom that extends far beyond rigid social classifications. They provide a framework for understanding the diverse yet equally necessary ways we contribute to society based on our natural tendencies and abilities.

- The four *varnas—brahmana, kshatriya, vaisya, and sudra—* represent different expressions of human nature, rather than hierarchical social positions. They highlight the wisdom-seeker, the protector, the creator, and the executor, all essential aspects of a functioning whole.

- The Gita makes it clear that actions determine these qualities, not birth. Realization liberates us from rigid social structures and invites us to discover and express our authentic nature.

- In our modern context, we often embody different aspects of all four *varnas*, adapting our expression to what each situation requires. Such flexibility aligns perfectly with the Gita's emphasis on discerning and fulfilling our dharma, which is our righteous duty in each moment.

- The more profound spiritual teachings remind us that by performing our natural duties with dedication and without excessive attachment to the results, we advance on our path toward self-realization. It's not about what work you do, but the spirit in which you do it.

Understanding *varna* in this way helps us appreciate the diverse ways we all contribute to life's tapestry. It encourages respect for all forms of work and contribution rather than elevating some and diminishing others. And it invites each of us to discover and express our authentic nature as our spiritual practice.

The understanding transcends cultural, religious, and temporal boundaries, speaking to our universal human need to find meaningful work that aligns with our nature and contributes to the greater good.

Start Today: Your First Step

If there's one action I encourage you to take right now, it's this: **Reflect on Your Natural Work Alignment.**

Here's how to begin:

Take a moment, even five minutes, to sit quietly and reflect on the type of work that brings you the most fulfillment and aligns with your true nature. Ask yourself these questions:

- Which of the four *varna* qualities do I express most naturally?

- Wisdom-seeking and ethical discernment (*brahmana*)

- Protection, leadership, and courageous action (*kshatriya*)

- Creation, organization, and resource management (*vaisya*)

- Execution, service, and reliable implementation (*sudra*)

Are there activities I'm currently engaged in that feel misaligned with my natural tendencies? How might I approach these with a different perspective, shifting my energy to work more in alignment with my goals? Then, identify one small action you can take tomorrow that honors your natural *dharma*.

It could be carving out time for learning and reflection if you resonate with *brahmana* energy, standing up for someone if you feel *kshatriya* qualities, initiating a creative project if *vaisya* aspects call to you, or bringing exceptional care to your work if *sudra* elements speak to you.

By honoring your natural tendencies while recognizing and respecting the different yet equally necessary qualities in others, you participate in the profound interdependence that Krishna describes —the foundation of a harmonious society and a fulfilled individual life. What will your dharma look like tomorrow?

REMEMBER, THE BEAUTY OF GITA'S TEACHING IS THAT YOUR DHARMA ISN'T SOMETHING DISTANT OR ABSTRACT; IT'S AVAILABLE TO YOU RIGHT NOW, IN THIS MOMENT, THROUGH THE CHOICES YOU MAKE AND THE SPIRIT IN WHICH YOU MAKE THEM.

PART SIX

Awakening Your Yogic Potential

The Silent Termites of the Mind

THE FIVE-STEP PATH TO DESTRUCTION AND HOW TO AVOID IT

SELF-IMPROVEMENT TYPICALLY FOCUSES on recipes for success, like how to achieve more, accumulate wealth, find happiness, or cultivate better relationships. Bookstores are filled with guides promising the secrets to a better life. But have you ever considered studying the path to destruction? It might sound counterintuitive, but understanding exactly how we sabotage ourselves can be one of the most powerful ways to avoid those very pitfalls.

Chapter 2, verses 62 and 63 of the Bhagavad Gita, provide us with exactly what we're looking for. A detailed roadmap of mental deterioration that Krishna describes as a five-step path to destruction. It's like having access to a detailed diagram of every trapdoor and hidden danger in a challenging journey. With this knowledge, we can navigate life with greater awareness and intentionality.

Let's Dive Deeper

I've come to think of the Gita as the ultimate MBA program for life management. While traditional MBA programs teach us how to manage businesses, the Gita teaches us how to manage something far more complex, our minds. And when it comes to mental management, understanding the diseases of the mind is as crucial as understanding healthy mental states.

These diseases are hazardous because they're difficult to diagnose. Unlike physical ailments that prompt us to seek medical attention, mental afflictions often go unnoticed until significant damage has occurred. With physical illness, the patient and the doctor are separate, but with mental afflictions, they're the same person. How can we objectively diagnose ourselves when the very tool we're using for diagnosis, the mind, is what's compromised?

In this chapter, we'll explore this five-step path to destruction that Krishna outlines, not to become experts in failing but to become skilled at recognizing the early warning signs of mental deterioration before we've gone too far down that path. Then, we'll discover the practical steps we can take to avoid these pitfalls and cultivate mental clarity and peace instead.

The Five-Step Path to Destruction

Krishna's wisdom reveals a cascading process that begins subtly but ends catastrophically. Let's trace this path step by step:

Step 1: Contemplation of Objects

It all begins innocently enough, starting with our attention. Our focus shapes our minds, our desires, and, ultimately, our destiny. In today's world, our attention is constantly being pulled in numerous directions, including advertisements, social media, news, entertainment, and the endless stream of stimuli competing for our mental energy.

When Krishna speaks of "contemplation of objects," he refers to the fixation of our awareness of things outside ourselves. These include material possessions, status symbols, physical appearances, or experiences we desire to have. There's nothing inherently wrong with noticing these things. The problem begins when simple awareness transforms into persistent contemplation, when these objects occupy an increasing amount of mental real estate, or, as I like to call it, an expanding amount of "brain space". In this context, persistent undesirable contemplation marks the first seemingly innocent step on the path toward mental deterioration.

Step 2: Attachment

Continued undesirable contemplation naturally leads to attachment. We begin to develop emotional investment in these objects. We start thinking in terms of "mine" and "not mine," defining ourselves by what we possess or hope to possess.

The attachment doesn't appear to be dangerous. It often disguises itself as passion or commitment. After all, wouldn't you agree that without some level of attachment, how could we care enough about anything to pursue it with dedication?

However, there is a crucial difference between healthy dedication and attachment, as Krishna describes it. Healthy dedication enables us to work toward a goal while maintaining our perspective and inner balance. Attachment, on the other hand, begins to define our sense of self and worth based on external objects or achievements.

Step 3: Desire

From attachment springs desire, the intense craving to possess, experience, or achieve what we've become attached to. Desires in themselves aren't problematic; they're natural aspects of human knowledge. But when fueled by attachment, desires take on a different quality.

They become less about natural preference and more about perceived necessity. The language of our inner dialogue shifts from "I would like this" to "I need this." The stakes feel higher, and the emotional investment grows deeper.

What makes this stage particularly tricky is that our society often celebrates unrestrained desire, equating it with ambition and drive. We're encouraged to "want more," never to be satisfied, and continuously to pursue the next thing. However, Krishna's wisdom reveals that when desire stems from attachment, it creates a troubling loop: momentary satisfaction upon achieving a desire quickly leads to increased craving, which in turn reinforces attachment, generating more desire.

Over time, this cycle transforms natural desire into something more problematic, manifesting as greed. We're no longer responding to authentic needs or healthy aspirations but to a compulsive drive that's never satisfied, regardless of what we acquire or achieve.

Step 4: Anger

When our desires meet obstacles, and they inevitably will, the result is anger. Such disturbance doesn't necessarily manifest as outward rage or violence. Krishna is referring to something more subtle: the disturbance of inner mental peace that occurs when reality doesn't align with our expectations.

Anger may manifest as frustration, irritation, resentment, or even depression. The common thread is that our inner harmony is disrupted by the gap between what we want and what is. The anger that Krishna describes is any form of internal resistance to the present reality.

Over time, this anger compounds. Each unfulfilled desire or unmet expectation adds another layer of dissatisfaction until it begins to color our entire worldview. We become more easily triggered, less patient, and increasingly dissatisfied with life as it is.

Step 5: Bewilderment Leading to Destruction

Here's where the real damage occurs. Krishna tells us that anger impairs our perspective, decision-making, and judgment. It's like a layer of dust covering a mirror, obscuring our clear view. Our emotions take center stage, overriding rational thought.

Impaired judgment creates a state of bewilderment, characterized by feelings of disorientation and confusion, where we struggle to make sense of our experiences. Our intellectual capacity to function effectively begins to erode. Like silent termites, this mental disarray creeps into our faculties, gradually compromising our ability to think clearly and make wise choices.

The ultimate result is what Krishna calls destruction, not necessarily physical death, but the death of peace, perspective, and purpose. Happiness becomes distant, while fear, insecurity, dissatisfaction, hatred, and a complaining mindset take over. We've arrived at the destination of the five-step path, and it's a place of suffering, akin to a living hell.

The Loop of Mental Deterioration

What makes this process particularly dangerous is that it doesn't move in just one direction but creates a self-reinforcing loop.

Bewilderment leads to poor decisions, which produce more unfulfilled desires, which in turn generate more anger, which further deepens bewilderment. The cycle accelerates, pulling us into an increasingly negative spiral.

Due to the accelerating cycle, many people find themselves stuck in patterns of unhappiness despite their best intentions. They're caught in this loop without realizing it, trying to treat the symptoms (sadness, stress, anxiety) without addressing the root cause, which is the initial contemplation and attachment that set the entire process in motion.

The Way Out: Krishna's Solution

What's the solution? Should we renounce all desires and live like ascetics, avoiding any attachment to the world? Not according to Krishna. In verse 64, he offers a more nuanced approach that acknowledges the reality of living in the world while maintaining inner freedom.

The key lies not in giving up our engagement with life but in changing our relationship with it. Krishna advises us to be fully engaged, utilizing our senses and faculties, but without becoming entangled in the web of attachment and aversion.

In a simple sense, we can pursue goals, enjoy experiences, and even own possessions, but we do so without allowing these things to define our identity or sense of self-worth. We maintain a healthy distance between who we are and what we have or do.

Think of it as the difference between swimming in the ocean versus being swept away by it. Both involve being in the water, but one is a position of engagement with control, while the other is a state of helplessness.

Practical Steps to Avoid the Path of Destruction

While Krishna's solution is profound, it can also seem challenging to implement. How exactly do we engage with the world without becoming attached? How can we desire things without letting them control us? Let me offer some practical steps that can help us begin this journey:

1. Practice Incremental Detachment

Begin by releasing attachments to at least some aspects of your life. You don't need to become a renunciate overnight—begin with small steps. Identify one or two things that you can let go of today and gradually increase that portfolio over time.

The key is to start with something small but meaningful, something that pleases your senses but isn't essential to your overall experience. Perhaps it's reducing your intake of sweets, delaying the impulse to buy something when you walk into a store, or spending one evening a week without checking social media.

Each small act of letting go helps weaken the habit of attachment and strengthens your capacity for inner freedom. Over time, these small acts accumulate into a significant shift in how you relate to the external world.

2. Create Space for Spiritual Connection

Even if it's just a few minutes a day, redirect your mind toward spiritual pursuit. Apply the brakes to your busy life and step out of the rat race of the transactional world. Spiritual connection doesn't necessarily mean formal religious practice. It could be meditation, contemplative reading, time in nature, or any activity that connects you with something larger than your concerns.

The crucial element here is not just learning spiritual concepts but applying them. Knowledge without implementation remains merely theoretical. Choose one principle or practice that resonates with you and commit to integrating it into your daily life.

Regular spiritual connection helps recalibrate your awareness, pulling it back from excessive contemplation of objects and redirecting it toward more lasting values and perspectives.

3. Engage in Selfless Service

Dedicate an hour each week away from your routine to help someone else or contribute to your community selflessly. Selfless service directly counteracts the self-centered focus that drives the path to destruction.

When we serve others without expectation of personal gain, we temporarily step outside the loop of desire and attachment. We experience a different kind of satisfaction, one that doesn't feed the cycle of craving but helps dissolve it.

Selfless service also provides a valuable perspective shift. Many of our attachments and desires shrink in importance when we witness the challenges others face and experience the joy of making a positive difference in their lives.

Summary: Conquering the Mental Termites

As we've explored in this chapter, the Bhagavad Gita offers us profound insights into how our minds can either lead us toward peace and clarity or down a path of destruction.

- The five-step process Krishna describes—contemplation of objects, attachment, desire, anger, and bewilderment— creates a cascade of mental deterioration that ultimately robs us of happiness and purpose.

- But understanding this process gives us power. By recognizing the early warning signs, especially excessive contemplation of external objects and growing attachment, we can interrupt the cycle before it gains momentum. We can choose a different relationship with our desires, engaging with life fully while maintaining inner freedom.

- The practical steps we've discussed: incremental detachment, spiritual connection, and selfless service, provide concrete ways to begin this journey. These aren't just techniques; they're invitations to a fundamentally different way of living—one where we're no longer driven by attachment and craving but guided by wisdom and purpose.

- The mental illnesses that Krishna describes are indeed challenging to diagnose, especially since the patient and the doctor are the same person. But with the map he provides, we can develop greater self-awareness and catch these mental termites before they cause severe damage.

Start Here: The Attachment Inventory

If there's one action I encourage you to take right now, it's this: **Conduct what I call an Attachment Inventory.** Your inventory isn't about judging yourself or forcing yourself to give up things you care about. It's about developing awareness of where your mental energy is flowing and how that flow might be affecting your peace and clarity.

Here's how to begin:

Set aside 15-20 minutes of uninterrupted time with a blank sheet of paper.

- Create three columns on your page: "Object of Attachment," "Nature of Desire," and "Emotional Response When Blocked."

- In the first column, list the things, experiences, or outcomes you find yourself thinking about frequently. These might be material possessions, achievements, relationships, or even certain emotions or states of being you crave.

- In the second column, describe the quality of your desire for each item. Is it a gentle preference or a consuming need? Does it feel like something that would be nice to have or something you must have to be happy?

- In the third column, honestly assess how you react when your pursuit of each item is blocked or delayed. Do you experience mild disappointment, or does it trigger significant anger, frustration, or dejection?

- Now, review your list and circle the items where your desire feels intense, and your emotional response to obstacles is strong. These are your current danger zones—areas where the five-step path may already be in motion.

- Choose just one circled item to work with over the next week. Practice consciously loosening your grip on this particular attachment. When you notice yourself contemplating it, gently redirect your attention. When you feel desire arising, acknowledge it without feeding it. If you encounter obstacles, practice accepting them with equanimity.

By starting with just one attachment and practicing a different relationship with it, you begin to develop the inner muscles needed for the kind of engagement Krishna describes, fully present but not bound by craving and aversion.

Try this attachment inventory today and revisit it each month. Over time, you'll likely notice a shift not only in specific attachments but in your overall relationship with desire and expectation. You'll be taking a concrete step off the path of destruction and onto the path of freedom and clarity that the Gita illuminates.

REMEMBER, THE GOAL ISN'T TO ELIMINATE DESIRE OR DISENGAGE FROM LIFE. IT'S TO ENGAGE IN A WAY THAT MAINTAINS OUR FREEDOM AND CLARITY. IT'S TO SWIM IN THE OCEAN OF EXPERIENCE WITHOUT BEING SWEPT AWAY BY IT. IT'S TO ENJOY THE WORLD WITHOUT BECOMING ENSLAVED BY IT.

The *yogi* and *sanyasi*

ACTION WITH DETACHMENT

TWO SEEMINGLY CONTRADICTORY IDEAS about spiritual life often create confusion for sincere seekers. On the one hand, we hear about renunciation and withdrawal from worldly affairs. On the other hand, there is guidance that we can be spiritual while fully engaged in the world. Which path is correct? Must we choose between being in the world or apart from it?

These questions aren't new. For years, there has been debate, and this is especially relevant today when many of us are seeking deeper meaning while navigating busy and complex lives. The good news is that the ancient wisdom of the Bhagavad Gita offers clarity on this very dilemma through its exploration of two spiritual archetypes: the *sanyasi* and the *yogi*.

In this chapter, we'll explore these two paths, with a particular focus on the *yogi's* path. Why focus on the yogic path? For three important reasons:

> First, the yogic state represents an elevated stage in anyone's spiritual journey.

> Second, and perhaps most importantly for most of us, we can aspire to become a *yogi* while continuing our daily work and responsibilities.

> And third, as Krishna clearly states in the Gita, the *yogi* is considered superior to the *sanyasi* or ascetic.

Let's Dive Deeper

This exploration will be liberating for many of you who've felt that profound spirituality is incompatible with an engaged life. Let's discover together how action with detachment can transform ordinary living into a spiritual practice of the highest order.

The Way of the *sanyasi*: The Path of Renunciation

Before we dive deeply into the yogic path, let's first understand what it means to be a *sanyasi*. A *sanyasi* is someone who has renounced work motivated by desire and greed. Their lives are reduced to the bare essentials needed to sustain physical existence, with no explicit pursuit of worldly goals or achievements.

The primary focus of a *sanyasi* is to be established in the Yoga of Knowledge—the precepts and components of a meaningful life guided by *dharma* and righteousness. They study scriptures, contemplate philosophical truths, and immerse themselves in spiritual practices that cultivate direct knowledge of reality.

In essence, the defining characteristic of the *sanyasi* is the practice of continued renunciation. They withdraw from worldly engagement to focus exclusively on spiritual realization.

The Way of the *yogi*: The Path of Engaged Detachment

In contrast to the *sanyasi*, a *yogi* maintains engagement with the world while transforming the nature of that engagement. A *yogi* not only performs the minimal work needed for physical sustenance but also engages in activities that pursue various worthwhile goals. These are actions that benefit society, create prosperity for oneself and one's family, and contribute to the greater good.

What distinguishes a *yogi* from any ordinary person isn't the outward activities but the inner attitude. The *yogi* considers every activity to be both the means and the end in itself, practicing detachment from results while remaining fully present in the action. Through this detachment, the *yogi* follows the path of righteous action (Karma Yoga).

Unlike the *sanyasi*, who explicitly focuses on the Yoga of Knowledge through study and contemplation, the *yogi* embodies that knowledge through action. The *yogi* does not make a special effort to learn spiritual wisdom because they demonstrate such wisdom through their daily actions and lifestyle. You might say that a *yogi* has a direct, experiential understanding of the true nature of life itself.

Selfish interests and motivations aren't traits of a *yogi*. While the means for becoming a *sanyasi* is renunciation, the means for becoming a *yogi* is activity, but activity of a particular quality.

The great philosopher Bhagavad Ramanuja expressed this beautifully when he said, "You can describe a person as rich not because of the wealth in lockers but the life of peace and contentment the person leads." Just as hoarding wealth has no meaning for a person of contentment, the *yogi* doesn't hoard theoretical and scriptural knowledge but demonstrates spiritual maturity through living a righteous life.

The Two Essential Practices of a *yogi*

The yogic life is maintained through two main practices that every *yogi* executes daily:

Following a meditative path

Practicing moderation

Let's explore each of these in more depth.

The Meditative Path

The great philosopher Acharya Madhwa explains, "Relinquishing thoughts and attachment to sense objects, you enter a realization of all being under the control of divine energy, and in that stage, you have reached the goal of the meditative path."

This doesn't mean that a *yogi* sits in meditation all day. Instead, as the *yogi* focuses on the self and the supreme through regular meditation practice, they become aware of an incomparable and priceless enjoyment. The deepening of such tranquility allows the *yogi* to maintain detachment and freedom from desire throughout ordinary activities.

The *yogi* achieves a practical meditative state that persists throughout daily activities. Even while doing regular work, their energy is channeled toward self-inquiry and directed to the divine. Krishna in the Gita compares this meditative state to a bright lamp in a windless place, steady and without flicker, emitting light all around and dispelling darkness and ignorance.

In this meditative state, love and devotion envelop the individual. The characteristics and activities of such a person are termed "*archana*" or "to honor." The *yogi* brings honor to all activities by infusing them with meditative awareness.

The Practice of Moderation

The second essential practice of a *yogi* is moderation, which, by its very nature, requires restraint. When restraint is by choice rather than force, the individual develops the ability to control their senses and their attachment to sense objects.

Think about it like this: just as a tortoise pulls itself into its shell when needed, the *yogi* develops the ability to pull inward at will. Like a bird that flies in all directions but then comes to rest on its perch, the *yogi* brings their sense organs to rest when appropriate. Physically, the *yogi* remains present, but spiritually, they can withdraw like a tortoise.

When this practice of moderation matures, the *yogi*'s mental and physical states become saturated with unalloyed, unadulterated, and unperturbed happiness, like the fragrance of perfume or the embers from an incense stick filling a room.

At regular intervals throughout the day, the *yogi* explicitly tries to "pull into a shell" while still engaged with the world. It is not a permanent withdrawal but a temporary recalibration that refreshes their connection to deeper realities.

The Yogic State: A Gradual Process

Entering the yogic state is a gradual process that begins with settling into a proper posture. The *yogi* prepares for meditation by sending subtle commands to the intellect to take control. The intellect then takes over the command center of the brain and starts disengaging the sense organs from their objects, one sense at a time.

After all the sense organs are disengaged, the *yogi* enters a blissful and tranquil state that cannot be described in words but only experienced; this is the "yogic state" in its fullness. In this state, an internal cleansing begins that eradicates indecisiveness, lack of mental peace, agony, and other forms of mental suffering (what some traditions broadly label as "sins").

As this cleansing progresses, the undesirable material modes of passion (*rajas*) and ignorance (*tamas*) get destroyed, leaving only pureness (*sattva*). The *yogi* can emerge from this state at will by letting each sense organ re-engage with the world, like a process of reverse osmosis.

Remarkably, even after emerging from the formal yogic state, the individual continues to experience tranquility and bliss. The qualities cultivated in deep meditation keep rising to the surface and radiating through the *yogi*:

- Their face shines with a special radiance

- A sense of calm prevails around them

- Their voice becomes soothing and melodious

- Anxiety takes a back seat in their presence

- Profound sorrow shies away from making an appearance, bowing to the resolute powers of the *yogi*'s intellect

This yogic state represents the purest form an individual can experience, yet it's not disconnected from everyday life. It transforms life from within.

The Foundation: Understanding Your True Nature

Before closing our exploration, we must address a critical question: Can you ever become a *yogi* if you're still stuck in the quagmire of thinking that the body is the real "you"?

Krishna's answer is clear: Never. To become a *yogi*, the first step is to remember that the body is like your car, and the real you is the fuel that powers it. Without this foundational understanding, all spiritual practices remain superficial.

Summary: The Path of the *yogi*

Let's take a moment to gather the essential insights from our exploration of the yogic path.

- The way of the *yogi* offers a spirituality that doesn't require withdrawal from the world but rather a transformation of how we engage with it.

- Unlike the *sanyasi*, who renounces worldly activity to focus exclusively on spiritual knowledge, the *yogi* embraces activity while maintaining inner detachment. Such detachment isn't cold indifference but rather full engagement with presence and commitment while letting go of attachment to results.

- The yogis maintain their path through two essential daily practices: following a meditative path and practicing moderation. Through meditation, the *yogi* cultivates a tranquil awareness that begins to permeate all aspects of their activities. Through moderation, they develop the ability to control their senses and withdraw their attention inward at will, like a tortoise pulling into its shell.

- As these practices mature, the *yogi* enters the yogic state—a condition of profound tranquility and bliss that cleanses the mind of agitation and negativity. The yogic state initially requires conscious effort to achieve, but eventually becomes the *yogi*'s natural way of being, radiating through their presence, voice, and actions.

- Importantly, the foundation for all yogic development is the recognition that you are not your body. Without this understanding, true yogic consciousness remains inaccessible. With it, the journey unfolds naturally, allowing you to engage fully with life while maintaining inner freedom.

The beauty of the yogic path is that it's accessible to everyone, regardless of life circumstances. You don't need to retreat to a monastery or abandon your responsibilities. You need to transform how you relate to those responsibilities, infusing them with awareness and detachment. As Krishna emphasizes in the Gita, this makes the path of the *yogi* superior to that of the *sanyasi*—it's spirituality that embraces life rather than withdrawing from it.

Start Today: Your First Step

If there's one action I encourage you to take right now, it's this: **Create a "Daily zone experience"** where you deliberately enter a yogic state, even if just for a few minutes. No elaborate preparation or perfect conditions are needed. You can begin right where you are.

Here's how to begin:

Choose a specific time each day—perhaps first thing in the morning, during your lunch break, or before bed, and set aside 5-10 minutes. Find a comfortable seated position, close your eyes, and begin by acknowledging that you are not your body but the consciousness that animates it.

Then, systematically withdraw your attention from external stimuli. Notice sounds without attaching to them. Feel bodily sensations without judgment. Observe thoughts as they arise without following their stories. Gradually, like the tortoise pulling into its shell, draw your awareness inward to a still point of quiet observation.

Don't worry about achieving a perfect state of meditation. The aim isn't to achieve some idealized experience but to practice the deliberate withdrawal and focusing of attention that characterizes yogic consciousness. Even a few minutes of this practice daily will begin to cultivate the qualities of a *yogi*. Start today right where you are, and trust in the natural unfolding of your yogic potential.

REMEMBER KRISHNA'S ENCOURAGEMENT: "WHEN POSSIBLE, GET INTO THE ZONE OF RELINQUISHING THOUGHTS AND ATTACHMENT TO ENTER A STATE OF REALIZATION." THE EFFORTS AND EFFECTS ARE CUMULATIVE—IT'S NOT ALL OR NOTHING.

Yogic Evolution

MOST OF US KNOW THAT BECOMING A YOGI means changing how we see the world, but the actual steps along the way aren't always clear. It's like starting a hike without knowing the trail markers. Luckily, the ancient yogic traditions don't leave us guessing.

The Bhagavad Gita, amplified by the great seer Shri Yamunacharya, outlines a clear progression of four distinct stages that mark the yogi's evolution. The stages show us how we transform from beginners to fully awakened beings. Consider it to be your spiritual roadmap, revealing not just where "you're headed" but also "how to recognize" when you've reached important milestones along the way.

Let's Dive Deeper

Let's embark on this exploration together, examining each stage with care and contemplating its meaning for our spiritual journey. Whether you're just beginning your practice or have been on the path for decades, understanding these four stages will provide valuable context for your experiences and aspirations.

I invite you to approach this chapter with patience and an open mind. As with many profound spiritual teachings, these concepts are usually not absorbed in a single reading. You might find yourself returning to these pages multiple times, discovering new layers of meaning with each visit. That's perfectly normal and even expected when exploring the depths of yogic wisdom.

Stage One: Recognizing Unity in Diversity

The first stage of yogic evolution marks a fundamental shift in how we perceive ourselves and others. At this stage, the yogi begins to see themselves in all other selves and all other selves in themselves.

Let me explain what this means. Ordinarily, we move through the world with a strong sense of separation, thinking "I am me, and you are you." We emphasize differences in appearance, personality, abilities, and beliefs. But the first-stage yogi begins to recognize something deeper beneath these surface distinctions.

It's like a gemologist examining different diamonds. A novice might focus on the apparent differences, noting that one is larger, another has a different cut, and a third has a slight tint. But the trained gemologist sees beyond these variations to recognize their essential sameness: "The second one is the same as the first one but of a different shape, size, and characteristics," knowing very well that in themselves, they are all diamonds.

Similarly, the first-stage yogi has mastered the art of discrimination, not in the sense of judgment or prejudice, but in the sense of discerning the true nature of things. They recognize that while our actions and karma make us unique individuals, we share a common essence. We are different expressions of the same fundamental reality.

Once recognized, equanimity naturally establishes itself in the yogi's heart. They no longer react differently to different people based on superficial characteristics or personal history. Instead, they perceive the interconnectedness of all beings, like various threads woven into a single, seamless fabric. Different colors and textures, yes, but all parts of the same cloth.

However, the yogi doesn't become blind to individuality. Instead, they hold two truths simultaneously: the truth of our unique expressions and the truth of our shared essence. Balanced perception becomes the cornerstone for all subsequent stages of yogic development.

Stage Two: Discovering the Divine Presence

Building on the insights of the first stage, the yogi now expands their contemplation from individual beings to the divine itself. Having recognized the common essence in all individuals, they begin to explore the relationship between this essence and the supreme divine.

The yogi contemplates: If the supreme divine is undisturbed by karma or actions, meaning it is free from karma, then isn't an individual soul that is severed or disconnected from karma also like the divine? A revolutionary insight emerges: the yogi begins to see all beings as part of the divine and the divine in all beings.

But the contemplation doesn't stop there. The yogi goes a step further and realizes: "If I see the divine in all beings and all beings in the divine, how can the divine ever be out of my sight?" At once, the yogi's relationship with spirituality undergoes a complete transformation. The yogi stops searching for the divine as something distant or separate and recognizes its immediate presence.

Like a curious child, the yogi then wonders: "Does the divine see me the same way I see the divine?" And their spiritual maturity provides the answer: "Yes, the divine is in all beings. I'm always connected to the divine. The divine entity is always seeing me, and I am never out of its sight." In this second stage, the yogi experiences a profound sense of being held in the divine gaze. The burden of "finding God" is lifted as they realize they have always been found, always been seen, and always been known by the divine. Deep peace and security naturally follow.

A significant shift occurs in the yogi's relationship with spirituality. As the great philosopher Bhagavad Ramanuja beautifully expressed: "When you surrender to divinity in a name and form like *narayana,* it is his responsibility to take care of you and not your responsibility to seek His protection."

Stage Three: Understanding Universal Energy

Having moved from recognizing the common essence in individuals (first stage) to awareness of divine presence (second stage), the yogi now explores the very nature of the soul or energy that animates the universe.

In this third stage, the yogi comes to a profound realization: the pervasiveness of an atomic soul like ours occurs through a flow of energy. When severed or detached from karma or action, that pervasive knowledge is the same for the individual soul, any other soul, or even a supreme divine soul.

In simpler terms, the yogi recognizes that the fundamental energy driving the universe is common to all beings. Beyond mere intellectual understanding, direct experience emerges through meditation. The yogi experiences the unified field of consciousness that underlies all apparent diversity.

What's remarkable about this stage is that the learning becomes so deeply ingrained that it persists even outside of formal meditation. The yogi's mind remains in unison with everything around them during ordinary activities. As the yogi's awareness stabilizes in this unified perspective, the boundaries between meditation and daily life begin to dissolve.

Previous insights now reach profound new depths. Unity isn't just a philosophical concept or a momentary experience during meditation, but rather the yogi's ongoing reality. They live from the awareness of the common energy that flows through all forms of existence.

Stage Four: Transcending Duality

In the fourth and highest stage, the yogi attains complete liberation. They can reason out and apply all the previous three stages under any physical or emotional condition. Neither sorrow nor joy can mask or distort their perception of reality.

A great seer once said that in this fourth stage, the yogi is beyond pain and pleasure: "The experience from the loss of his son is no more harsh or painful than the loss of the son of a stranger." Individual differences remain visible to the awakened practitioner. Instead, their compassion extends equally to all beings without the usual intensification that comes with personal attachment.

At this level, the yogi has reached the highest elevation of spirituality and can be considered a mystic. Preferences, attachments, or aversions no longer cloud their perception. They see reality as it is, without the distortions of personal desire or fear.

An individual who has become a yogi and passes through all four stages is completely liberated and realizes they have attained *moksha*. They remain in the world but are no longer bound by its limitations. Their consciousness has expanded beyond the confines of individual identity to embrace the totality of existence.

The complete fulfillment of the yogic journey arrives in the fourth stage. It is what the ancient texts refer to as self-realization or enlightenment. While it may seem distant from our current experience, tradition assures us that it is the natural culmination of consistent practice and progressive development through the earlier stages.

Summary: The Ladder of Spiritual Ascension

The journey of a yogi unfolds through four distinct stages, each building upon the insights and stability of the previous ones. Each stage unfolds organically, reflecting the expansion of consciousness through dedicated spiritual practice.

- In the first stage, we recognize the common essence that unites all beings despite their apparent differences. We see ourselves in others and others in ourselves, establishing an initial sense of unity and equanimity. Armed with foundational insight, we can move beyond the rigid boundaries of separate identities that cause so much conflict and suffering.

- The second stage deepens this understanding as we begin to recognize the divine presence pervading all existence. We realize that the divine isn't something distant to be sought but is immediately present in all beings, including ourselves. No longer do we search for something distant; instead, we recognize what has always been present.

- In the third stage, we come to understand the nature of the universal energy or consciousness that animates all forms. Moving beyond intellectual understanding, the insight becomes a lived experience, persisting even outside formal meditation. The boundaries between spiritual practice and daily life begin to dissolve as we remain established in awareness of this universal essence.

- Finally, in the fourth stage, we transcend all remaining limitations of conditioned perception. Neither pleasure nor pain, gain nor loss can disturb our recognition of the underlying reality. We achieve complete liberation, or *moksha*, by living in the world but free from its bondage, seeing clearly without the distortions of personal preference or aversion.

We begin to see the elegant design underlying yogic spiritual development. It isn't a matter of all-or-nothing enlightenment but a gradual unfolding of awareness through discernible stages. Each stage represents a significant shift in perception, a widening of the lens through which we view existence. While the fourth stage may seem distant from our current experience, the Gita assures us that it is attainable through dedicated practice and the grace that naturally flows from sincere spiritual effort.

Start Today: Your First Step

If there's one action I encourage you to take right now, it's this: **Foster Common Thread Vision.**

Here's how to begin:

Each day for the next week, deliberately look for the common essence in the people you encounter. A simple willingness to look beyond surface appearances is all that's required. No special techniques or philosophical knowledge are necessary.

When you interact with someone—whether a family member, colleague, stranger on the street, or even someone you find challenging—pause internally and say to yourself: "The same essence that animates me also animates this person. Beneath our differences, we share a common nature."

Don't worry about whether you're "feeling" this connection immediately. Make a conscious mental observation and notice what happens over time. This simple practice gradually shifts your perception and opens you to experiencing the first inklings of what the texts describe as the first stage of yogic development.

Begin today. In your very next interaction, pause and recognize the shared essence. Consistency in practice, however simple, can transform your entire experience of life and relationships.

REMEMBER, ANYONE CAN ENGAGE IN CONSCIOUS RECOGNITION, REGARDLESS OF THEIR STAGE IN THE SPIRITUAL JOURNEY OR MEDITATION EXPERIENCE. IT PLANTS THE SEED FROM WHICH YOUR DEEPER YOGIC AWARENESS CAN NATURALLY GROW.

Yogi

BECOMING ONE

IS BECOMING A YOGI POSSIBLE FOR YOU? Has this question likely crossed your mind, or do you feel overwhelmed with the thought, especially during those moments when spiritual advancement feels out of reach?

When I speak of a *yogi* here, I'm referring to Krishna's definition. Someone who lives with balanced awareness and detachment while engaging fully with life, not necessarily someone who has renounced everything (for more on this distinction, see the chapter on "The Path of *yogi* and *sanyasi* - Action with Detachment"). You're not alone in this doubt. Even Arjuna, speaking directly to Krishna on the battlefield, expressed this same concern.

After hearing Krishna's profound wisdom, Arjuna found himself simultaneously inspired and doubtful. He prostrated before the divine and voiced the very concern many of us share today: "Is it even practical to rise to the stage of a *yogi* where I can see all souls within you and the universe as one common fabric?"

It's a fair question. We live in a world of division and distinction. Our minds constantly separate, categorize, and judge. Transcending these mental habits seems daunting. Arjuna acknowledged this in chapter 6, verse 34, when he admitted that "controlling the mind is probably even more difficult than controlling a gale of wind."

We can all relate to that sentiment. Each time we try to focus, our mind wanders. We commit to meditating for ten minutes, and within seconds, we're planning dinner or reliving an awkward conversation from years ago. The mind is indeed fickle and resistant to our best efforts at control.

But what if becoming a *yogi* isn't about perfect mental control? What if there's a more accessible path forward? Let's explore what the Gita reveals about this journey that makes it possible for each of us, regardless of our current position.

Let's Dive Deeper

The *yogic* path often seems reserved for the exceptional few—those rare individuals who can sit in meditation for hours without distraction or who've seemingly mastered every aspect of their lives. However, the Bhagavad Gita presents a much more inclusive and practical approach to spiritual development.

When we examine Krishna's response to Arjuna's concerns about the difficulty of mind control, we find something remarkable. Instead of dismissing Arjuna's struggle or suggesting that only the extraordinary can become *yogis*, Krishna acknowledges the universal challenge of taming the mind while offering practical wisdom that makes the path accessible to all.

A more approachable understanding of yogic development isn't about achieving an overnight transformation or acquiring superhuman mental abilities. It's about working intelligently with our natural tendencies, trusting in the cumulative nature of spiritual growth, and recognizing that the journey continues even beyond our current lifetime.

In the following sections, we'll explore these reassuring principles that make the yogic path accessible to everyone, regardless of current spiritual development. We'll see how the obstacles that seem most insurmountable, such as the fickleness of the mind, can become doorways to a more profound understanding when approached with the wisdom of the Gita.

The Nature of the Mind

When Arjuna expressed his frustrations about mind control to Krishna, the response he received was both realistic and hopeful. Yes, the mind is difficult to control. This isn't just your struggle but a universal human condition. However, the mind has a fascinating quality that we can leverage, which tends to channel back to familiar territory.

A gambler's mind naturally drifts back to thoughts of gambling. A champion swimmer's thoughts return to the pool. Someone who habitually criticizes others will always find new faults to focus on. Similarly, a kind person naturally tends to revert to compassion.

We can apply the same concept to spiritual practice. When we consistently direct our minds toward the divine, even if our focus occasionally strays, our thoughts will naturally return to spiritual contemplation. It's like training a puppy—it may wander off repeatedly, but with gentle, persistent guidance, it learns to stay closer to us.

Understanding the mind's natural patterns changes everything. Instead of seeing the yogic path as requiring superhuman mental control, we can approach it as a gradual training of the mind's natural tendencies. As our focus increases through regular practice, our control over the mind naturally strengthens, bringing us closer to the yogic state.

What About Failure?

Arjuna's concerns didn't stop with the difficulty of mind control. He also worried about what would happen if we failed to persevere on this path. There is a powerful metaphor that describes someone who starts the yogic journey but doesn't complete it as "a breakaway cloud in the sky, left on its own, surrounded by enlightened ones." What becomes of such a person? Is all their spiritual effort wasted? The Gita's answer is profoundly reassuring. Spiritual effort of any kind is never a waste. If someone deviates from the yogic path at an early stage, they'll continue their spiritual journey in subsequent lives, being born into pious, spiritually wealthy, and prosperous families. Being born into these supportive environments allows them to resume their spiritual evolution from where they left off.

For those who deviate at a later, more mature stage of yogic development, the Gita promises an even more auspicious rebirth. They will be born into a family of yogis. Such births are rare and reserved for souls who have already made significant progress on their spiritual journey. These individuals often rise to become transformative figures who benefit humanity through their wisdom and compassion.

The great philosopher Bhagavad Ramanuja explains this continuity beautifully: "Like a person waking up from sleep and remembering earlier happenings, the individual resumes his spiritual quest." Having already reached an advanced stage in a previous life, these individuals naturally gravitate toward spiritual practices in their current life, requiring relatively little effort.

It works like that because karma yoga and good deeds are cumulative. They're like spiritual capital that continues to grow and yields returns across lifetimes. The merit earned over previous births continuously purifies the soul, washing away obstacles and ultimately leading to the fulfillment of the yogic journey.

The Progressive Stages

As mentioned in the chapter on "The Four Stages of Yogic Evolution," the path unfolds progressively. Each step builds upon the last, creating a natural evolution of consciousness. We don't need to worry about achieving the final state immediately, but focus on taking the next step from our current position.

Even if progress seems slow, remember that each moment of practice, each kind of action, and each attempt at self-control contributes to your spiritual development. Every effort counts and accelerates your journey, if not in this lifetime, then certainly in those to come.

Understanding the journey gradually helps to alleviate the pressure of immediate perfection. You don't need to master every aspect of yoga at once. Just as a child learns to crawl before walking and walk before running, your spiritual journey unfolds in natural stages. Your only responsibility is to take the next step with sincerity and persistence.

Summary: The Accessible Path to Yogic Consciousness

Let's pause and gather what we've learned. Becoming a *yogi* is indeed challenging. Arjuna wasn't wrong about the difficulty of controlling the mind. However, the path is made accessible through several reassuring principles that the Gita reveals to us.

- Rather than fighting against the mind's fickleness, we can work with its natural tendency to return to familiar territory. By consistently directing our thoughts toward spiritual contemplation, we gradually train our minds to make this their default state. It's like walking through a dense forest. At first, the path is barely visible and requires effort to navigate, but with each journey, the path becomes clearer, more defined, and increasingly familiar until you can traverse it almost effortlessly, even in the dim light of dawn.

- Every step on the yogic path adds to our spiritual development. Nothing is lost, even if we temporarily deviate or don't reach the highest stages in this lifetime. Think of it as making deposits in a spiritual bank account: each meditation, each act of compassion, and each moment of self-awareness contributes to a growing balance that remains yours forever.

- If we don't complete the yogic transformation in this life, we'll be born into circumstances that facilitate our continued spiritual growth. The Gita assures us that we'll find ourselves either in pious families that support our development or, for those more advanced, directly into families of yogis. Our spiritual journey continues uninterrupted, merely changing form as we move from one life to the next.

- When we resume our spiritual journey in subsequent lives, we don't start from scratch. We pick up where we left off, often with a natural inclination toward spiritual practices. Have you ever met someone who has been drawn to meditation or philosophical inquiry since childhood? This could be the result of significant progress made in previous lives.

- The yogic path, as described in the Gita, isn't an all-or-nothing proposition. It's a gradual, cumulative process that unfolds throughout lifetimes if necessary. Seeing the journey as continuous across lifetimes removes the pressure of immediate perfection. It replaces it with a more sustainable approach, one that is a consistent effort in the right direction, trusting in the cumulative nature of spiritual growth. When we understand this, the journey itself becomes more peaceful, more joyful, and paradoxically, more likely to reach its destination.

Start Today: Your First Step

If there's one action I encourage you to take right now, it's this: **Make a daily commitment to directing your mind toward whatever represents the divine for you.** It might be formal meditation, contemplative prayer, mindful breathing, or even conscious acts of compassion. The specific form matters less than the consistency and intention behind it.

Here's how to begin:

Set aside time to cultivate higher awareness consciously. When your mind inevitably wanders (and it will), gently bring it back without judgment or frustration. Remember, you're working with the mind's tendency to form habits. Each time you redirect your attention, you're strengthening this positive pattern.

As Krishna advised Arjuna, don't worry about perfection or immediate results. Trust in the cumulative nature of this practice. Begin today. Not because you need to achieve yogic consciousness immediately, but because every moment on this path enriches your life and contributes to the ultimate transformation that awaits you. What are you waiting for? The journey of a thousand miles begins with a single step, and the yogic path starts exactly where you are right now.

REMEMBER, EVEN IF PROGRESS SEEMS IMPERCEPTIBLE DAY BY DAY, THE EFFECTS WILL COMPOUND OVER TIME. AND WHATEVER PROGRESS YOU MAKE IS YOURS FOREVER, CARRIED FORWARD EVEN BEYOND THIS LIFETIME

.

PART SEVEN

Confronting Mortality

Death

MANY PEOPLE BELIEVE OUR DEATH date is predetermined when we are born. But here's what might surprise you: the timing of death isn't predetermined. The Bhagavad Gita and the Upanishads don't teach that our death date is fixed at birth or written in some cosmic ledger. You might find yourself surprised by this perspective, maybe even relieved or unsettled, but it's an understanding I've developed through years of studying these ancient texts alongside the evidence of our lived experience.

To be clear, I'm not suggesting we can indefinitely postpone death. As the old saying goes, "death and taxes are certain," though I would add that taxes reliably arrive on schedule, while death keeps its timing a mystery. The body will indeed die someday. But when? Death is a complex interplay of factors that we'll explore together in this chapter.

The timing of our death touches something much more profound than abstract speculation. It explores how we perceive fate and free will, how we make sense of tragedy, and, ultimately, how we choose to live. If death's moment is fixed and unalterable, why bother with health practices, safety precautions, or medical interventions? Yet most of us intuitively recognize that our choices matter when it comes to matters of life and death.

Let's explore what the ancient wisdom of the Gita and Upanishads teaches about this profound mystery, balanced with what we observe in our modern world. The answer might offer not just philosophical clarity but practical guidance for living with greater awareness and purpose.

Let's Dive Deeper

Before diving into the philosophical teachings, let's ground ourselves in what we observe in the world around us. If death were predetermined at an exact moment, wouldn't we expect to see relatively consistent life expectancies across time and cultures?

Yet the data from various public news sources tells a different story. Global life expectancy was just 47 years in 1900, rose to 68 years by 1950, and reached nearly 79 years by 2019. Between 2000 and 2019, global life expectancy increased by more than six years. Far from small fluctuations, these numbers represent dramatic shifts in the typical lifespan of human beings.

What caused these changes? Advances in nutrition, clean water, sanitation, healthcare, antibiotics, vaccines, and public health initiatives, along with improvements in living standards, economic growth, and poverty reduction, have contributed to significant progress. Human invention, discovery, and choice have demonstrably extended life spans.

We've also seen life expectancy move in the opposite direction. During the COVID-19 pandemic, public news sources reported that U.S. life expectancy fell to 77 in 2020 and further dropped to just over 76 in 2021. COVID-19, drug overdoses, and accidental injuries accounted for about two-thirds of this decline, with heart disease, liver disease, and suicides also contributing significantly.

The changing patterns demonstrate that death's timing responds to human choices—both collective decisions (like public health investments) and individual ones (like health behaviors or risk-taking). If you develop a life-threatening illness, you are likely to seek medical treatment rather than passively accepting it as your "time to go." When retirement planners advise you to prepare financially to live until at least 85 or 90, they acknowledge that modern humans typically live much longer than their ancestors, not because fate has changed, but because our circumstances and choices have.

The Wisdom of Ancient Texts

Now, let's turn to what the Gita and Upanishads teach about the timing of death. Far from promoting fatalism, these texts present a nuanced understanding of time, karma, and human agency.

Ancient teachings view time as cyclical rather than linear. Within these vast cosmic cycles, human life unfolds through predictable stages of birth, growth, decay, and death. But the precise timing and circumstances of death arise from a complex interplay of factors, including your karma (actions), the karma of others that affects you, external factors beyond human control, and your spiritual evolution.

Consider a simple but tragic example: A careful, sober driver traveling within the speed limit gets killed instantly when a drunk driver swerves into their lane. Was this death predetermined? The Gita would suggest not. Instead, it resulted from the intersection of choices, including the victim's decisions and the harmful choices of another person. The Gita and Upanishads grant all beings the freedom to choose their actions, and these choices inevitably intersect and influence one another.

Central to these teachings is the concept of *karma,* the law of cause and effect that governs the operation across lifetimes. Your past actions, until the present moment, create tendencies and consequences that shape your present circumstances, while your current choices generate new karma for the future. Part of this accumulated karma, known as *prarabdha karma,* manifests in your present life, influencing events, including your eventual death.

But *karma* isn't rigid predestination. The texts acknowledge our genuine free will to make choices in the present moment. Sometimes, these choices help us transcend or transform the effects of past karma; other times, either our actions or those of others create such powerful new consequences that they overwhelm other factors.

There's also the simple reality of the body's natural limitations. A patient might die during surgery despite a doctor's best efforts because the body has reached a point where it can no longer heal or sustain itself. When facing such painful realities, people often take comfort in the idea that "it was meant to be" or "their time had come." But according to the more profound teachings, this isn't true. It's just that multiple factors converged in a way that resulted in death at that moment.

God's Larger Plan

You might wonder about the role of divine will or cosmic planning in all this. The Upanishads and Gita do acknowledge a cosmic order (*dharma*) that governs all existence. However, this isn't a rigid script that predetermines every event but rather a set of universal laws within which countless possibilities unfold.

Think of it like the laws of physics. Gravity doesn't dictate exactly what you'll do, but it does establish certain constraints within which you make your choices. Similarly, the cosmic order establishes specific patterns and principles while leaving room for genuine choice and contingency.

What about the idea that everything is part of "God's plan"? The texts suggest a more subtle understanding. The divine consciousness witnesses and upholds the cosmic order, but it doesn't micromanage every event. Just as parents establish boundaries for their children while allowing them to make meaningful choices within those boundaries, the divine allows for genuine freedom within the cosmic framework.

The most compelling evidence that death isn't predetermined comes from the texts' emphasis on spiritual practices that can transform one's life and death. The performance of righteous deeds (*dharma*), spiritual disciplines (*sadhana*), and devotion (*bhakti*) are ways to mitigate negative karma and potentially alter the timing and circumstances of death.

Most dramatically, the texts describe great seers who could choose the time of their death. Through advanced spiritual practices, these masters attained such profound control over their life force that they could consciously release it from the body at a time of their choosing. The ability to choose one's death contradicts any notion that the moment is predetermined from birth.

Preparing for the Inevitable

While the Gita doesn't teach that death's timing is predetermined, it places tremendous emphasis on how we should prepare for this inevitable transition. In chapters 7 and 8, Krishna provides detailed guidance for the dying process, including developing a single-minded focus, withdrawing the senses inward, detaching from the external world, and channeling one's life energy upward in a controlled manner.

Of course, Krishna recognizes that most of us won't have the luxury of a peaceful, controlled death like the great seers. Death often comes unexpectedly, without time for elaborate spiritual practices. For precisely these reasons, the Gita stresses the importance of cultivating spiritual awareness in daily life rather than waiting until death draws near.

The texts encourage continuous devotion, regular contemplation of the divine, and maintaining sacred mantras "on your lips at all times." By integrating spiritual awareness into everyday life, you prepare yourself for death whenever and however it comes. This is why traditional practices like the *pancha kala kriya* (spiritual activities performed at different times of the day) are considered so important—they maintain a steady current of awareness that can carry through even sudden or traumatic death experiences. In the earlier chapters, I provided a detailed discussion of the practice of *pancha kala kriya*.

The presence of spiritual support at the time of death is also emphasized. Being surrounded by holy beings, hearing sacred mantras and prayers, and having guidance from realized teachers can create an uplifting environment for the departing soul. Cultivating meaningful spiritual relationships enables us to establish a foundation of support that becomes invaluable in life's final stages. As Krishna states in the Gita,

> *For one who is born, death is inevitable, and for one who has died, birth is certain. Therefore, in the unavoidable discharge of your duty, you should not lament*

Rather than fixating on death's timing, we're encouraged to focus on living virtuously, growing spiritually, and recognizing our true nature beyond the limitations of birth and death.

Summary: A Dance of Destiny and Choice

The Gita tradition offers a more nuanced perspective on death than simple predestination. Death's timing arises from a complex interplay of past *karma*, present choices (both our own and those of others), cosmic laws, and spiritual development.

- Rather than a predetermined endpoint fixed at birth, death comes as the culmination of countless factors converging in a particular moment. Some of these factors lie beyond our control, arising from past actions or external circumstances. Others remain very much within our influence—our current choices, spiritual practices, and the consciousness we cultivate daily.

- The view provides us with both empowerment and solace. We have genuine agency or role in shaping our lives and potentially influencing when and how our death occurs. At the same time, we're part of a larger cosmic order that gives meaning and purpose to our existence beyond individual control.

- The evidence from our lived experience aligns with this teaching. The human lifespan has increased dramatically due to advances in medicine, public health, and living standards, demonstrating that our collective and individual choices significantly influence the timing of death. Yet despite these advances, death remains inevitable and often unpredictable, reminding us of the limits of human control.

- What matters most is not trying to predict or control the precise moment of death but living in a way that prepares us for this transition whenever it comes. By living righteously, practicing spiritual disciplines, and cultivating divine awareness, we create the conditions for a conscious death and favorable transition, whether death comes gradually as we age or suddenly in an accident.

Ultimately, the question of whether death is predetermined points us toward a deeper inquiry: How shall we live in the face of mortality? The wise response isn't fatalistic resignation ("everything is predestined") or anxious control ("I must prevent death at all costs"). Instead, it is conscious engagement with life's flow, making meaningful choices while acknowledging the larger mystery in which we participate.

Start Today: Your First Step

If there's one action I encourage you to take right now, it's this: **Start a daily reflection on life's impermanence.**

I'm not suggesting you become consumed by thoughts of mortality or live in constant anxiety. Quite the opposite. Life's impermanence, practiced wisely, brings extraordinary clarity and appreciation to life. When we acknowledge that life is impermanent and death is not predetermined, but rather the result of the confluence of countless factors, we naturally begin to live with greater presence, purpose, and peace.

Here's how to begin:

Each morning, when you wake up, take a moment before rising to acknowledge both the gift of another day and the reality that this day could be your last. Say to yourself: "I have the precious gift of another day of life. Let me live it fully, wisely, and with an open heart." Then, each night before going to sleep, take a moment to practice the concept of impermanence.

- Lying in bed, consciously relax your body from your toes to the top of your head. Release the day's stress. Withdraw your awareness from the outer world.

- Focus your attention on your heart center or between your eyebrows and recall whatever represents the divine to you— a name, form, light, or simply a sense of boundless awareness.

- Fall asleep holding this awareness.

These brief morning and evening rituals accomplish several important things. It harnesses the power of impermanence to clarify your priorities and eliminate trivial concerns. It gradually reduces the fear of death by making it familiar rather than foreign. Most importantly, it creates a habit of consciousness that can serve you at the actual moment of death, whenever and however it comes.

So, begin today. Don't postpone this vital practice. Death's timing may not be predetermined, but its inevitability is certain. By practicing conscious transitions daily, from waking to sleeping, you prepare yourself for the ultimate transition when it comes.

REMEMBER KRISHNA'S TEACHING: WHATEVER STATE OF BEING ONE REMEMBERS AT THE TIME OF DEATH, THAT STATE THE PERSON SHALL ATTAIN. THE WISEST RESPONSE IS NEITHER DENIAL NOR DREAD BUT CONSCIOUS PREPARATION THROUGH HOW YOU LIVE EACH DAY.

Is Death Justified?

THE NEWS CAME WITHOUT WARNING. An old friend, someone I'd known since college, had suddenly passed away. As I sat with this reality, I found myself cycling through the familiar stages of grief—denial, anger, and sadness. But beneath these emotions, more profound questions surfaced: Why do we die? Is death ever justified? How should we understand this universal yet profound personal experience?

Like many of you, I've noticed an increased awareness of mortality in recent years. Whether from the pandemic, natural causes, or accidents, the news of someone's passing seems to arrive with unsettling frequency. Perhaps you might have found yourself at a funeral or memorial service, contemplating the meaning of it all.

Death is the great equalizer, touching every life regardless of wealth, status, or achievement. Yet, despite its universality, we often struggle to make sense of it. Through various cultural and religious frameworks, we hope to understand death, but when we lose someone close to us, these explanations can feel hollow or insufficient.

Let's Dive Deeper

In this chapter, I aim to explore death through the lens of the Bhagavad Gita—not as an abstract philosophical concept but as a practical understanding that can transform how we experience loss and live our lives. What I've found in these ancient teachings isn't just comfort in times of grief but a radical reframing that challenges our most basic assumptions about life, death, and what it means to exist.

Let's embark on a journey together into one of life's greatest mysteries, not to eliminate the pain of loss but to see it within a broader context that might change everything about how you understand your existence and the passing of those you love.

The Cycle of Physical Existence

Have you ever watched the seasons change and noticed how everything in nature follows a cycle? The sapling becomes a tree, which eventually withers and returns to the soil, nourishing new life. According to the ancient scriptures, our physical bodies follow a similar pattern, moving through six distinct stages:

- Conception or Initiation — The beginning of the physical form

- Period of Fertilization — When the form takes shape

- Period of Growth — Expansion and development

- Phase of Transformation — Changes in form and function

- Decay — Gradual deterioration

- Destruction — The end of the physical form

Think about your own body. It's constantly changing, cells die and are replaced, tissues heal and regenerate, and systems adapt to new conditions. You're not physically the same person you were ten years ago or even one year ago. Your body is in a state of perpetual flux, transitioning through these stages in subtle ways every day.

However, here's where the Gita offers a perspective that differs from our typical Western understanding: According to Hindu scriptures, the soul (also known as the *atman*, spiritual energy, or spirit), your true essence, attaches to a material form from the moment of conception. The soul exists before your body takes shape and continues after your body returns to dust. Instead, it moves on and gets assigned to another material form.

Your future form emerges from conscious choices, not chance. Gita teaches that it depends on your actions and intentions. In this way, the six-stage cycle continues, with the soul taking on new forms based on its prior experiences and choices.

When we understand this cycle, we begin to see death not as an ending but as a transition—a movement from one form to another. The question then becomes not "Is death justified?" but rather "What is death? And does one truly die?"

Krishna's Perspective on Death

In the Bhagavad Gita, Krishna offers a fascinating response to these questions. He challenges Arjuna (by extension, us) with a logical explanation that upends conventional thinking about death.

Krishna asks:

> *If you think that the soul, which is not even an object, is being slain, isn't that ignorance?*

He continues with a profound observation:

> *The body is non-existent before having a life. It is absent after losing a life. How can such a body then be slain? Isn't that ignorance?*

Let's take a moment to consider Krishna's message. He points out that the physical body doesn't exist in the same form before birth or after death. It emerges temporarily and then dissolves back into its elemental components. The only constant is the soul, the consciousness that animates the body during its existence.

From this perspective, death is simply a break in the relationship between the soul and one particular material manifestation. The soul, your true self, continues its journey, taking on a new form based on your actions and choices in this life.

But this raises an important moral question: If there is "no one to slay or no one to be slain," as Krishna suggests, does this mean anything goes? Can people harm others without consequence? Can murderers go unpunished? Not at all. Let's examine Krishna's message more closely.

The Moral Dimension of Death

Krishna's teachings don't eliminate moral responsibility. They deepen it. While the soul is indestructible, the break of the relationship between the soul and the body matters tremendously.

Nature's law dictates that this break must occur in harmony with morals and be natural. In Hindu tradition, this natural law is called *dharma*—the cosmic order that underlies right action and ethical behavior. Anyone who violates *dharma* faces the consequences on a spiritual level. Consider these two contrasting scenarios:

> A murderer who intentionally takes another person's life

> A doctor who performs surgery to save a patient but is unsuccessful

In both cases, someone dies, and there's a break in the relationship between a soul and its material body. But the "how and why" of that break makes all the difference.

The doctor was following their *dharma* —their duty to heal and protect life. Even though the outcome was death, moral principles guided the intention and action.

The murderer, however, violated *dharma* by intentionally causing harm. Understanding the difference shows us that death may be natural, but how it occurs matters deeply.

The contrast reveals that while dying is inevitable, the manner of dying carries spiritual significance. We have a responsibility to respect the natural cycle of life and death, allowing it to unfold according to *dharma* rather than violently disrupting it.

The Soul's Journey After Death

What happens to the soul after death? According to the Gita, it depends on how the person lives their life.

If someone dedicates their life to honorable acts, their soul will attach to a different and potentially more exalted body. Think of it like clothing, you wouldn't discard practical old clothes for ones of poorer quality. You'd look for something newer and better. Similarly, a soul that has lived with honor may move to a form that allows for greater peace and spiritual growth. On the other hand, if someone lived with hatred and wrongdoing, death allows for a reset. The soul gets a fresh start in a new body, a chance to correct itself and live more honorably.

Nature provides endless opportunities for the soul to realign with its highest purpose. Like a GPS that recalculates when you take a wrong turn, the soul continues cycling through the six stages until it aligns with its ultimate destination, connection with the supreme or divine.

But even with this understanding, we can't deny the sorrow we feel when someone dies. The loss is real and painful. How can we reconcile this spiritual perspective with our very human experience of grief?

The Body as a City of Nine Gates

To understand our relationship with the physical body, the Gita offers a beautiful metaphor: the body is compared to a "city of nine gates."

These nine gates are the openings in our body: two eyes, two ears, two nostrils, one mouth, and the two excretory and reproductive openings. Through these gates, we interact with the world, taking in experiences and expressing ourselves.

In this metaphor, the soul is a temporary inhabitant, a guest visiting this particular city for a time. When the body dies, the soul moves to another town. The quality of that new "city" is influenced by three factors from yogic philosophy: *sattva* (purity), *rajas* (passion), and *tamas* (inertia).

True detachment allows us to love more freely without the desperation of clinging. Everyone you meet is, like you, a soul temporarily inhabiting a city of nine gates. We are all eternal beings visiting different "cities" for a time.

Death, then, is merely the fall of one city, making way for another to take form. Think about how doctors declare someone dead. They pronounce the death of a person with a name and form, the physical body. They cannot declare the soul dead because the soul continues its journey.

Relationships and Attachment

True detachment allows us to love more freely without the desperation of clinging. But this perspective might raise another question: If we're all just souls temporarily inhabiting separate "cities," what about our relationships? Do our connections to others matter, or should we adopt a cold, detached approach to life?

At the fundamental level, each soul is indeed unique, eternal, and housed in its separate city of nine gates. However, these "cities" don't exist in isolation. They're part of a larger ecosystem called nature. The individual souls and bodies are all integrated within this ecosystem, connected by the same divine energy that pervades everything.

The equilibrium of the entire ecosystem depends on individual "cities" and souls being in harmony. In this context, relationships matter since they're part of the interconnected web of existence.

Death is an event in the cyclical life of a soul. Our attachment to the physical form of that soul and the manner of its passing influences whether we see a particular death as justified or not. We tend to feel that the death of a loved one is entirely unjustified, while remaining indifferent to thousands or millions of people dying with whom we have no connection. Yet, in reality, no death is more or less important than another from the cosmic perspective.

Finding Peace with Death

When someone you care about experiences pain or approaches death, recognize that while you must help them, becoming attached to their suffering won't serve either of you. The only way to remain objective and truly helpful is to maintain some degree of spiritual detachment.

Rather than losing yourself in questions of fairness or waves of despair, you can anchor yourself in love while honoring their sacred transition. It means offering support without becoming overwhelmed by grief to the point where you can no longer be present. As part of your responsibility to help someone in need, you can offer prayers on their behalf, connecting with divinity and helping them continue their life cycle with peace.

Rather than losing yourself in questions of fairness or waves of despair, you can anchor yourself in love while honoring their sacred transition, supporting their journey with love and spiritual awareness.

A person on the path of spiritual maturity develops the discriminating intellect to understand the relationship and differences between the soul and the physical body (the city of nine gates). For such a person, the veil of ignorance disappears, just as the sunrise dispels the darkness of night.

Your heart will still ache when you lose someone you love—and that's perfectly human. Grief is a natural human response to loss. However, understanding death from this spiritual perspective can transform your grief, lending it context and meaning within a larger cosmic framework.

Summary: A New Understanding of Death

Let's bring together the key insights we've explored about death from the perspective of the Bhagavad Gita:

- The physical body goes through six stages: conception, fertilization, growth, transformation, decay, and destruction. Every physical manifestation follows a predictable and inevitable pattern.

- The soul or spiritual energy attaches to a material form from conception, but is eternal. It existed before this body and will continue after it. At death, the soul transitions to a new form based on one's actions in this life.

- Death is not the end of existence but a break in the relationship between the soul and a particular material manifestation. The soul itself is indestructible.

- The circumstances of death matter morally. Natural death, by *dharma* (cosmic order), is distinct from death caused by the violation of *dharma*, and each carries different consequences.

- The body can be understood as a "city of nine gates" that the soul temporarily inhabits. At death, the soul moves to a new "city."

- While each soul is unique and separate, we're all part of an interconnected ecosystem. Relationships are crucial for maintaining harmony within this larger system.

- When someone is suffering or dying, we can best help them by offering support without becoming overwhelmed by attachment to their pain. Prayer and connecting them to divine energy can help their soul's journey.

- Spiritual maturity involves developing the discernment to distinguish between the eternal soul and the temporary physical form.

We can fully embrace each moment while remembering that we are more than any single moment. When we recognize death as a transition rather than an ending, we can honor our loved ones' continuing journey even as we mourn the loss of their physical presence in our lives.

Death remains one of life's greatest mysteries, but the Gita offers us a framework for approaching it with wisdom, compassion, and spiritual awareness. *You dance fully in this life, knowing you're the eternal dancer, not just the dance.*

Start Today: Your First Step

If there's one action I encourage you to take right now, it's this: **Practice gentle detachment in your daily life.** Detachment doesn't mean being careless or withdrawing from relationships; it simply means being mindful of one's own needs and priorities. Instead, it means loving and engaging fully while remembering the temporary nature of all physical forms—including your own body and the bodies of those you love.

Here's how to begin:

- Take a few minutes, preferably in the morning, to sit quietly and contemplate—I am not this body. I am the eternal soul temporarily inhabiting this city of nine gates.

- As you go about your day, when you interact with others, silently acknowledge: "This person too is an eternal soul, temporarily inhabiting their city of nine gates."

- When you find yourself becoming stressed, anxious, or overly attached to outcomes, gently remind yourself: "This situation involves temporary forms and circumstances. My true self, and the true self of everyone involved, transcends these temporary conditions."

Conscious detachment enhances, rather than diminishes, your engagement with life. It simply means maintaining awareness of the deeper reality beneath physical appearances. By remembering the eternal nature of yourself and others, you can engage more fully with life while holding your experiences in a broader spiritual context.

Over time, this practice of conscious detachment cultivates a profound shift in perspective. You'll likely find yourself less frightened by the prospect of death (your own or others), less controlled by fear and attachment, and more able to act from a place of wisdom and compassion.

REMEMBERING, AWAKENING IS A JOURNEY OF MANY SMALL MOMENTS RATHER THAN ONE DRAMATIC REVELATION. EACH MOMENT OF REMEMBERING YOUR TRUE NATURE AS AN ETERNAL SOUL BRINGS YOU CLOSER TO THE PEACE AND CLARITY THAT COMES WITH SPIRITUAL MATURITY.

The Final Thought

WHO WE REMEMBER AT DEATH

WHAT OCCUPIES YOUR MIND in your final moment on earth? It's a profound question that most of us avoid contemplating. Yet according to the Gita, that final thought occurring in just a fraction of a second before our consciousness leaves this world may be one of the most significant moments of our existence.

I often think about this mysterious final moment when the flame of life reaches its brightest intensity just before it's extinguished. In that instant, what face will appear in your mind? What name will echo in your consciousness? What feeling will envelop your being? It's a question without a definitive answer, as those who have crossed that threshold can't return to tell us their experience. Yet the Bhagavad Gita offers us a profound insight:

> *Whichever state of being one remembers at the time of death, that state the person shall attain without fail*

This teaching suggests that our final thought doesn't just mark the end of one journey, it potentially shapes the beginning of another. The entity or quality we remember in our last moment may influence our soul's next destination or form of embodiment.

What makes this teaching so powerful isn't just its spiritual implications but its practical invitation to live more consciously in the present moment. The truth is, we don't suddenly remember something random at death—our final thought is simply the culmination of all our previous thoughts, actions, and meditations.

Let's Dive Deeper

In this chapter, we'll explore this profound teaching together and discover how it might transform not just our understanding of death but, more importantly, our approach to living.

At the moment of death, whether it comes gradually after a long illness or suddenly in an accident, a remarkable phenomenon occurs. In that last flickering instant, the flame of life intensifies before it's extinguished. During this brief yet eternal moment, a thought arises. The final thought doesn't occur by chance. It springs from the most ingrained habits of our mind.

Krishna tells us something remarkable about this moment in the Gita. He says that whatever entity or quality we remember at the time of death shapes our next existence. If we die thinking of worldly possessions, those attachments follow us. If we die with hatred, those qualities manifest in our next embodiment. And if we die with our consciousness fixed on the divine, we either attain liberation or take birth with elevated spiritual attributes.

Krishna's wisdom is not to make us fearful about dying or frantically worried about our last thoughts. Instead, it highlights a profound truth: what occupies our mind at the moment of death is a reflection of what has occupied our mind throughout life. We don't suddenly remember Krishna at death if we've never thought about divinity during life. We remember what has become our natural state of consciousness through consistent practice.

When we grasp this truth, death shifts from being our greatest fear to becoming our most profound spiritual gateway. However, to make the most of this opportunity, we need to be prepared. And that preparation isn't something we postpone until old age—it's the very substance of a spiritually meaningful life.

Three Paths for Three Types of Seekers

As we explored in the chapter on "The Four Devotees", believers approach their relationship with the divine in distinctly different ways. We examined how the Acquirer, the Inquirer, and the Knower represent progressively deeper levels of spiritual engagement during life. Now, we'll see how these same spiritual personality types approach the most profound transition of all: death itself.

Our temperaments, inclinations, and levels of spiritual maturity differ significantly, and these differences don't disappear at death's threshold. Recognizing this diversity, Krishna provides specific guidance tailored to each type of devotee, offering practical methods that align with their natural inclinations. Each type has a unique approach to remembering the divine during this pivotal moment, drawing on the same essential qualities that characterize their spiritual practice throughout life.

The Acquirer's Path

Accumulation is the hallmark of the acquirer. People with this temperament instinctively amass collections—material goods, life experiences, or personal accomplishments. Rather than trying to eliminate this tendency (which could create internal conflict), Krishna suggests channeling it in a spiritual direction.

If you recognize yourself as an acquirer, Krishna offers specific guidance: Cultivate divine memories with the same enthusiasm you bring to collecting material possessions. Visualize Krishna not as an abstract concept but as a majestic, radiant being whose splendor outshines a million suns. Make this visualization a daily practice so that at the time of death, it becomes your natural focus.

The technique involves directing your life energy upward at the moment of death, focusing your consciousness on this magnificent vision of the divine. You must cultivate the technique through consistent practice throughout your life, not as a last-minute improvisation. The acquirer essentially "hoards" divine memories, creating such a wealth of spiritual impressions that they naturally predominate at the time of death.

The Inquirer's Path

The quest for understanding drives the inquirer. People of this nature continuously investigate truth, examining how the self relates to both the material world and ultimate reality. For the inquirer, Krishna isn't primarily a person to be visualized but a principle to be contemplated.

If you identify as an inquirer, your approach involves a more meditative practice. You might focus on a sacred symbol such as the *om*, using it as a doorway to transcendental awareness. Your spiritual practice resembles that of an ascetic, withdrawing attention from external distractions to focus on inner reality.

At the time of death, the inquirer follows a systematic process similar to a pilot shutting down an aircraft's systems. You methodically withdraw from sensory experience, disconnecting from external objects and then from the senses themselves. With significant focus, center your awareness on the middle of the eyebrows; this way, life energy moves upward through a central channel that connects to the crown. Chanting *om*, you enter a state of tranquility (*samadhi*) and depart with your consciousness fixed on the divine. In the reflection exercises for this chapter, I will guide you through a meditative practice that helps you cultivate this awareness pattern.

The Knower's Path

The knower has reached a level of spiritual maturity where remembering the divine isn't an effort but a natural state. For this type of devotee, awareness of Krishna permeates every moment, every action, every breath.

If you've reached this level of devotion, you no longer need special techniques for your final moments. Your entire life has become an unbroken meditation on the divine. You've established a relationship with Krishna as a pure devotee, friend, servant, parent, or lover. This relationship has become so central to your identity that it naturally dominates your consciousness at all times, including the moment of death.

The knower's devotion isn't motivated by fear of death or desire for a favorable rebirth. It flows from pure love, the same unconditional love a parent has for a child. Non-devotees may consider such love fanatical, but for the spiritually realized, it's as natural as breathing.

Death as Transition, Not Tragedy

Many religious and philosophical traditions depict the world as a place of suffering from which we seek escape through liberation. While there's truth in recognizing life's difficulties, this perspective can lead us to devalue the precious gift of human existence. This magnificent universe isn't inherently a place of agony, but it's a divine manifestation offering countless opportunities for growth and service.

Our experience of the world as pleasant or painful largely depends on our karma, choices, and attitude. When we recognize life's spiritual purpose, even challenges become opportunities rather than obstacles. Yes, liberation from the cycle of birth and death offers eternal bliss, but that doesn't mean we should disparage the world we currently inhabit.

Instead, we can embrace our present existence as a purposeful and meaningful one. Our task is to fulfill our *dharma* (purpose) while simultaneously cultivating divine awareness. In this way, we transform ordinary living into yoga by maintaining a continuous connection between individual consciousness and universal consciousness.

For those who haven't developed a spiritual perspective, this approach might seem like religious fanaticism or mere flattery of God. But genuine devotees understand it differently. Their devotion isn't about gaining divine favor through obsequiousness, but it's about expressing the soul's natural love for its source. Just as a parent cares for a child with spontaneous affection rather than calculated self-interest, the mature devotee remembers Krishna with pure love.

Preparing for the Inevitable

Death remains the one certainty in all our lives. It's not a matter of "if" but "when." And contrary to what we might prefer to believe, death often comes without warning. Death's certainty shouldn't terrify us but should inspire us to take our spiritual development seriously.

The state of consciousness we maintain throughout life creates momentum that carries into our final moments. If we've spent our days focused on material acquisition, worldly status, or sensory pleasure, these concerns will likely dominate our awareness at the moment of death. If we've cultivated hatred, fear, or resentment, these emotions may color our final thoughts. But if we've practiced remembering the divine throughout our lives, whether through visualization, meditation, ritual, or loving service, this remembrance will naturally arise when our time comes. Ancient sages recognized this truth, leading them to stress the vital importance of consistent spiritual habits. It's not just about living well; it's about dying well.

The beautiful paradox is that by learning to die consciously, we learn to live more fully. When we recognize each day as practice for our final day, we bring greater awareness, intention, and gratitude to every moment. What begins as preparation for death becomes a transformation of life.

Summary: The Thread That Binds Life and Death

As we've explored together, the teaching about remembering the divine at death reveals a profound continuity between how we live and how we die.

- Our final thought doesn't emerge randomly—it arises from the patterns of consciousness we've cultivated throughout life.

- Krishna offers guidance for different temperaments—the accumulator, the questioner, and the realized soul, but the essence of the teaching applies to everyone: what occupies your mind habitually will ultimately occupy your mind. Grasping this principle calls us to be more deliberate about the thoughts and concerns we habitually entertain.

- Rather than viewing death as merely the end of life, the Gita tradition sees it as a pivotal transition that can lead either to liberation or another form of embodiment. The quality of this transition depends mainly on the state of consciousness we've developed. Just as a river flows naturally toward the ocean, our consciousness flows naturally toward what we've most consistently cherished.

- Krishna's guidance doesn't require abandoning worldly engagement or escaping into philosophical speculation. Instead, it invites us to live fully while maintaining awareness of our divine connection. We fulfill our specific purpose (*dharma*) in the world while simultaneously cultivating remembrance of our universal source.

- The practice of divine remembrance doesn't diminish our engagement with life. It enhances it. By maintaining awareness of the eternal amidst the temporal, we bring greater presence, purpose, and peace to our daily activities. We learn to see each moment as both complete in itself and as preparation for our final moment.

- Ultimately, this ancient wisdom offers us a profoundly practical insight: by remembering what's most essential throughout life, we ensure that it becomes our final thought at death. And in this remembrance lies the seed of our continued evolution.

Start Today: Your First Step

If there's one action I encourage you to take right now, it's this: **Start each day by keeping the divine in your thoughts.** Before your day gets busy and your mind becomes cluttered, take a moment to consciously connect with the divine in whatever form resonates with your heart.

Here's how to begin:

If you're visually oriented, you might create a mental image of divine radiance or beauty. If you're more conceptual, you might focus on a sacred word or phrase, such as *om* or feel the presence of universal consciousness. The specific form matters less than the regular practice of turning your attention toward what's eternal within and beyond you.

Don't worry about getting it perfect. What matters is consistency, not perfection. Each time you practice, you're creating a neural pathway, a groove in your consciousness that will deepen over time. You're establishing a pattern that will become increasingly natural and spontaneous, eventually extending beyond your formal practice into your daily activities.

As you continue this practice, you will likely notice subtle changes in how you perceive and respond to life's challenges. Situations that once seemed overwhelming may appear more manageable. Once automatic, reactions may become more conscious and deliberate. A sense of underlying peace may emerge, even amidst external turbulence.

Start today. Right now. Take a few slow, deep breaths, close your eyes, and turn your attention toward the divine presence that sustains all existence. By regularly connecting with what's most essential, you bring greater awareness, compassion, and wisdom to every dimension of your existence. What begins as a spiritual discipline gradually becomes your natural state of being.

REMEMBER THAT THIS PRACTICE ISN'T JUST ABOUT PREPARING FOR DEATH—IT'S ABOUT TRANSFORMING LIFE. LET THIS MOMENT BE THE BEGINNING OF A PRACTICE THAT WILL ENRICH YOUR LIFE AND PREPARE YOU FOR DEATH, WHENEVER AND HOWEVER IT COMES.

PART EIGHT

Now It's Your Turn

Now It's Your Turn

YOU STARTED THIS JOURNEY living two lives—going through the motions of religion and tradition while secretly questioning everything. Dealing with real-world challenges one way, then falling back on karma explanations when things didn't work out— struggling with confusion. **That ends now.**

The common thread weaving through every exploration in this book has been your power to choose. Not just once, but every single day. Even the decision to apply what you've learned is itself a choice, and it's the most important one you'll make.

Choice is what moves you from reaction to response. Your default mechanism is to retreat to that ancient part of your brain that only knows fear. The more you rely on this as your command center, the more you become a victim of inherited beliefs and mechanical reactions.

But when you consciously choose to engage your thinking mind, everything changes. You shift from fear to faith, from victim to victor, from reaction to thoughtful response. You learn to see beyond surface appearances to what's really happening.

This is your Arjuna transformation, and it's precisely what this book has guided you toward.

The Journey We've Taken Together

We began with the basics: What is the difference between spirituality, religion, and tradition? You discovered that each serves a purpose, but clarity about their distinct roles prevents the confusion that keeps people living divided lives.

We explored how to find authentic guidance without surrendering your discernment. You learned to distinguish between teachers who illuminate your inner wisdom and those who create dependency. The most profound spiritual insights come from intelligent inquiry, not blind acceptance.

Through worship and prayer, you moved beyond transactional approaches. True prayer isn't about getting what you want from God, whereas it's about aligning yourself with divine will while maintaining your essential human agency.

When we confronted mortality, you discovered that understanding impermanence frees you to invest more fully in what's eternal: your consciousness, your choices, and your capacity for love and wisdom.

The practical wisdom sections equipped you with tools for daily living that honor both spiritual principles and worldly responsibilities. You learned how to address daily challenges in relationships, work decisions, and conflicts while maintaining your spiritual center. You've discovered that detachment doesn't mean withdrawal. Instead, it means engaging fully while maintaining a clear perspective on outcomes.

Through traditional and spiritual practices, you have learned how to create a sacred space in your ordinary life without making dramatic lifestyle changes. Spiritual discipline enhances rather than restricts your freedom.

Finally, by awakening your yogic potential, you glimpsed the possibility of living with such internal mastery that external circumstances lose their power to determine your peace and happiness.

The Choice That Changes Everything

Here's what you now understand:

Religion is necessary but not sufficient

Religion and Tradition provide valuable scaffolding but cannot replace your personal experience of the divine. Spiritual practices offer powerful tools, but they must be wielded with wisdom rather than mechanical repetition.

Your spiritual destiny is in your hands. You have the capacity for divine connection, the tools for authentic inquiry, and the discernment to distinguish between what serves your growth and what merely perpetuates comfortable illusions.

The choice before you is clear: Will you drift through unquestioning religious traditions and mechanical practices, or will you consciously choose authentic spirituality that liberates you in your everyday living?

Will you allow fear to dictate your spiritual choices, or will you respond from faith? Will you remain a victim of inherited beliefs, or will you become the victor of your spiritual inquiry?

No More Two Lives

The crossroads moment isn't behind you—it continues with each choice you make. Every morning presents you with the opportunity to choose a response over a reaction, faith over fear, and authentic inquiry over borrowed beliefs.

The Gita and Upanishads you've explored aren't new dogmas but tools for your ongoing liberation. Use them wisely, question them thoroughly, and apply them practically. They point toward truth, but you must walk the path yourself.

This book ends, but your real journey has just begun. You now possess something invaluable: the ability to distinguish between spiritual practices that serve your authentic growth and those that merely provide comfort through familiar routine.

Most importantly, you've learned to trust your capacity for spiritual discernment while remaining open to genuine guidance. You know that authentic spirituality enhances your engagement with the world rather than requiring an escape.

The seven paths we've explored together are now yours to walk. Some days you'll find yourself on the path of the seeker, others on the path of the devotee, still others on the path of practical wisdom. Spiritual growth unfolds organically, always returning to familiar themes at deeper levels of understanding.

Your spiritual development and practical effectiveness can work in tandem. Your inner strength supports you in facing outer challenges. Your authentic spirituality serves your real-world relationships and informs your decisions.

Your Arjuna moment is here, and it's ongoing. Choose wisely, act consciously, and remember: the goal was never to become someone else but to become fully yourself. You are now grounded in timeless wisdom and perfectly equipped for the modern world.

THE PATH FORWARD IS YOURS TO WALK, WITH ONE INTEGRATED LIFE AND THE CLARITY THAT COMES FROM AUTHENTIC SPIRITUAL STRENGTH. DEVELOP YOUR SPIRITUAL CORE.

SECRET OF THE ARJUNA WAY

THE FINAL CALL

LET GO & BE LIBERATED

सर्वधर्मान्परित्यज्य मामेकं शरणं व्रज ।
अहं त्वां सर्वपापेभ्यो मोक्षयिष्यामि मा शुचः ॥

sarva-dharmān parityajya mām ekaṁ śaraṇaṁ vraja ahaṁ tvāṁ
sarva-pāpebhyo mokṣayiṣyāmi mā śucah

Chapter 18 | Verse 66 of The Bhagavad Gita

KRISHNA SAID

THE SPIRITUAL CLIMAX: YOU'VE HEARD IT ALL—every path, every duty, every philosophy. Now I'm telling you the heart of it: Let go of all those duties and identities you're clinging to. Just come to Me. Trust Me completely.

I'll take care of your past, the present, and the future, your mistakes, and your fears. You no longer need to carry the weight. Surrender, and I'll liberate you.

REFLECTION EXERCISES

TWENTY EXERCISES FOR CONTEMPLATION AND PRACTICE

Foundational

EXERCISE 1: PERSONAL RELIGIOUS REFLECTIONS (REALITY OF RELIGIONS)

Set aside 20-30 minutes in a quiet space with a journal. Reflect on your personal history with religion:

- What religious traditions were present in your family or community growing up?
- What positive or negative experiences did you have with religion?
- How have your views on religion changed over time?
- What aspects of religious thinking might still influence you today?

If possible, write about the key moments that shaped your understanding of religion. Conclude by reflecting: How might your personal history influence how you view different religious expressions today?

EXERCISE 2. THE SACRED PAUSE PRACTICE (TRUE SPIRITUALITY)

Identify three trigger situations where you typically react automatically (criticism, being late, tech problems, etc.). For two weeks, practice the Sacred Pause (three conscious breaths + awareness) when these triggers arise.

- Track each successful pause
- Note what you observed during the pause and how it affected your response
- Also note when you forgot to pause, and the result

After two weeks, review your patterns and insights. Refine your practice by adding new triggers or deepening your awareness during pauses.

EXERCISE 3. DIVINE ATTRIBUTES EXPLORATION (THEISM)

Review these divine attributes and add any others that speak to you: Compassion, Wisdom, Strength, Peace, Unconditional love. For each attribute, briefly consider:

- When have I experienced this quality?
- How might I cultivate this in myself?
- What images or names represent this quality?

Choose the 2-3 attributes that evoke your strongest response. Create a simple affirmation or prayer using your chosen attributes. Spend 5-10 minutes daily for one week contemplating these qualities, noticing how your connection deepens.

Daily Practice & Integration

EXERCISE 4. OBSERVING ENERGY PATTERNS (A DAY WITH GOD)

Think of a recent emotionally charged situation and consider:

- What material elements were involved? (People, places, objects)

- How was the energy flowing—freely or blocked?

- How did your characteristics and tendencies shape what happened?

- Where did you try to control outcomes instead of surrendering?

Choose something you're currently attached to achieving, then reflect: What do I want, and why does it matter? How would it feel to release attachment to this specific outcome while staying committed to the highest good?

EXERCISE 5. FOUR-PERSPECTIVE PROBLEM SOLVING (PURPOSEFUL LIVING)

Think of a current challenge. Write it at the top of a page, then divide it into four sections for each mindset:

- **Student Mindset:** How would I approach this as a learning opportunity?

- **Householder Mindset:** What responsible action and contribution are needed?

- **Retired Mindset:** How can I step back to observe the broader context?

- **Renounced Mindset:** How can I act without attachment to outcomes?

Develop an integrated approach using insights from all four perspectives.

EXERCISE 6. GOALS TO OBJECTIVES SHIFT (FROM GOALS TO OBJECTIVES)

For each of your current goals, ask:

- What outcome am I attached to?
- What daily actions are within my control?
- How can I find satisfaction in these actions regardless of results?

Rate yourself 1-10 on the Four Medicines:

- Eliminating Hatred: Do I separate people from their behaviors?
- Nourishing the Body: Am I mindful of eating and movement?
- Health Consciousness: Do I know my body's current state?
- Spiritual Learning: Do I consistently engage with spiritual teachings?

For any area scoring six or below, identify one improvement you can make this week.

Relationship &
Compassion

EXERCISE 7. DIVINE ENERGY IN RELATIONSHIPS
(UNDERSTANDING DIVINITY)

Select three people you regularly interact with. Reflect on each person:

- What unique divine qualities do you observe in them?
- How do their expressions differ from yours?
- What qualities do they bring out in you?

Practice for one week: Before interactions, set an intention to recognize the divine essence in others. During conversations, maintain awareness of this shared energy. After each interaction, note how this perspective affected the exchange.

EXERCISE 8. ROLE AWARENESS
(DANCE OF COMPASSION)

List 3-4 key roles you play in life (parent, professional, friend, citizen). For each role, note:

- Core responsibilities
- What righteousness looks like in this role
- Where do you feel tension between compassion and duty

Recall a situation where you felt torn between compassion and righteousness. Take 10 minutes to have a written dialogue between your "conflicted self" and your "wise guidance" about a current moral dilemma.

Devotion & Practice

EXERCISE 9. CROSS-TYPE EXPERIENCE (THE FOUR DEVOTEES)

Practice embodying each spiritual personality type for one day:

- **Day 1 - The Distressed:** Identify a challenge and ask the divine for help. Allow vulnerability.

- **Day 2 - The Acquirer:** Perform spiritual practices with clear intentions for what you wish to receive.

- **Day 3 - The Inquirer:** Question your assumptions about reality. Meditate on your eternal essence.

- **Day 4 - The Knower:** Maintain continuous awareness of divine presence. See everything as a divine manifestation.

Reflect: What did you learn from each type? Which felt most challenging? Most natural? Most enlightening?

EXERCISE 10. FROM TRANSACTIONAL TO CONNECTIONAL PRAYER (TRANSFORMING PRAYER)

Identify three current situations where you typically pray for specific outcomes. Before your next prayer about these situations, shift from asking for outcomes to connecting with divine attributes:

- Instead of "Please give me..." ask "Help me embody..."

- Focus on qualities like wisdom, strength, compassion, or peace

- Notice how this changes your prayer experience

Example transformation:

- Before: "Please help me get this job." After: "Help me connect with confidence, clarity, and purpose."

EXERCISE 11. RIVER MEDITATION
(SANATANA DHARMA)

Settle in a quiet space. Visualize a mighty river flowing from mountain springs through diverse landscapes. See this river as *sanatana dharma*:

- Mountain springs = Prehistoric gratitude toward nature
- First channels = Vedic ritualistic expressions
- Deep gorges = Philosophical depth
- Broad valleys = Storytelling reaching more people
- Mature river = Integrated spiritual practice

Stand on the riverbank. What's your relationship to this flowing tradition? Which part of the river do you feel most drawn to? This reveals your natural spiritual inclination.

EXERCISE 12. FIVE-STEP SPIRITUAL DISCIPLINE
ASSESSMENT
(THE FIVE-STEP PATH)

Create your morning and evening spiritual routine plan:
Morning: Decide on the time for connection (*abhigamana*), preparation (*upadana*), and offering (*ijya*)? **Evening:** Decide on the time for study (*svadhyaya*) and meditation (*yogadhyana*)? Reflect on:

- Do I start with confidence and gratitude or worry and haste?
- What obstacles might interfere, and how will I handle them?
- How will I monitor my consistency?

Choose one insight to implement immediately in your spiritual practice

Mind & Mental Patterns

EXERCISE 13. DESIRE WITHOUT ATTACHMENT (THE SILENT TERMITES)

Choose something you want but feel a strong attachment to. For one week:

- Set intentions without fixating on results
- Daily reminder: your worth doesn't depend on this outcome
- Notice shifts in your pursuit experience

Create space between stimulus and response: Choose a regular trigger (social media, store windows, work emails). When triggered, pause for 30 seconds before responding. Consciously decide whether and how to engage. Practice for one week, noting pattern changes.

EXERCISE 14. RESPONSIBILITY VS. REACTION (THE END OF SUFFERING)

Examine your current challenges:

- What external challenges are you facing right now?
- Can you distinguish between the external event and your internal response?
- Where do you react instinctively rather than respond thoughtfully?
- How might reframing a situation as your "duty" change your emotional response?

Reflect on incorporating compassion, charity, and self-restraint into daily life: How can you express greater compassion toward yourself and others today? What resources could you share more generously with others? Where would greater self-restraint reduce your suffering?

EXERCISE 15. CHAIN REACTION AWARENESS (FATE)

Choose a significant life event and trace backward:

- What specific actions or choices did you make that contributed?
- What actions by others played a role?
- What environmental factors influenced the event?
- What chain reactions did this event set in motion?

Practice shifting from fate consciousness to responsibility consciousness. Before making essential decisions, pause and ask: What values guide this decision? What effects might this action have? After deciding, release attachment to specific results while staying committed to responding wisely.

Self-Inquiry

EXERCISE 16. STATES OF CONSCIOUSNESS (FINDING YOUR PATH)

Recall moments when you experienced:

- **Non-duality:** Seeing beyond names and forms to the underlying unity
- **Qualified non-duality:** Recognizing distinctions while perceiving a common source
- **Duality:** Perceiving separation while feeling devotion that bridges the gap

How did each experience feel? What insights emerged? In your current situation, do you require additional instruction or guidance? Why?

EXERCISE 17. BODY-SOUL DISTINCTION MEDITATION (IS DEATH JUSTIFIED)

Sit comfortably with spine straight and eyes closed. Take several deep breaths to center yourself.

- Visualize your body as a beautiful city with nine gates—your two eyes, two ears, two nostrils, mouth, and two lower openings.
- Imagine yourself as a traveler visiting this city.
- Notice that you can observe the city from both inside and outside. If you can observe it, you must be something different from it.

Spend 5-10 minutes appreciating the city's complexity while maintaining awareness of your distinct identity as the traveler. Set an intention to carry this awareness throughout your day.

EXERCISE 18. TENDENCIES ASSESSMENT (DREAMS)

Categorize your daily activities into three columns:

- **Sattvic** (balanced, harmonious): meditation, peaceful music, positive conversations, fresh food
- **Rajasic** (active, agitated): rushing, multitasking, anxiety, spicy food, action movies
- **Tamasic** (dull, negative): oversleeping, procrastination, processed food, violent content

Which category dominates your typical day? Does your dream tone match your predominant tendencies? Make one simple change: choose one tendency to reduce and one to increase. Notice any changes in your dream experiences.

EXERCISE 19. THE LAMP IN THE WINDLESS PLACE (ADVANCED MEDITATION)

Create a distraction-free meditation space (optional: use an actual lamp or candle). Sit comfortably with steady breathing.

- Visualize a steady flame at your chest or eyebrows— unwavering, bright, radiating warmth.
- When thoughts arise (the "wind"), notice them without letting them disturb your inner flame.

Practice for 10-15 minutes, then contemplate:

- What disturbs your inner flame most?
- What helps your awareness remain steady?
- How can you cultivate this steadiness in daily activities?

This practice cultivates the mental stability that spiritual traditions describe as essential for a fulfilling life.

EXERCISE 20. EXAMINING YOUR BELIEFS ABOUT DEATH'S TIMING (DEATH)

Take a moment to reflect on your current beliefs about mortality and timing:

- Do you believe the moment of death is predetermined? What shaped this belief?

- How might your view of life change if you saw death's timing as influenced but not predetermined?

- When you hear of someone dying "before their time," what does that phrase mean to you?

Assess your current level of preparation:

- If you died suddenly today, what unfinished business would you leave behind?

- What spiritual practices might help you maintain awareness during the dying process?

- Who would provide spiritual support at your deathbed?

- What name, image, or concept of the divine might you focus on at death?

This reflection helps clarify your relationship with mortality and identify areas for spiritual preparation.

Glossary of Sanskrit Terms

SANSKRIT WORDS - CONSOLIDATED REFERENCE

Divine Concepts & Names

paramatma - The Supreme Soul, divinity; supreme consciousness; the divine energy that pervades everything

brahman - The Absolute; an impersonal form best visualized as an energy grid pervading the entire universe; also referred to as the Supreme; a holistic and complete entity with no lack. When referred to as the supreme soul, it is the same as *paramatma*

ishvara - Divinity with personal form that encompasses everything; divine energy given a name and form

bhagavan - Divinity with personal form that encompasses everything, another name for *ishvara*

narayana - The abode of everything, the space where everything and everyone dwells. The supreme personified

atman - Your true self, your soul; the soul, spiritual energy, or spirit; self-energy or individual thread energy

deva - Deity

devas - Deities (plural)

lakshmi - Supreme deity emphasizing motherhood, compassion, forgiveness, and nurturing aspects. Always seen as a pair with *narayana*

rudra - Deity representing the eleven sense faculties

shiva - Interpretation of rudra

ganesha - Deity associated with clearing paths and removing impediments

ganapati - Deity associated with clearing paths and removing impediments

vishwaksena - Deity associated with removing obstacles in Narayana tradition

krishna - Divine figure, representing the supreme, *paramatma*, *ishvara*, *bhagavan*, *narayana*, and the sage imparting the Gita.

vishvarupa - Universal form - Krishna's cosmic form that encompasses all of existence, as revealed in the Bhagavad Gita

Spiritual Practices & Concepts

dharma - Natural law, duty, or righteous way of living; cosmic order and righteousness; righteous duty; one's authentic purpose and responsibility aligned with their nature; the cosmic order that underlies right action and ethical behavior; righteousness; meaningful life guided by moral and spiritual principles

sadhana - Persistence - acting with mindfulness and awareness, finding fulfillment in the process rather than the outcome; spiritual disciplines or practices

tapasya - Conviction - acting with unwavering conviction toward a specific outcome; goal-oriented practice

bhakti - Devotion (to the divine); the devotion with which you live out that knowledge; the path where "the artificial boundary between the spiritual and the mundane dissolves"

jnana - The knowledge you acquire and apply; complete knowledge

prapatti - Your surrender to the process—doing your best while releasing attachment to specific outcomes; complete surrender

moksha - Spiritual liberation; the ultimate spiritual goal of complete freedom; self-realization or enlightenment

yoga - Union; spiritual practice

yogic - Relating to the path or practice of yoga

yogi - A spiritual practitioner who maintains engagement with the world while transforming the nature of that engagement through detachment; someone who lives with balanced awareness and detachment while engaging fully with life

sanyasi - Someone who has renounced work motivated by desire and greed; focuses on the Yoga of Knowledge through withdrawal from worldly engagement; someone who has renounced everything

adhyatma - Spiritual inquiry - using beliefs and faith as starting points for deeper exploration and direct experience

sadhak - One who performs actions with persistence and conviction without linking them to specific outcomes

Knowledge & Understanding

vishwas - Belief - a conclusion reached based on information gathered; intellectual and rooted in learning

shraddha - Faith - when belief is elevated to absolute truth in mind and heart, it becomes unquestionable

sravana - Listening (part of spiritual learning process)

manana - Contemplation (part of spiritual learning process)

nidhidyasa - Experiencing (part of spiritual learning process)

vichara - Intellectual inquiry and understanding

abhyasa - Constant, dedicated repetition; consistent practice

shravanam – Listening (part of spiritual learning process)

svadhyaya - Spiritual learning through listening, reading, and contemplation

Social & Cultural Framework

parampara - Lineage or family heritage; the specific family line you come from

sampradaya - The set of traditional practices within a family unit; family-specific traditions that create a distinctive identity

samajam - The broader social sphere that extends beyond the family; the larger community context

sanatana dharma - Eternal religion or eternal way; dynamic, ever-evolving spiritual tradition; the eternal/universal religion or way of life

purushartha - The objective of human life; the four-fold framework encompassing *artha, kama, dharma,* and *moksha*

dharma – *already defined*

artha - Material prosperity and growth; pursuing material value

kama - The pursuit of desire and gratification; fulfillment of desires

moksha – *already defined*

Life Stages (*asramas*)

asramas - Life stages; the four traditional stages of life described in the Bhagavad Gita

brahmacharya - The student (life stage); first of the four *asramas*, representing the student mindset

grihastha - The householder (life stage); second *asrama*, representing engaged responsibilities

vanaprastha - The forest dweller or retiree (life stage); third *asrama*, representing thoughtful observation

sannyasa - The renunciate (life stage); fourth *asrama*, representing inner detachment

varna System (Natural Classifications)

varna - Categories of human nature; not a rigid caste system but classification based on actions, tendencies, and innate qualities

brahmanas - Those whose primary purpose involves seeking truth, cultivating wisdom, and sharing knowledge; wisdom-keepers

kshatriyas - Those with natural tendencies toward courage, leadership, protection, and decisive action; passionate protectors

vaisyas - Those whose work involves creation, organization, entrepreneurship, and resource management; engines of growth

sudras - Those whose natural gifts involve consistent, precise execution and reliable service; the power of execution

guna - Natural qualities; one of the factors (along with *karma*) that defines *varna*

karma & Cosmic Law

karma - The universal law of cause and effect; actions and their consequences that create an endless chain reaction; spiritual debt or consequences of actions from past lives; actions; one of the factors (along with *guna*) that defines *varna*

sanchita karma - Your cosmic ledger and savings account—every accumulated deed from previous incarnations stored until the moment is right for expression

prarabdha karma - The "monthly withdrawal" from your karmic account—the portion of *sanchita karma* you're assigned to experience in your current life; part of accumulated karma that manifests in your present life, influencing events including your eventual death

agami karma - Every action you perform today that creates newly formed cause-and-effect relationships contributing to your karmic inventory

samsara - The cycle of birth and death; wandering through cycles of existence; riding the rollercoaster of experiences as part of existence

maya - Ignorance that drives our perception of separation and difference

Three *gunas* (Modes of Nature)

sattva - Goodness, purity; one of the three modes of material nature; one of the three factors from yogic philosophy; material mode of goodness/pureness

rajas - Passion, activity; one of the three modes of material nature; one of the three factors from yogic philosophy; material mode of passion

tamas - Ignorance, inertia; one of the three modes of material nature; one of the three factors from yogic philosophy; material mode of ignorance

sattvic - Pure, harmonious, balanced

rajasic - Active, passionate, restless

tamasic - Dull, lethargic, negative

Spiritual Qualities & Virtues

dama - Self-control; self-restraint

daya - Compassion

dana - Charity or generosity

daana - Charity; giving

seva - Service

pranipaatena - Humility

achara - Disciplined living

archana - "To honor"; characteristics and activities of a person in a meditative state who brings honor to all activities

Mental States & Consciousness

samskaras - The characteristics you develop and embody; mental tendencies and impressions

vasanas - The tendencies and inclinations you manifest; mental tendencies and impressions (alternative term for *samskaras*); innate spiritual tendencies carried from previous experiences

prana - Life force that flows through the body

jagarithastanah - The waking state

svapnastanah - The dream state

suṣuptasthānah - The deep sleep state

taijasa - A conscious life filled with light (wakeful state as described in the Upanishads)

samadhi - State of tranquility; meditative absorption

Stages of Spiritual Development

sthitha prajna - "Firm wisdom" - a state of being where decisions flow naturally from inner clarity and spiritual alignment

yatamaana samjna - "Awareness Before Action" - the first stage of developing the ability to pause before reacting

vyatireka samjna - "Emotional Balance" - the second stage, involving restraint from excessive likes and dislikes

ekendriya samjna - "Proactive Mindset" - the third stage, where one develops a proactive rather than reactive approach to life

vaseekara samjna - "Unwavering Concentration" - the fourth stage, characterized by unwavering concentration and focus

aparoksha jnani - A person with the ability to perceive direct knowledge without being judgmental

Worship & Ritual

puja - Worship; honor (derives from root word *puj*); prayer/worship room

abhisheka - Bathing and decoration ritual

homa - Fire ceremony

aarti - Ceremonial worship with lamps, often accompanied by singing *agni* - Fire; the most visible manifestation of energy

surya - Sun

varuna - Water

yajnas – Sacrifices

Three Sacred Fires

gaarhapatya - The householder fire; always kept burning as a constant source of energy for the home

ahavaniya - The fire used for offering sacrifices and invoking the power of deities, creating a direct channel of communication with the divine

dakshinagni - The southern fire; served as a protective and spiritual fire used for ancestral crematory rites, maintaining a connection between the living and those who had passed away

pancha kala kriya (Five Daily Practices)

pancha kala kriya - Spiritual activities performed at different times of the day; a five-step process that combines spirituality and ritual, segmenting your day into meaningful touchpoints with the divine

abhigamana - Approaching divinity; means "approaching near" to our true self, a deity, God, or the overall divinity

upadana - Preparation and collecting; preparing for the variations and movements of the day ahead

ijya - Worship; the actual act of worship to a deity

svadhyaya - spiritual learning

yogadhyana - Body-mind connection; establishing the connection between body and mind

Worship Offerings

pushpam samarpayami - "I offer flowers" - offering flowers and garlands to the deity

dhoopam samarpayami - "I offer incense" - lighting incense and circling it three times

jalam samarpayami - "I offer water" - providing water to the deity

snanam samarpayami - "I offer bath" - bathing the deity with water and special substances *vastram samarpayami* - "I offer cloth" - wiping and dressing the deity with cloth

deepam samarpayami - "I offer lamp" - lighting oil lamps before the deity

phalam samarpayami - "I offer fruit" - presenting fruits to the deity

naivedyam samarpayami - "I offer food" - presenting food offerings to the deity

naivedyam - Food offerings

prasadam - Grace of the divine (food offerings become this when consumed after worship)

Worship Stages

mantra-asana - First stage of worship - invocation to connect with the divine

snana-asana - Second stage of worship - symbolic water offering to the deity

alankara-asana - Third stage of worship - decorating the deity with flowers and lighting the lamp

Sacred Sounds & Mantras

om - The primordial sound/vibration from which all creation springs; the "seed mantra"; sacred sound/symbol used as a doorway to transcendental awareness

tat - "That" - refers to the divine reality within and beyond all things

sat - That which is genuine, authentic, and unchanging; truth and existence; purity

asat - Unreal (opposite of *sat*)

om tat sat - The three fundamental syllables representing spiritual reality; a powerful mantra described as "in many ways, the only prayer you need"—used to shift the center of gravity from self to divine; acknowledging that divinity exists everywhere, including within you

om krishnaya namah - "I offer my salutations to Lord *Krishna*" *om kleem krishnaya govindaya gopi jana vallabhaya* - A mantra offering to *Krishna*, sending vibrations that connect to the supreme energy

karagre vasathe lakshmi, karamadye vignana, kare mule sthitho govinda, prabhate karadarshanam - Extended mantra recognizing that auspiciousness, knowledge, and divine sustenance exist within you

vasudeva sarvam iti sah mahatma sudurlabah - "Very few understand him" - refers to the rare souls who recognize that *Vasudeva* (*Krishna*/divinity) is everything

mantras - Sacred sounds or phrases used in spiritual practice

Devotional Practices

bhajans - Devotional songs; devotional songs chanted during worship

kirtans - Chanting

laali - Lullaby/melodious music for "putting the deity to bed"

satsang - Spiritual gatherings; company of the pure, pious, like-minded, and compassionate (*sat* = purity, *sang* = company); being in the company of the pure, pious, like-minded, and compassionate

katha - Storytelling

harikathas - Evening gatherings where people come together to hear stories

pravachana - Philosophical and devotional stories shared during worship

yoga nidra - Practice of expressing appreciation for the physical vessel or this body that enables spiritual experience

bhaagavatha - The divine as it appears; devotion to the divine manifested in human form

Philosophical Terms

nama - Name (as in giving names to aspects of divinity)

rupa - Form (as in providing forms to aspects of divinity)

nama-rupa - Name and form; names and forms - the theistic approach of giving tangible attributes to infinite divine energy

neti neti - Not this, not that

dvaita - Dualism (Madhwa's philosophy)

vishishtadvaita - Qualified non-dualism (Ramanuja's philosophy)

advaita - Complete non-dualism (Sankara's philosophy)

dravya - Substance; foundation; the supportive environment where spiritual qualities can emerge and grow

tattvas - Characteristics (as referred to in the scriptures)

puranas - Stories that convey spiritual principles through narrative

puranic - Relating to the *Puranas*; the period when the concept of temples evolved into what we recognize today as part of modern Hinduism

agama - Scriptures that prescribed detailed standards for temple construction, including deity height, temple dimensions, structure shape, and sanctum specification

vishnu sahasranama - A scriptural book

Light & Illumination

divya jyoti - Divine light; the supreme light showing the path of inquiry

atma jyoti - The light of the self; the divine spark within us

gu - Sanskrit root meaning "darkness"

ru - Sanskrit root meaning "dispeller"

Action & Being

upavishathi - Sitting

uttishthati - Getting up

tishtathi - Standing

chalathi - Moving

ishvara iccha - The Divine's wish or will

bhagya - The divisible share of modifying effects from a chain reaction

Word Components & Roots

tap - Root meaning "to heat" or "to burn" (root of *tapasya*)

sadh - Root meaning "to accomplish" or "to perfect" (root of *sadhana*)

hrudayam - Heart (composed of three syllables)

hr - To take

da - To give

yam - Giving through knowledge, thought, and feeling

puj - Root word meaning "honor"

Epic References

pandavas - One of the two groups of cousins in the Mahabharata war

kauravas - The other group of cousins in the Mahabharata war

partha – Another name of Arjuna, the one with noble lineage and a sense of duty to family,

gudakesha - Another name of Arjuna, the one who is a "Conqueror of sleep" - highlights discipline and vigilance

kaunteya - Another name of Arjuna, referencing his mother Kunti - reminds of family values

dhananjaya - Another name of Arjuna, the one who is the "Winner of wealth" - refers to worldly achievements and successes

savyasachin - Another name of Arjuna, the one who is an ambidextrous archer - speaks to exceptional skills and abilities